D1307408

PORTRAIT OF AN AMERICAN BUSINESSMAN

One Generation from Cotton Field to Boardroom

UNIVERSITY

MERCER UNIVERSITY PRESS

Endowed by

TOM WATSON BROWN
and
THE WATSON-BROWN FOUNDATION, INC.

PORTRAIT OF AN

AMERICAN BUSINESSMAN

One Generation from Cotton Field to Boardroom

CARL WARE

with Sibley Fleming

MERCER UNIVERSITY PRESS
Macon, Georgia
1979–2019
40 Years of Publishing Excellence

MUP/ H977

© 2019 by Lucky Feather Media, LLC
Published by Mercer University Press
1501 Mercer University Drive
Macon, Georgia 31207
All rights reserved

9 8 7 6 5 4 3 2 1

Books published by Mercer University Press are printed on acid-free paper
that meets the requirements of the American National Standard for
Information Sciences—Permanence of Paper for Printed Library Materials.

Printed and bound in the United States.

This book is set in Adobe Caslon.

ISBN   978-0-88146-715-4
Cataloging-in-Publication Data is available from the Library of Congress

Dedicated to my parents,
Lois Missouri Wimberly Ware and Ulas B. Ware;
my wife, Mary Clark Ware;
my son, Timothy Alexander Ware;
my grandchildren, Aaron Alexander Ware
and Renita Johnson Ware;
and my great-grandson, Tayden Alexander.

CONTENTS

Foreword by *Archbishop Desmond Tutu*   ix

Introduction   1

1: Daddy   3

2: The Wares   10

3: Prayer Rock   16

4: Sharecropping Years   23

5: A Better Life   31

6: Buying the Land   37

7: Find a Way   41

8: Cradle of Civil Rights   48

9: Meeting Mary   52

10: Becoming an Urbanologist   59

11: Praying for Guidance   64

12: "Carl Cares"   73

13: The 25-Percent Policy   84

14: Bringing Dr. King's Dream to Life   93

15: Coca-Cola University   100

16: A Better Company   107

17: "Leave no stone unturned"   119

18: Temperature Rising   129

19: South Africa, At Last   135

20: An Encounter with a Spiritual Icon   143

21: The Coke Way   154

22: Kilimanjaro   162

23: At the Leeds Castle Meeting and the Dakar Conference   169

24: Meeting Two South African Presidents   181

25: The Making of Clark Atlanta University   188

26: Becoming Coca-Cola's Africa Group President   204

27: Inauguration of President Nelson Rolihlahla Mandela   214

28: "We believe in Africa"   227

29: The Ware Report   244

30: There Is Life after Coke   253

31: Just Business   261

Afterword   271

Acknowledgments   275

Index   279

FOREWORD

by Archbishop Desmond Tutu

In our long struggle to end apartheid, we needed every ally we could get. I sought the support of international companies, asking them to stop doing business in South Africa. We wanted to cut the flow of corporate tax revenues to a government whose goal was to deny 35 million people of color their freedom, their hope, their very humanity in order to keep them subservient to 5 million whites. I spoke often to businessmen. One after the other, they acknowledged the evil of apartheid and said they wanted it to end. But, in the end, the bottom line for them was their company's bottom line. They wanted to strike a blow against apartheid as long as doing so didn't cut into their profits.

Black South Africans needed business people who truly understood the desperation of our plight and the justice of our cause. I prayed that they would see that apartheid was killing my country and destroying its soul. I wanted them to realize that profits and apartheid could not coexist for long, because the urgent question before us was not whether their companies could continue to do business in South Africa; the question was whether there would continue to be a South Africa in which to do business if the corrosive effects of racial oppression and injustice were allowed to cause the country to crumble into chaos. Therefore, it was imperative that we find corporate leaders who would place the desperate plight of our people ahead of profits.

Experience had taught me that only those who themselves have been victims of oppression and discrimination could know that the ultimate evil of apartheid is not the suffering, excruciating as it may be, which it metes out to those who are God's children. The ultimate evil of the oppression, certainly of that oppression so ruthlessly carried out by the South African government, is the way it makes a child of God doubt that he or she is a child of God.

Carl Ware was amongst a few who walked the corridors of power of international commerce who both understood the situation in South

Africa and possessed a sense of personal identity which gave him empathy for oppressed people.

Growing up black in the segregated American South is not exactly the same as growing up black in South Africa under apartheid. But, from what I know, there are similarities. Both experiences require a willingness to struggle against the forces that are aligned against you and designed to grind you down. Therefore, the black children of America's segregated South and the black children of South African apartheid are like people who speak different dialects of the same language. The more they speak to each other, the better they understand each other.

I have spoken to Carl Ware many times over the more than thirty years that I have known him. And as our conversation continues, I understand more and more why he had the ability to identify with our struggle against apartheid and why he was so willing to support our efforts to create and maintain a democratic, nonracial South Africa. In interacting with and giving counsel to anti-apartheid leaders such as Nelson Mandela, Oliver Tambo, and Thabo Mbeki, Carl has been invaluable to our successful struggle. Nelson Mandela wrote to Carl and said, "When the history of our struggle is properly reviewed in the near future, only then will the world be privy to fully understand your catalytic role in that struggle. We know of countless contributions made to innumerable individuals and organizations in our country through your direct intervention. This you did, not only in your capacity as one of the decision-makers within Coca-Cola, but also in your own right as a conscientious human being of African descent."

The life lessons Carl learned while on his trek from the sharecropping fields he worked as a child to the corporate boardrooms in which he eventually sat prepared him for his work in South Africa and for the many other challenges he faced as a student, a civil rights activist, a politician, and a businessman. I know him as a man who is firmly rooted in the values his parents taught him and who is guided by God.

As is the case with all of us, Carl has had his ups and downs as he has made his way. Even as he and I searched together for a strategy to demonstrate the Coca-Cola Company's unequivocal opposition to apartheid, there were bumps in the road. But I have seen in him the strength of character and the calm under pressure that allows him to chart the smoothest course for himself and the people he leads.

Now Carl is telling his story in a way that reveals how his experiences prepared him for success. He also shows others how what he has learned can help them achieve their goals. He has a powerful message about the benefits of the black experience. He moves us beyond victimhood to an embrace of our affirmative duty to build on the lessons of those who came before us and to use everything that befalls us as a teaching tool that makes us wiser.

The case Carl makes resonates with me because its affirmation is demonstrated by the history of my own country. We South Africans are stronger for what we have survived. Having rejected what we once were, we have a clear vision of what we should be. In overcoming hopelessness, we have proclaimed our right always to believe that there is hope.

Carl Ware's journey through life illustrates that our planet is becoming a smaller place. He has seen corners of the globe and met with people from more diverse cultures and backgrounds than he ever could have imagined while growing up in rural Georgia. In writing this book, he has plotted a course to success that others can follow in a world where the flow of information, products, and people is impeded less and less by those imaginary barriers we call borders. There is no doubt that globalization is the wave of the future. The question is whether it will benefit the masses or the few, whether it will unite humanity or be a wedge that further divides us. Carl draws on his personal experiences to show people can move into the global marketplace without shedding their ethics, their moral compass, or their humanity.

Carl does not only understand *Ubuntu,* the Africa philosophy of humaneness, he lives it and applied it to the corporate, educational, social, political, and religious environment in which he played decision-making roles. *Ubuntu* is described in an African saying that translates, "A person is a person through other persons." It means that a solitary human being is a contradiction in terms. A totally self-sufficient human being is ultimately subhuman. We are made to be complementary. I have gifts that you do not; you have gifts that I do not. We need each other to become fully human.

Carl brought his considerable gifts to South Africa and shared them with us. He became part of the process that helped make us fully human in our own land. He became our brother, and he has continued to be our brother ever since. There is a saying from the American civil rights movement that says, "He can talk the talk, but can he walk the walk?" I love these words because they so clearly articulate the difference between rhetoric and action. Of course, we need a combination of the two. You will see in the following pages that Carl Ware has that combination. He can talk the talk. He has always walked the walk. Listen to his words; follow in his footsteps.

PORTRAIT OF AN AMERICAN BUSINESSMAN

One Generation from Cotton Field to Boardroom

INTRODUCTION

I was born at home, a tiny shack next to a railroad track in Coweta County, Georgia. My parents were sharecroppers who worked other people's land, laboring alongside their twelve children. From such humble beginnings I rose to become the highest-ranking African American executive at the Coca-Cola Company, the most recognizable brand in the world.

My careers as a community activist, politician, businessman, and philanthropist also played out against a backdrop of radical change, beginning with the shift from Jim Crow laws to the ascendancy of black political power in the South. At the same time, corporate America was opening up at the highest levels for people like me who had education, managerial training, and political savvy to contribute to the global expansion of American business.

My life as an international businessman started in an era of unprecedented geopolitical events. Shortly after the fall of the Berlin Wall and the collapse of the Soviet Union in 1991, I was promoted to the position of deputy group president of North East Europe/Africa and assigned to work out of Coca-Cola's Windsor, England, office with direct responsibility for the Africa business.

I witnessed postcolonial Africa's struggle with the ravages of war, tribal conflicts, famine, and disease. In some of these countries, I worked in the midst of transitions to democratic principles and free-market economies. I saw firsthand the heinous crimes against humanity under the system of apartheid in South Africa.

My most difficult experience, however, may have been the journey of writing this book. As you read, I hope you come to understand what motivated me to keep going and complete this daunting task that began in 2003.

There is no question I have been blessed beyond measure, and I have lived a life with profound inspirations, from my high school principal and pastor to my personal contacts with such great men as Roberto Goizueta, Warren Buffett, Colin Powell, Desmond Tutu, and Nelson Mandela.

Like many American success stories, the most critical period I cover in this book is my childhood. My greatest advantage indeed was having devoted and God-fearing parents who gave me a solid moral foundation. Lois and Ulas Ware were engaged parents who instilled in me the value of hard work, preparation, and humility—habits I would need to beat seemingly impossible odds, seize opportunity, and eventually to use my power to make a difference in the lives of others.

In the end, telling my story is important because it illustrates a fundamental truth: whatever the circumstances of your birth, you, too, can succeed. No matter where you come from, you can make a difference in your time on this earth.

1

DADDY

My mother must have worried mightily on the day my father went to vote. I can picture her rising before the crack of dawn—as she always did—building a fire in her black cast-iron cookstove, rolling out the soft, light dough for her famous brown biscuits, and filling the house with the mouthwatering smell of streak o' lean.

I wonder if deep down, as Mamma went about her morning routine, she didn't harbor the wish that it was somebody else's husband going off to face imminent danger.

If such thoughts did cross her mind, I never heard anything about it. I do know that while Mamma was forthright in her opinions, in the end, Daddy's word was law. And he was already keenly aware of the dangers he faced and all that he put at risk by attempting to cast his ballot at the Coweta County Courthouse. Doing so in 1949 would make him the first African American to vote in Georgia's Fifth Congressional District since Reconstruction, the period just after the Civil War, from 1865 to 1877, when the South was rebuilding under military rule ordered by Congress.

Daddy was escorted to the courthouse by Sheriff Lamar Potts. As my longtime friend and former Coweta County commissioner Robert Wood put it, Potts "controlled Coweta County like Matt Dillon controlled Dodge City" for more than twenty years.

Potts is still remembered as being "colorblind." Lamar and his brother, J. H., who was also in law enforcement for the county, were a "different breed" of white people. That's according to my brother Walter Ware, now seventy-seven and our family's most revered historian. Walter was ten when Daddy cast that vote.

Walter remembers the Potts brothers well and says they didn't have this "hatred passion" for black people. They believed in treating everyone fairly, regardless of race, and in upholding the law, which largely revolved around catching people who were making and running illegal moonshine.

The most vivid example of how Potts ran things took place in 1948, when he investigated the murder of a white tenant farmer named Wilson Turner. Turner was the tenant of a wealthy and powerful landowner in neighboring Meriwether County. What was unusual about the case was that John Wallace, the wealthy white landowner accused of the murder, was condemned to die in the electric chair on the testimony of two black men, whom Potts protected throughout the trial. The sensational story received national attention and was made into a book, *Murder in Coweta County*, by Margaret Anne Barnes, as well as a CBS television movie starring Johnny Cash and Andy Griffith.

Potts, along with J. H. and two other deputies, escorted my father to the polls. They met him in Sargent, about a mile away from our home, and drove him to the county courthouse some six miles away, in downtown Newnan.

When they arrived, my father only had to walk past the cement statue of a Confederate soldier. There were no white-hooded Klansmen burning crosses on the lawn, nor was there an angry mob shouting words of hate or holding up signs emblazoned with racial epithets. That kind of thing didn't happen with Lamar Potts in charge of the situation.

Then again, as my brother Walter notes, racists typically didn't just come out openly as they do now—then, it was a whole different ballgame. If people wanted to intimidate or terrorize you, they'd do it behind your back, under cover of night, or in a sneak attack where they could catch you off guard when you were alone—Klan style.

If they did come during the day, they would be hidden beneath a sheet. And you really couldn't tell who it was—it might be the store owner who accepted your hard-earned dollars. It might be your landlord...anybody.

But many people around Sargent didn't feel that way. In fact, Daddy had been encouraged to vote by Ellis Peniston, president of Arnall Mills, the cotton mill in Sargent. Peniston was married to the daughter of former Arnall Mills president Alton Wynn Arnall. The family was directly related to Newnan native and progressive Georgia governor Ellis Arnall, whose accomplishments between 1943 and 1947 included repealing the poll tax, lowering the voting age from twenty-one to eighteen, and creating eight constitutional boards to reduce the power of the governor.

Ellis defeated three-term governor Eugene Talmadge, who wielded almost unlimited power in the state. The one-term victory was possible only because Talmadge, who has been likened to a dictator, had egregiously overstepped his authority by firing Georgia university system administrators, professors, and members of the Board of Regents—in short, anyone who didn't support his view of segregation. As a result, state-supported white colleges lost accreditation.

Governor Arnall led efforts to restore accreditation, among many other praiseworthy reforms. It was this progressive white community, Walter recalls, that had sort of "latched on" to Daddy, encouraging him to vote and even offering protection.

My father was thirty-eight years old when he cast the ballot. Although just a humble mill laborer, he had earned a reputation among blacks and whites for his hard work, intelligence, and honesty. No matter how little he had, Daddy shared with people who were less fortunate, teaching his children that giving back was a privilege rather than an obligation.

He was also a community leader and role model. He chaired the deacon board and managed the business affairs and spiritual issues at Oak Grove Baptist. He also served as an active member of the Newnan lodge of Prince Hall Masons, founded in the 1700s in Boston by Prince Hall, an African American abolitionist.

After Daddy cast his ballot, Sheriff Potts drove him back to Sargent, where news of the vote spread quickly. Men who worked on the docks, loading cotton onto the trains, asked him incredulously, "How did you get by?"

"I just walked in there and voted," my father replied. Then, according to Walter, he encouraged other men who had felt it too risky to do the same. Following his example, other men began to cast their ballots, one by one. Walter still remembers the names of the next six men who followed Daddy: Cody Turner, Cody Freeman, J. W. Kirkland, A. C. Barber, John "Fris" Bohannon, and Robert Calhoun.

Coweta County voter records show that my father, Ulas B. Ware, registered to vote on October 1, 1949. Forty-two years later, in 1991, Coweta County would honor him with a proclamation citing the historic vote. I have no memory of Daddy voting, as I had just started the first grade, but the act was of such significance in our family that it left a lasting impression on Walter, who vividly remembers Daddy walking through the door and telling Mamma that he had voted.

The day must have been full of tension for everyone, given there was a very real concern for our father's safety. The significance of my father's actions can fully be understood by looking at the history of the black vote, beginning with emancipation. In the late 1860s, Congress took a series of important steps that were of major importance to blacks, including the ratification of the Fourteenth Amendment in 1868, which gave African Americans citizenship and protected them from discriminatory state laws. Two years later, the Fifteenth Amendment gave African American men the right to vote and to run for political office.

In Coweta County the population was closely split down the middle by race, while the state of Georgia overall was predominantly white. With the right to vote, in 1870 a black man named Sam Smith won a seat in the Georgia legislature. Nationally, between 1870 and 1901, black voters across the South elected twenty-two black politicians—two senators and twenty representatives—to the US Congress.

However, by the time my father was born, in 1911, "inalienable rights" such as the right to vote and equal protection under the law had been systematically stripped away from African American men in the South by Jim Crow laws, which were enforced by a terroristic system of violence, intimidation, and segregation.

It's remarkable to think that although it happened more than 100 years ago, the magnitude of that institutionalized system of violence against blacks is still not fully known. Ongoing research by Alabama nonprofit Equal Justice Initiative, as of the writing of this book, revealed that some 4,075 racial terror lynchings took place between 1877 and 1950. I say "to date" because, as the investigations continue, the number of murders continues to rise.

First and foremost, of course, these lynchings served to intimidate and keep African Americans "in their place." Sickeningly, they were also used as public entertainment, with crowds of white spectators sitting on picnic blankets as the victim was tortured, lynched, and sometimes burned.

In the 1899 case of Sam Hose, which happened in Coweta County, newspapers reported that the skin on the face of the victim was removed along with his ears, fingers, and genitals. The man was then tied to a tree and burned. As if that torment weren't enough, the white crowds fought over his body parts, which they sold as souvenirs on the streets of downtown Newnan.

The terror tactics worked, almost completely disenfranchising the black population. From 1904 to 1910, black voter registration in Georgia fell from 28.3 percent to 4.3 percent. In 1905, Coweta County's voter roll in the registrar's office listed 3,375 whites and 577 blacks; by 1925, it listed just seven black men and two black women.

Remembering Ernest "Buster" Brown

Yet the horrors continued, even after my father voted.

The very next year, 1950, an event occurred in Coweta County that hit close to home. U. B. Ware had graduated to the title "Mr. U. B.," a sign of respect in the South, mostly expected of black folks toward white folks. Even though there were good people in the white community, the undertow of violence was strong, its victims real.

For instance, four of my mother's brothers—Sam, J. S., Lamar, and Levi Wimberly—had to flee Coweta County after getting the best of some Klansmen in a fight near the town of Sargent. They were on a train headed north to Detroit before daybreak. The sheriff came looking for them the next day, but they were already long gone, never again to call this place home.

These stories abound. When I set out to gather my family stories for this book, one of our most enduring legends from that era centered on the death of Ernest "Buster" Brown, a twenty-year-old black man who worked in the Arnco mill.

To feed a family the size of ours, my father had to be a jack-of-all-trades, which included running a barbershop from our home. As it happened, one Friday evening in 1950, Buster Brown came for a haircut. It was the last time any of us saw him alive.

What we learned the next day was that, on his way home, Buster had been attacked by a group of whites in an area we called "The Line," where the white mill and cotton gin workers lived.

My brother Walter still recalls seeing Buster's mutilated body. Walter and Daddy had just loaded up the wagon with corn and watermelon to peddle in Newnan. On the way, my brother and father passed through the small village of Sargent, which had a cotton gin, warehouses, and a general store, all situated near a railroad track.

A huge crowd had gathered around the track, several hundred yards from the loading dock. As Walter and Daddy approached, they saw Dan Moten, the black undertaker from Roscoe Jenkins Funeral Home, in the process of recovering Buster's body. It had been completely severed in half by the train.

One of my big sisters, Mildred, sometimes assisted Daddy by holding a lamp for him while he cut hair. She still recalls overhearing the men discussing the murder the next day. "They put Buster up against the tree, pulled his clothes off, and cut off his privacy," Mildred said. "And then they took him and threw him across the railroad track. They said that the train had run over him.

"That was the talk amongst the blacks because they knew he had been at our house and had left to go home," Mildred said. Buster's body was soaked in moonshine. From the "evidence," so the legend went, the sheriff deduced that the young man had obviously gotten drunk and then just stumbled onto the train track, where he passed out.

Mildred did not repeat the story she overheard to anyone at that time, not even her brothers and sisters. "What we heard, we kept our mouths closed," she reminded me. Furthermore, I found no evidence it was ever reported in the local paper.

Maybe the details of this young man's death didn't stand out as being unusual because black folks had seen it so many times before. It was a known tactic of the Klan to beat up a man, pour alcohol down his throat and over his clothes, and then leave him on the railroad track. They knew that the death would be ruled an accident or suicide, never homicide or a lynching.

Over the years, the story of Buster's death lingered in my mind. Eventually, my curiosity led me to look for answers with anyone still living who might remember Buster.

I decided to stop by Roscoe Jenkins Funeral Home, Newnan style, unannounced. It is one the oldest and nicest funeral homes in town, and its personnel handled Buster's body. I thought it reasonable to expect that they would have a record of the death.

Roscoe Jenkins, the patriarch of the family, was highly respected and had a reputation for being a Southern gentleman. When I rang the bell, I expected to see his daughter, Octavia Jenkins, whom I knew from high school. Instead, I was greeted by a very poised young woman in a tailored suit. She introduced herself as Linette Ward and explained she was Octavia's new partner and would help me if she could.

In a reception room filled with comfortable antiques and soft Persian rugs, Linette listened as I told her the story of Buster. She asked a few questions, jotted down some notes, and told me that she'd talk to Octavia, as well as do a little research of her own, and get back to me.

A week later, Linette called and told me she was leaving the Coweta County Probate Court, where she found the death certificate of an Ernest Brown who was killed on the railroad track in Sargent on July 7, 1950. I listened briefly and, later that day, met her at the funeral home.

This time, when I rang the bell, Octavia greeted me with a warm embrace, and then Linette handed me the death certificate. I stood there in the foyer, trying to make out the scrawl. I borrowed Octavia's reading glasses and held the paper under a lamp.

"Oh, my God," I said. "This is Buster's death certificate." As I looked at the description of his body, I almost froze. 'Body was cut into parts. Killed by a train. Body was cut into parts on the railroad.' This was noted by the coroner as the underlying cause of death.

Buster had indeed died on a Friday, as Walter had remembered. What I didn't know, as the death certificate revealed, was that Buster had been buried two days later. That was unusual back then because it normally took at least a week or two to get word out to family members.

Buster Brown's lynching was the reality of life growing up in the Jim Crow South. It is my hope that remembering him as part of my family history will help to bring some dignity to his death.

9

2

THE WARES

My father, Ulas B. Ware, was born June 15, 1911, to Peter Walton and Besora Ware. Following Southern tradition, they gave him a middle initial that didn't stand for anything. It was "B" and nothing more.

That same year, the National Urban League was founded to help blacks migrating from the South to the big cities in the North adjust to their new lives. The National Association for the Advancement of Colored People was also incorporated in 1911.

While researching my family's history, dating back to slavery, I drove down to Franklin, Georgia, the Heard County seat, and Hogansville, located in Troup County, looking for anyone who had information on the Ware family. My father told me that's where our ancestors got their start in this country.

When I told the librarian at the public library in Hogansville what I was looking for, she lit up. "You need to talk to Miss Jane," she said. "She's a direct descendant of the white Wares of Troup County, and she may know something about your ancestors."

"Miss Jane" was Jane Ware Strain. If, as the librarian suggested, Miss Jane's ancestors held my ancestors in slavery, she might have something valuable to tell me.

As I drove to Miss Jane's house, I thought of my first visit, in 1992, to Goree Island in Senegal, the notorious site of the slave trade where some 20 million African men, women, and children were warehoused, traded, and dispatched from West Africa as if they were livestock.

Miss Jane lived in a beautiful old antebellum home accented by a pretty flower garden and a manicured front yard. The woman who opened the door looked to be in her early eighties, but she was clear-eyed and sharp. "You look just like the Wares," she said warmly but without preamble.

"I am one of the Wares," I said. With that, she opened the screen door and invited me into her living room.

I told her I was searching for family history, which was enough to get her going. Genealogy was one of Miss Jane's passions, and she was able to take the story all the way back to the early 1600s, when Robert Ware first sailed to America from England with his sons Robert Jr. and Peter.

From that group sprang Ware families who settled in Virginia and Maryland. Over several generations, the Wares made their way down to South Carolina and, just before the Revolutionary War, into Georgia. A Henry Ware Sr. and his sons fought the British in Georgia.

A generation later, John Ware and his wife, Lucy, settled in a part of Coweta County that later became Heard County. According to Miss Jane, the family arrived around 1827 with five enslaved people, though my ancestors were not in that group.

Eventually, the Wares met the Waltons of Heard County. A cholera epidemic had devastated the Waltons' plantation, and they were facing financial ruin. Desperate for money, they sold all of their land and holdings, including my great-grandparents, Peter and Mary Walton, to the Wares. Miss Jane also confirmed what my father had told me, which was that my great-grandparents were buried in a cemetery for enslaved people that stood across the road from the white Liberty Baptist Church on Highway 17, near Hogansville.

With the transfer of property ownership, Peter Walton became Peter Walton Ware. The white Wares, owners of a 700-acre plantation and thirty-eight enslaved people to work it, prospered as the Civil War approached.

Miss Jane didn't know any of the particulars on the black Wares, especially after emancipation, but I can pick up the story from what I know and what I learned from my father.

A Much Right Man

My grandfather, whom we called Grandpa Pete, was born in 1871, after the end of American slavery. Family lore has it that when he married, Grandpa Pete "stole" his bride, fifteen-year-old Besora

Beasley. He was twenty years her senior.

Besora was born in 1891, the daughter of Annie Beasley, who was one of two sisters married to John Beasley—at the same time. It was a strange and unusual arrangement, to say the least. But John Beasley and his two wives, Annie and Dolly, otherwise carried on their lives as good Christians, so the community apparently accepted them as they were. Each sister bore him fifteen children.

Grandpa Pete called himself a "much right man." He simply refused to fit into the accepted profile of a black man and thumbed his nose at the absurdities of Jim Crow when he felt like it. He neither turned his eyes away nor stepped aside for any man.

My grandfather was a traveling minstrel who beat a drum and played a flute that he carved out of sugarcane stalk. He performed at baseball games, juke joints, and other places where crowds gathered for entertainment.

Sometimes he was paid in a little folding money by the proprietors of the places he played, but most of his pay was coins from customers and spectators. Because he traveled the back roads so frequently and always had cash, Grandpa Pete carried a revolver for protection. Legend has it that he was one of two black men in the county allowed to carry a gun openly, which probably added to his image as a man you didn't want to tangle with.

According to family history, on a hot summer day in the early 1940s, Grandpa Pete went to the general store in Sargent. There was an open keg of water outside that had been steeping in the sun. The sign above the keg read: "COLORED." He was thirsty, so he had walked right past it and into the store, where he drank a dipper of cold water from the barrel marked "WHITES ONLY."

"Boy," said one of the white men standing around the store. "What are you doing at our fountain? Get out there to your keg if you want some water!"

Grandpa Pete turned around and said, "Now, listen to me, white man, I am a much right man. I have just as much right to drink this water as you."

The store owner stepped in. "Y'all better leave that fella alone," he said. "That's Peter Walton Ware."

It was unheard of back then for a black man to have a reputation that white people knew about, something that gave them pause. But Grandpa Pete had earned that reputation.

န

Baseball diamonds were often carved out of grassy fields and had seats set up for spectators, along with concession stands selling barbecue or fish sandwiches and sodas cooled in washtubs full of ice—but the scene wasn't always pastoral.

Rivalries between small-town teams could be intense. The winners were always euphoric, but the losers were sometimes angry, looking for some post-game payback. A few fans might get worked up after drinking something a little harder than soda pop during the game, so the chance of a brawl always existed.

Juke joints, the nightclubs of the rural South, were worse. They were mostly shacks on the black side of town or hidden down some dark country road. People came to unwind after a long workweek, listen to songs on the jukebox, dance, and drink moonshine whiskey, often the only alcoholic beverage available. Grandpa Pete didn't drink illegal moonshine, though. He drank an over-the-counter tonic called Hadacol that was marketed as a vitamin supplement but had a 12-percent alcohol content.

Trouble was routine, given the volatile mix of folks at close quarters, drinking, and dancing...sometimes with the wrong partners. Grandpa Pete, who was there to provide live entertainment, often found himself in the middle of it. During his travels, he got into more than one brawl and more than held his own.

Actually, I know of one time that Grandpa Pete got the worst of it. It happened at a ballgame where he was entertaining, and he ran into his archenemy, a man named Edmond Dunston. In no time, the two were fighting, getting so tangled up they couldn't throw punches or use their hands at all. At the end of it, Grandpa Pete had bitten off Dunston's ear, and Dunston had bitten off part of Grandpa Pete's thumb.

Grandpa Pete didn't go looking for trouble, but he was always ready when trouble found him. He was no bully, and he didn't try to dominate or humiliate people. For him, it was about being treated with respect.

He always carried himself with dignity, and there was no one whose eyes he could not look into directly. He embraced self-reliance and industriousness, and he would always make a way out of no way. Grandpa Pete worked to develop his music talent and earned a living from it. He knew he was as good as anyone else, and no one could convince him otherwise.

Grandpa Pete passed on those characteristics to my father, and my father passed them on to me.

A Country Schoolteacher

Ultimately, the person who had the most influence in making my father the man he became may not have been Grandpa Pete. According to Walter, that honor goes to a schoolteacher named Miss Rose Trailor, who taught at Mount Zion Elementary, a one-room schoolhouse near my grandparents' home.

Miss Trailor had a home with her husband in Newnan, but she lived with my grandparents in the country during the week because she didn't have transportation to make the journey to town and back every day. Instead, she boarded with my grandparents, who lived just a short skip down a path from the schoolhouse.

When Miss Trailor moved in with the family, Walter pointed out, Daddy was the only child in the house. In the evenings, she taught him everything she could by lamplight, from good penmanship to how to understand different situations in the world around him.

When Grandpa Pete walked off and left the family, the teacher continued to encourage and motivate Daddy to do good, to work the crops in order to provide for his mother, who was dependent on him because she was with child.

The teacher's influence had a lasting effect. Daddy became the type of man who didn't throw away anything. "If it was a pencil that was short, he would take it and put it up because he said somebody might need it," Walter recalls. "He was always thoughtful in that way, to be a preserver of what he had. He wouldn't throw anything away, but he would give you his heart if you needed it. That came from Miss Trailor." Before she died in 1935, at age forty-four, my grandmother would have two more sons—my uncles Eddie Benjamin Ware and William Henry Ware.

My father began his way in the world with a seventh-grade education, strong Christian faith, a solid work ethic, and the will to survive. Back then, if you finished the seventh grade, you were educated, because rural blacks and whites didn't typically get more schooling than that. Somehow it was enough, because Daddy was always considered a smart man, someone who could figure out anything, from rebuilding an old truck engine to making sorghum syrup. He would do much more than that.

3

PRAYER ROCK

My parents, Ulas B. Ware and Lois Missouri Wimberly, were married on March 27, 1932, at Mount Zion Baptist, a small country church on Old Carrollton Highway. Their faith must have been strong, given the fact that at one point in the congregation's history its nearest neighbor was a KKK meeting hall. Mamma was seventeen and Daddy was twenty-one.

The Ware children came in sets that totaled twelve from 1932 through 1951. The eldest was Willie. Then came Louise, Julia, and Mildred by '37. Then Walter, Thomas, Eugene, and I by '43. The boys were followed by more girls: Barbara, Evelyn, and Joyce. The last Ware child was named Ulas B. after Daddy, but he lived only a day.

Mamma's secret to managing such a large brood? Delegating. She trained each child to take care of the next one down, and so on.

Jones Quarter

As a part of the research to write this book, I attempted to retrace the steps of my family's early history in Coweta County. A large part of that process consisted of picking the brains of my oldest siblings and driving the old county roads in my pickup truck to locate physical remnants of old homesteads, schools, mill buildings, cemeteries, and churches.

One of my first drives was down Dyer Road to the site of the plantation where my parents lived and worked when they were first married. It was a roughly 1,500-acre farm known as Jones Quarter, only a few miles from my birthplace.

The overseer of Jones Quarter was a vicious and dangerous white man. My sisters Mildred and Louise still recall the dark rumors that circulated about him whipping and even crippling black workers for disobeying his orders.

This man didn't like our father and, according to Mildred, "It was understood you had to get off of his land, or otherwise he would get rid of you. He didn't like the fact that Daddy was smart." It wasn't just the threat of violence that the overseer used to intimidate people. My older siblings remember the time in 1938, before I was born, that Daddy was in downtown Sargent, running errands with my sister Julia, then a three-year-old toddler. The overseer initiated some type of physical altercation, one that Daddy tried to defuse by locking himself and his daughter in the cab of his truck. The raging man then smashed out the windows with the two of them inside. Fortunately, Daddy was able to drive away, and neither he nor Julia was injured. Fearing for his own life and the safety of his family, he moved Mamma and the children to a house close to Mamma's parents' home, and he fled to Atlanta, where he stayed in hiding for two weeks.

I tried to envision the old plantation as I passed Georgia Power Plant Yates, which now occupies that landscape and is bordered to the north by the Chattahoochee River.

As I drove, I thought, *I didn't know that overseer, but I did know Gene Yates, the first president of Southern Company, for whom the plant is named.* I knew Gene because I served on the board of directors for Georgia Power Company for twenty-two years.

Gene was a prankster, a fact I learned soon after joining the board. During my orientation, we were in a small prop plane together, touring plants. Gene sat in the copilot's seat, and I sat one seat back from the cockpit. Once we reached cruising altitude, he reached under his seat and pulled out what appeared to be a bottle of Smirnoff vodka. He handed the bottle to the pilot, who took a swig and passed it back to Gene.

"You've got to be kidding me!" I said. I wasn't wild about the idea of flying tanked up on booze and then touring power plants. It did not seem to me like a good orientation lesson for a new director. Gene took another swig and burst out laughing.

I was not amused—until he poured a bit of the "vodka" into a small cup, passed it to me, and said, "Smell it. Taste it."

It was water.

I laughed all day long.

❧

Walter told me I could find the site of the old Jones Quarter share-cropper settlement by locating the plant's current-day boiler and a gravel pit. There wasn't much to see, but I pulled my truck over, alongside the Chattahoochee River Bridge, on the northern border of the old plantation site, and got out to stretch my legs. I had fond childhood memories of fishing for catfish there on Saturday afternoons.

As I pondered what my parents must have gone through to give me a better life, I began humming an old black hymn: "How I got over, how I got over," with its refrain, "My soul look back and wonder how I got over."

Ma Fannie's Saturday Night Suppers

Back in my truck, not far down the road, I saw on the left a small house with a shiny tin roof. I must have passed it hundreds of times over the years, but it was on this trip that the sight of it jogged my memory: I could see an image of my mother walking the dirt road to pick up the laundry of the white family who lived there.

Mamma didn't have a washing machine or electricity or running water. To "do" the laundry, one of the boys built a fire around the big cast-iron wash pot filled with water drawn from the well. After boiling the clothes with potash soap, Mamma scrubbed them on a homemade wooden washboard, rinsed them in a second pot of hot water, hung the clean laundry on a clothesline to dry, and then pressed the garments with a cast flatiron that she heated on a wood cookstove. A day or so later, Mamma returned the basket of clothes to the white family.

They were farm people who wore out their clothes in the fields just as much as we did. But Mamma accepted their hand-me-downs with gratitude, and she diligently washed and patched the frayed garments before we wore them. It didn't matter how little she had to work with—my mother always made sure that her children left the house clean and neat and presentable.

The next stop on my driving tour was a visit to the old home site of Mamma's parents, "Papa Joe" Wimberly and "Ma Fannie" Pollard

Wimberly. The land is still a farm, now owned by prominent Atlanta developer A. J. Land.

I felt comfortable entering the property off Sewell Mill Road, and I drove a few hundred yards to the old home site. The chimney and hearth are still standing above the millpond. I got a warm feeling remembering how Ma Fannie had adored me and my first cousin David. She treated us like princes, calling David "Big Honey" and me "Little Honey."

Ma Fannie was an independent businesswoman whose life was a testament to the strength and ingenuity of the matriarchs of my family. As a child, I wasn't allowed to visit there much without my mother because Mamma was a teetotaler and didn't one-hundred percent approve of Ma Fannie's enterprises.

My grandmother's business was Saturday night suppers in her home, where she offered fish sandwiches, pig-ear sandwiches, and home brew for sale. The home brew process entailed fermenting potato peels and yeast in a big clay pot and then straining through a cheesecloth the final product, which she bottled in fruit jars and sold.

My sister Louise recalls Ma Fannie once being taken to the county jail in downtown Newnan by her good friend Sheriff Lamar Potts. She wasn't kept long, and nothing ever came of it. Besides, as long as she paid her "taxes" and nobody got cut up or shot up, she could carry on business as usual.

The business operated from Saturday night through Sunday morning, when Ma Fannie opened her doors for some of the church brethren on their way to Jones Hill United Methodist, my mother's family church on Walt Carmichael Road, about a mile away.

My sister Mildred, who inherited our grandmother's tenacious business acumen, said Ma Fannie was always the last one through the church door on Sunday. She would sit in the back row, a sharp, well-dressed woman wearing one of her beautiful hats tilted stylishly to one side.

I was close to my grandparents and loved them all, but there was friction between Grandpa Pete and Papa Joe, who was a Geechee descended from the African people who lived on the barrier islands off the coast of Georgia and South Carolina. Whenever Papa Joe came around, Grandpa Pete would say, "There come that ol' Geechee man." But to me, Papa Joe was the kindest, gentlest, and sincerest human being I ever knew. Mamma inherited Papa Joe's gentle spirit and calm nature, which she passed on to me.

Papa Joe had only a second-grade education, yet he was a very intellectual man. I don't just mean he had wisdom or common sense; he had a way of working things out in his mind by applying logic and sound reasoning, and he became a peanut specialist. I remember trailing behind him in the fields where he planted and harvested peanuts and Irish potatoes, which sounded like "iceman taters" through his Geechee accent. Everybody wanted Papa Joe's peanuts and potatoes.

A Big Head

After taking a few snapshots of the old homeplace with my iPhone, I headed down the road toward the small unincorporated community of Arnco, location of the old Arnall Mills buildings, long shuttered. The gates to the property stood wide open. The main building itself was abandoned. The old mill office, a small red-brick structure with broken windows, stood a little off to the side, nestled in undergrowth.

The landscape, with the railroad track and the millpond, had not changed much. I immediately recognized the site of the home of my birth, one of a handful of shacks for black mill workers.

Around the time of my birth, Daddy got a job in Arnall Mills as a day laborer. That might not seem like much of a job title by today's standards, but back then it was considered a plum job for black men, who made up just 2 percent of the textile industry workforce in the entire country.

Between the 1870s and 1960s, mills in the South provided the only opportunity for poor whites hoping to escape competition from blacks in the fields. So the "fortunate" few black men who were able to land mill jobs labored outside, handling 500-pound bales of cotton. If they got inside work, it was as sweepers or janitors. Black women weren't allowed even to do menial jobs at the mill, though they were allowed to work as domestics for the white mill workers, cleaning their homes and taking care of their children.

Even though Daddy was able to secure a mill job, it still wasn't enough to feed our family. Food came from the land, from family gardens and farms. My father scratched out a vegetable garden in the

20

derelict yard of the mill house, though it didn't yield much. Times were hard. Sometimes fatback meat and white rice or syrup and cornbread were all we had to eat.

I don't know why my father was unable to find employment on another farm, but we suspect that the malicious overseer spread word among other plantation owners in the area that Daddy was a "problem" worker.

Our fortunes depended upon my father's ability to provide, which was complicated by his asthma. It would get so bad some days that Daddy couldn't walk home after his job at the mill, just 600 yards away. Through sheer force of will, he'd put in a full day and then crawl on his hands and knees along the path beside the railroad track, where Mamma would meet him and help him get to the house.

It was in the living room of that three-room shack that I was born on September 30, 1943, at 3:30 A.M. After Mamma went into labor, a midwife came, as was the practice in those days among blacks in rural areas.

My elder siblings remember Mamma calling them to see me for the first time, explaining that I had just arrived in a suitcase. They also say I had a big head!

On my second day, I was taken to Dr. Elliott, a white physician in Sargent, to be circumcised. That is noteworthy because I was the first of my brothers to have the procedure, which was new to the black community in those days. On one of my driving tours, I found Dr. Elliot's house still standing, much as it did more than seventy years ago, a beautiful one-story clapboard with a large wraparound porch.

Two years later, we moved again to another tiny shack, not far from Jones Quarter plantation, Arnco, or Sargent. The shack stood at the intersection of Rex Hyde and Walt Carmichael roads, an area I know well because at one point I owned the vast timber acreage around there. I had seen the house in years past. But on that day, I could make out only a small patch of rusted tin roof peeking through the thick pine forest. I decided to investigate and picked my way through briars until I was standing under the roof of the front porch, which was half gone and slanting steeply toward the ground. Through the empty window casements, I noticed the floor was caving in around the edges, though still intact around the old fireplace, which would be the last thing to go.

We had moved to this humble shack with the help of my mother's brother-in-law, Uncle Alfonzo Paige. My brother Walter remembers the entire family and all of our possessions being packed and stacked high in the flatbed of Uncle Alfonzo's Model-T truck. The truck was so heavy that it wouldn't go up the hill on the way there. So Uncle Alfonzo went and got two mules and hitched them to the front of the truck. We were there in almost no time, and that story became part of family legend. We lived in that house until I was four.

My next stop was right next door, about 300 yards up the hill, at my mother's family church, Jones Hill United Methodist. Many generations of our Wimberly family members are buried there, but the church holds more meaning for me as the location where my father made a pact with God, after which Daddy's blessings began to multiply. I was looking for a relic connected to the story that has become known in my family as the "prayer rock."

A quick look around the churchyard revealed no boulder or slab substantial enough to be what my father described. As I was about to give up, I found it on the side of the hill, the only rock, prominently set off from the church, in a clearing in the woods, as if it had been placed there and arranged on purpose.

I knelt down in front of this altar and closed my eyes to remember what I had been told.

In 1945, my father was still suffering miserably from asthma and pleurisy. Just when it seemed nothing would make him better, he turned to God for help. Daddy was struggling to breathe but somehow managed to crawl on his hands and knees from the house in the woods up the hill to the church, where he found a large granite rock in the shape of an altar, and on his knees, facing east, he began to pray.

The prayer went something like this: "Lord, if you'll help me survive this illness—if you spare me—I will dedicate my life to you."

Daddy's health didn't immediately improve. But ever after when he told the story, he would remember how from that moment forward God showered him with blessings. He would return to that rock again and again to pray.

22

4

SHARECROPPING YEARS

Not long after my father turned to God for help, he moved his family once again, this time into a new house that he himself helped to build.

I was just four when Daddy struck a sharecropping agreement with Paul Smith, the owner of a 650-acre plantation near Sargent. Paul Smith bought the land after he returned from World War II, where he served as a lieutenant in the army.

The deal was that the entire Ware family—an army of field hands and laborers—could live in a small shack "rent free" in exchange for our labor in Paul Smith's cotton fields and cornfields. The split on the crops we produced was 50-50: one-half of all of the crop yields went to Paul Smith and one half to the Ware family.

The typical such arrangement was that of a sharecropper, who got to keep only a third of what he and his family raised. That meant if a sharecropper produced six bales of cotton, he could keep two while the owner took four; if he produced three wagonloads of corn, he kept one while the owner took two, and so on.

Sharecropping was what some called the "new slavery." Share-croppers lived at the forbearance of a landowner who could tell them to leave or change the crop split at any time for any reason. The pay-offs were often meager or nonexistent when the crops failed.

Soon after we moved to Paul Smith's plantation, he and my father built a new barn together. Paul Smith was so impressed with Daddy's abilities and work ethic that he offered to build a new house for our family as an added incentive for us to stay and work his crops. Paul Smith was unusual for a white man in that he stopped to explain to us what he wanted done, how he wanted it done, and why it was important that it be done that way.

But Paul Smith was really being pragmatic where the large Ware family was concerned. We were many, and we were disciplined, and we were hardworking. My sisters toiled in the fields just as hard as the boys.

Daddy was also pragmatic where the sharecropping agreement was concerned. For him, it was a means to an end, that being to save enough money to purchase our own farm.

That kind of thinking was counterintuitive to the times. While other black families were migrating away from the Jim Crow South, Daddy and Mamma made a conscious decision to stay. It was a matter of self-determination, of having the courage and the will to forge a future of their choosing, despite the obstacles. When Daddy met Paul Smith, our fortunes began to change.

The barn that they built was followed by a four-room house, which they also constructed together. Paul Smith helped Daddy to hone his carpentry skills and to learn concrete masonry through those two construction projects. Daddy then taught those trades to his sons.

Everyone had a job on the farm. My older brothers did the skilled labor, such as shoeing the mules, sharpening and repairing the farm tools, and greasing the axles on the wagon wheels. My job was to slop the hogs, feed the chickens, hay the cows, and look after the hunting dogs. I enjoyed taking care of the animals, and I was good at it. But my brothers Eugene and Thomas milked the cows, something I was not good at because I was afraid the cows would kick me, and milk cows are sensitive to people's emotions.

Apron Strings

When we were too small to be left alone, Mamma carted us out to the fields and spread a blanket at the end of a row of cotton where she could keep an eye on us. At home, Mamma kept a vegetable garden that provided ample fresh food for us and enough to fill the pantry for the winter. The boys prepared the garden for planting by tilling and fertilizing the soil. Mamma then sowed her seeds and set out rows of everything you can name: rutabagas, sweet potatoes, white potatoes, cucumbers, pole beans, butter beans, crowder peas, turnip greens, collard greens, cabbage, squash, sweet corn, and tomatoes.

Mamma loved her flowers, too. In the summer, she always had a cheerful bed of sunflowers alongside the house. She also had pink petunias, red roses, and orange daylilies that provided colorful accents. The yard was swept clean with a straw broom that left intricate patterns in the dirt.

Some of my earliest memories are clinging to Mamma's apron strings as she cared for her flower garden. And I stayed underfoot in the kitchen while she worked miracles on her wood-fueled cookstove, which had a reservoir in the middle to heat water for dishes and baths.

The delicious meals she cooked on that old stove remain legendary, whether it was breakfast, dinner, or supper. That was before "lunch" was invented and when "brunch" was being served only in England.

All of Mamma's meals were special, but Sunday dinner was a spectacular feast of soul food that reached from one end of the long table to the other. We had neck bones, fried chicken, turnip greens, macaroni and cheese, rice pudding, and Mamma's famous fried peach pies. Cornbread and biscuits were two of her baking specialties. She cooked both for each meal because Daddy didn't eat cornbread. He ate biscuits with every meal.

Mamma turned our new sharecropper house into a cozy home. All of the windows had ruffled curtains, which she made from cotton flour sacks that came in printed patterns for housewives to repurpose.

My sister Barbara, a retired schoolteacher in Suffolk, Virginia, remembers the old foot-pedal sewing machine that Mamma used to make our clothes. She stitched all of the girls' dresses from scratch, cutting patterns from pictures she liked in the Sears, Roebuck & Company catalogue.

All of my sisters learned how to sew on that machine, but my sister Julia, now deceased, went on to become a professional seamstress. Her clientele consisted predominantly of wealthy white folks in Buckhead. But I think her favorite client must have been her son, Bobby Lovelace, an original member of the R&B group Midnight Star, which had a string of hits in the eighties and still tours in the US, Europe, and Asia today.

Mamma could have written the book on home economics, though she had only a third-grade education. She could take five dollars and do more with it than another person who had twenty,

Barbara recalled. "On Friday, we sometimes had what Mamma called 'Girls' Pepsi Night,'" she continued. "Mamma would send me and my sisters Joyce and Evelyn to the kitchen to crack ice into three small glasses and one large glass. And then we would sit in a circle on the floor around her; she'd open a 16-ounce bottle of Pepsi, fill her glass, then fill each of ours, and still have some left."

Because Mamma was always on her feet, she needed sturdy shoes with support that didn't come ready-made off the shelf. She had to have them made at Robert's Shoe Store in downtown Newnan. She would go in to select her shoes and put down a layaway deposit. And then, just before Easter, when the shoes arrived, they were paid for.

Revival Week

The sharecropper house was 1,100 square feet and didn't have indoor plumbing. We drew water from a well in the yard. But even with our large numbers, we somehow managed to make it work.

No doubt it helped that the house had a large kitchen, where we also ate our meals. Next to the kitchen was a large pantry. A wall separated it from the boys' room, where Walter, Thomas, Eugene, and I slept. We also shared our room with Grandpa Pete, who spent most of his time as a traveling minstrel. A door connected the boys' room to Mamma and Daddy's bedroom. Next to the boys' room was the girls' room, where my sisters slept three to a bed. And then the living room doubled as a guest room for family and visiting preachers during Revival Week.

Christianity was a way of life for our family. We prayed before every meal and before bed. We sang spirituals, and Eugene and Walter banged out notes on Mamma's piano in the girls' room. There were often box suppers on Saturday evening at the church. And then we spent most of Sunday at church.

I was six years old when I joined Oak Grove Baptist Church. I was baptized in Cedar Creek, a small tributary of the Chattahoochee River. The creek is less than a quarter of a mile down Sewell Mill Road from the Oak Grove graveyard, where my ancestors are buried.

Directly across the road from Cedar Creek was Sewell Mill, where we took our corn to be ground into meal. On the other side of the creek is rich bottomland, where my father worked the cotton fields as a young man.

White-robed candidates for baptism were led from the church and down the road to the creek, while the congregation sang soulfully, "Take me to the water. Take me to the water. None but the righteous shall be baptized."

As each candidate was dunked under the water and baptized in the name of the Father and of the Son and of the Holy Ghost, the singing would pause a moment and then continue as the next person was brought forth and the entire ritual repeated.

After the baptism, we changed out of our wet clothes behind a bush or in the back of someone's car and returned to the church for the rest of the service. All eyes were on you, seated on the front pew, as the newest members of the congregation.

The first week in August was the busiest and the happiest week in the life of Oak Grove Baptist Church. People came from all over, with members coming down from up North as if it were an extended family reunion.

The highlight of the first Sunday service was the pastor's sermon, which started around noon. After the service, there was a dinner on the church grounds. All of the families brought large boxes filled with dinners and spread them out on picnic tables. When those spots were filled, congregants spilled into the church parking lot and tailgated their meals. It was a time to reminisce and embrace people you hadn't seen since last homecoming, or maybe longer.

The dinner was followed by a second church service that started at three o'clock and was conducted by a visiting church, including its choir and minister.

The success of Revival Week was measured by the number of new members joining the church and by how much money was raised. The weeknight services began around 7 P.M. with the deacons leading a devotion and prayer service. Old-fashioned, soul-stirring hymns followed—such music as "A Charge to Keep I Have" and "Amazing Grace," to warm folks up for the visiting preacher to deliver an inspiring message. And then the doors of the church were "open" for new members to join. It wasn't unusual for old members to rededicate themselves to Christ during this phase of the service.

The deacons would then pass a collection plate that, to me, resembled a pie pan. You literally could hear what everyone else was giving by the sound it made, whether it was pennies, quarters, or fifty-cent pieces. Checks were unheard of because most black folks didn't have checking accounts in those days. Money either came out of your pocket, or it came out of your war chest.

Although Revival Week was important, Oak Grove Baptist was at the heart of our family life year-round. Both of my parents were leaders in the church, with Daddy serving in many ways, including as chairman of the Deacon Board. The deacons managed the money and the business affairs of the church, and they served as the stewards of its doctrines. But the women ran the church.

Among those women, my mother, who served as the choir director, was a member of the Mothers' Board, which oversaw everything from ushers to hospitality. Mamma also organized fundraisers such as box suppers, where dishes were brought to the church on a Friday or Saturday evening and auctioned off to raise money for Bibles, choir robes, fans, and church supplies.

Mamma always sat in the Amen Corner, right up front by the pulpit and closest to the congregation, my sister Barbara recalls. When someone shouted and fainted and we were amused, Mamma didn't have to say a word—just a hard stare, daring us to laugh, frown, or make any kind of gesture.

Saturdays in Downtown Newnan

On Saturdays, Mamma made us clean the entire house inside and out. Louise and Julia, the two oldest girls, helped Mamma scrub the floors with lye soap. When the boys came in from the fields at noon, we helped with outside chores, including sweeping the yard and tending the weeds in her flower and vegetable gardens.

After the house and yard were spotless, we bathed in a tin washtub, put on our starched jeans, and made ready for a trip to downtown Newnan that we looked forward to in happy anticipation all week long.

Newnan was a segregated Southern town that had signs of racial separation in all public places, including soda fountains and the Alamo, the only movie theater in town. "Colored" seating was upstairs. The best hamburgers came from a place called Barber's Corner, right next to the old Newnan First Baptist Church. We could buy a hamburger, but we would have to eat it outside. Whether you were a happy customer or not didn't matter.

At Sprayberry's Barbecue, one of my very favorite restaurants, you'd have to go to the back door to place your order. Blacks couldn't park in the drive-in for curbside service or sit at the tables inside. We sold them hickory wood they used to smoke their meat.

Today, I'm one of their best customers. Sometimes when I sit down for lunch, I remind them of our shared history. One of my favorite items on the menu is the "Lewis Grizzard" special, named after the famous *Atlanta Journal-Constitution* newspaper columnist and native son.

On Saturdays, while Mamma and the girls did their shopping at Kessler's department store and Daddy headed to Johnson Hardware, Eugene and I would walk around with our buddies, looking into store windows and hanging out around the older men on East Broad Street.

For a kid, it was exciting just to sneak in and sit quietly in the back of the barbershop and listen to the older guys tell stories of their hunting dogs, their favorite baseball stars, the big fish they caught, and the pretty girls they courted.

One Saturday, I was sitting there quietly in the back with my buddy Leroy Stegall when the barbershop stories were interrupted by an old man who came begging for change. Earlier that day, I had noticed him on the street corner and thought he must be really in need to come begging from black folks.

His plight moved me deeply. I had about a dollar after my fun in town, and I reached into my pocket and gave the beggar fifty cents, half of my pocket change. Some of the older men in the barbershop grunted their disapproval of my gesture. Although we were poor, my parents taught us that there were people worse off than we were who needed help. The negative reaction made me somewhat despondent, and I left the barbershop wondering whether I had done the right thing. As I walked toward our truck, with my head hung down, I saw a shiny quarter, just lying there on the sidewalk. I looked around and saw no one to claim it, picked it up, and, as we drove back home, I knew I had done the right thing.

"I want to be a businessman"

In many ways I had an idyllic childhood. As the youngest boy, I loved trailing after my big brothers and sisters in the fields and picking berries and plums. I was a mischievous child, getting on the nerves of my siblings at every turn. I was curious about how things worked. I asked so many questions that at one point Mamma said, "Boy, one day you are going to be president."

My mother's faith in me inspired me to always believe in myself and to know that I could accomplish my dreams. One day, when I was about twelve years old, my Uncle Alfonzo asked, out of the blue, "Sport, what you want to be when you grow up?" We were bundling sorghum cane and loading it on a wagon to take to the syrup mill.

"I want to be a businessman," I said.

"A businessman?" my uncle said, surprised. "What do you know about business? You don't wanna be a teacher? You don't wanna be a preacher? You look like a preacher to me." Teaching and preaching were two of the highest professions that blacks aspired to. My uncle had paid me a high compliment.

"No," I said. "I want to be a businessman." Even at that age, I was an avid reader. I devoured everything I could get my hands on, including a rare copy of the *Atlanta Daily World*, the oldest black newspaper in Atlanta. Its stories revealed successful black businessmen who owned their own businesses, including restaurants, insurance companies, funeral homes, and drugstores.

At such a young age, I had no idea what my dream of becoming a businessman really meant. Or that I was already learning my most valuable business lessons from my parents.

5

A BETTER LIFE

I began the first grade in 1949 at Mount Zion Elementary, a one-room schoolhouse two and a half miles from our new sharecropper home. No school buses carried black children in Coweta County back then, so we walked.

The Ware kids lived the farthest away, and we "picked up" other children as we went. There was safety in numbers. As the white school bus passed, the white kids would make it a sport to throw rocks at us from the windows. When we heard the bus coming, we stepped off the red dirt road and waited in the ditch until the vehicle passed.

I'll never forget the day when we were walking to school and it was raining, and we heard the school bus coming. As the bus passed, the white kids began throwing rocks at us from the windows, as though it was a planned attack. We ran into the woods to escape the assault. It made me so angry that I wanted to throw a rock back at them. I didn't, because if I had, I wouldn't be sharing this story now.

At an early age, we were taught to be untrusting of some white folks. But none of the Ware children were paralyzed by fear. We played with the white kids on the farm as if they were kinfolk. They were the children of the owners and the white straw bosses. Interestingly enough, these children never called us by the N-word. They called us by our names, and we played and had fun together.

Walter and Mildred recall a night, around that time, when hooded Klansmen attempted to invade our home. They must have spent a long time talking about it before they acted, because word got back to Daddy, and he was prepared when they came.

All of us small children were tucked into bed, and the lights were out. Those who could shoot took positions out of sight, and then Daddy waited on the front porch with a double-barreled shotgun.

They told Daddy they were looking for another man and asked if he had seen him, to which my father replied, "No, I haven't seen who you're looking for. I wish you all would just go on and leave me and my family alone."

And they did.

Miss Sadie Allen

My teacher for first grade through fourth grade was Miss Sadie Allen, a tall, fair-skinned, gentle lady whose husband served in World War II. Miss Allen was Mount Zion's principal and lead teacher. She was also a strict disciplinarian who didn't tolerate foolishness.

The odds were stacked against her achieving even the most basic order, given that the student-teacher ratio was something like one teacher to fifty students. The school didn't have electricity, so we read by the natural light streaming through the windows. We were kept warm by a coal-burning potbelly stove that heated only half of the classroom. When temperatures dipped below 30 degrees, we rotated our seats throughout the day to be closer to the stove.

To educate so many children across so many grade levels and ages, Miss Allen paired us off. In first grade I was matched up with Robert Wood, a second grader who later would be elected as the second black Coweta County commissioner since Reconstruction. Robert's assignment was to teach me everything he knew, including how to write in cursive.

We shared our textbooks because there weren't enough to go around. The textbooks we did have were the white schools' hand-me-downs, tattered volumes with missing covers and pages. To compensate, Miss Allen wrote out our math, English, and other homework assignments on the blackboard.

Miss Allen never used the poor conditions of the school as a reason not to give every student the opportunity to learn. Little did I know Miss Allen was teaching us a lesson that extended far beyond basic reading, writing, and arithmetic. For me, that lesson was how to persevere and overcome adversity through self-discipline and self-reliance.

Miss Allen never lowered her standards. If you didn't master a subject, you weren't promoted to the next grade. Or, as my sister Mildred put it, "If you didn't know it, you couldn't get away with not knowing it. You had to learn because she was the teacher, and she was going to make sure she did her job, whether you liked it or not."

At the end of my fourth-grade year, Mount Zion Elementary closed, and we were sent to another country school, about three miles away, in the community of Roscoe. Roscoe Elementary was not much bigger than Mount Zion, but it did have electric lights. Even better, by then there were school buses in Coweta County for black kids.

In 1952, when Dwight D. Eisenhower was elected president of the United States, the writing was on the wall that all American schools, even ones in the South, would eventually be integrated the same way President Harry Truman integrated the military in 1948.

In response, Coweta County put forth a last-ditch effort to start making "separate but equal" actually appear to be "separate but equal" to the federal government. The county built several new segregated schools for black children, including Northside Elementary, which I attended after Roscoe Elementary.

I loved to learn. I wanted to know why things were the way they were, and I would read everything I could find, particularly the Bible. When I read a Bible verse, it was always a little complicated because I couldn't catch the true meaning of every word and put it all together into something coherent.

What I enjoyed reading about most, however, were current events, which I devoured in the school's periodicals and also picked up via the radio.

There really wasn't much on the radio, though we listened to a lot of farm news. We would tune in to Mamma's favorite soap operas, including *Stella Dallas*. Eugene and I liked to listen to episodes of the cliffhanger *Boston Blackie*. We also listened intently to Saturday afternoon broadcasts of Major League Baseball games and marveled at such black pioneers as Jackie Robinson, Willie Mays, and Roy Campanella.

Buying the Land

Mamma and Daddy kept alive the dream of owning our own land, and so our main occupation as a family was to earn enough money to make a $500 down payment. "We were moving up and buying property, something of our own," my brother Walter remembers. "In my mind, it was a godsend."

The land Daddy wanted was a fifty-acre tract that was part of the land we were already working. It was owned by a man named Rex Hyde, who was willing to sell us the land for $100 an acre, bringing the total cost to $5,000. Hyde would accept payments of fifty dollars a month until the acreage was paid off. The agreement was sealed with a handshake.

It took a couple of years of hard labor to save the down payment. How that played out in our daily lives was that the boys took over the farm work, leaving our father free to pick up carpentry and other odd jobs on the side.

My father was so determined to get the down payment that we tried just about everything we knew to make money, including salvaging scrap metal from abandoned cars and worn-out farm equipment. That entailed using a blowtorch and a hacksaw to disassemble a vehicle and break it down into sections that we could lift onto the truck.

When we gathered enough for a truckload, we hauled it up to Atlanta to a place called J. T. Knight's Scrap Yard in the Summerhill section of the city. I was in awe of the gigantic magnet that was guided by a crane. It sucked the scrap iron from the bed of the truck. The scrap was then weighed to determine how much we got paid.

Whatever the amount, Daddy would always carve out the savings for the land first. Then he would take what was left, and we'd stop at the nearby farmer's market in Forest Park to buy oranges and apples by the crate and bananas by the stalk. Daddy would allow each of us to eat a banana on the way home. That was a treat, and it was a reward for our hard work.

Our job was to keep Paul Smith's farm running like clockwork and then to work on other farms in our spare time. Although by 1955 our numbers were shrinking as the oldest children left home, the sons and daughters of U. B. and Lois were still a formidable force.

Willie was by then serving in the Korean War. Louise, the second oldest, who inherited Mamma's gentle nature and was like a surrogate mother to her siblings, left to become a housekeeper in Atlanta's chic Buckhead section of town. Her compensation included room and board and a small paycheck of $25 a week. It wasn't much, but she still managed to save enough money in a fruit jar to send back home for the land.

I was eleven years old when I got my first paying job. I worked with my brothers Eugene, Thomas, and Walter clearing the bottoms on a farm ten miles north of Roscoe, in South Fulton County, for a country physician who everyone called Doc Tanner. We were paid eleven dollars a week.

Clearing the bottoms meant removing all of the underbrush in the swampland and getting it prepared as grazing land for cattle. We wore boots to protect against snakebites, covered our arms to fend off wasp stings and mosquitos, and wore hats—no matter how hot it was—to protect against heatstroke.

I remember Daddy gathering us boys around the hog pen for a powwow. "Boys, I want to take $7.50 from each one of you, to put toward the down payment on the land." Daddy personally collected all of our earnings from Doc Tanner himself. After extracting the $7.50, our father doled out $3.50 to each of us, which still jingled in our pockets.

His decision to take away almost all of our hard-earned cash was the subject of much grumbling. When we were clearing swampland in 95-degree heat and beating back snakes and mosquitos, "because Daddy said so" didn't make it any better.

The whole situation riled my brother Thomas. In retaliation, he got a job at Mathis Furniture Store in downtown Newnan, making twenty-two dollars a week. True to Daddy's old habit, he picked up Thomas's first paycheck. Thomas, like all of us, believed in the dream of owning our own land. But at sixteen, he was a grown man by rural standards, and he felt that he should be able to collect his own paycheck.

The second time Daddy went to the furniture store to pick up Thomas's paycheck, Thomas became so infuriated that he quit his job, joined the army, and left home for Fort Benning, Georgia.

Ultimately, we understood that everything our parents did was to give us a better life. We could see it in big things, such as the decision to buy the land, and in little things, such as Daddy giving up smoking cigars, his sole vice. Daddy figured he could take the money he spent on cigars, buy one large candy cane, and cut it up into eleven pieces with his pocketknife so that each of us could have a bite.

We were taught never to be ashamed of our circumstances, so even when we couldn't get to school until October, after the crops were in, we didn't look at it as deprivation. There were kids who would make fun of us because we were a little behind, but we always managed to get caught up and shrug it off.

I used some of the money I had earned from Doc Tanner to have *The Atlanta Constitution* newspaper delivered to our home every Sunday. I was determined that we would have a newspaper to read. I was curious about the business section, which was packed with people and current events. I always read the comics first, but then I'd go back to the business section and read it from beginning to end, then finish off with the baseball scores.

The year before we finally saved enough money for the down payment on the land was also the year we lost Grandpa Pete, whom I loved dearly. I was twelve years old.

Throughout his eighty-six years on this earth, Grandpa Pete had been a wanderer, traveling from place to place, a free spirit who seldom had a place of his own to return to, so every once in a while he came home to stay with us. The last time he came, he was sick and soon became bedridden.

Among my daily chores were to keep Grandpa Pete fed and bathed, to change his bed sheets, and to sanitize the room.

After Grandpa Pete died, Mamma told me, "You are going to be blessed for the rest of your life because you care so much for people and you did so much for your grandfather."

From that point on, anytime something good happened to me, my parents would remind me that God was blessing me because of what I did as a little boy, taking care of Grandpa Pete.

And I believe God is blessing me still.

6

BUYING THE LAND

We bought the fifty acres from Rex Hyde and began laying out plans for what was to us a modern four-bedroom house. It would have indoor plumbing, a spacious kitchen with a dining area, and a large hallway that doubled as a music room, piano and all. It also featured the one thing Daddy had always wanted: a basement where he could store his hand tools and set up his power saws to make furniture and fix things.

We didn't use a contractor, but Paul Smith volunteered as our "consultant." What's more, Daddy knew how to build a house, and he had four strong sons to help him.

Just as we didn't buy our meat or vegetables at the grocery store, Daddy's plan to frame the house didn't include buying timber from the lumberyard. By age forty-seven he was a master at recycling. Where others saw a falling-down house, Daddy saw potential building materials. Whenever he found an abandoned house, Daddy negotiated with the owner to tear it down in exchange for the salvaged lumber.

Much of the timber we used to build our house came from an old antebellum home in downtown Newnan. We salvaged two-by-fours, two-by-sixes, and two-by-eights that we used to frame walls, rafters, and floors.

My brothers and I learned valuable skills while building the house, skills that my father honed from the time he built the small sharecropper house with Paul Smith. We learned masonry, carpentry, and basic plumbing and electrical wiring.

We also learned how to frame and construct a hardwood floor— the hard way. Daddy had meticulously shown Eugene and me how to lay the hardwood flooring, fitting each tongue and groove until it was flush and ready to be nailed. Then he left us to work and went to town to take care of some other job.

Without Daddy there to oversee us, we ran into some glitches, specifically, getting each strip of flooring to fit flush. Still, Eugene and I forged ahead with our hammers, damaging the wood instead of taking our time to figure out what we were doing wrong.

When Daddy got home and assessed the damage, he made us rip up the entire floor and start all over. He said, "It takes as much time to do a job the wrong way as it takes to do it the right way." In other words, do it right the first time.

After we poured the concrete for what was to be a garage but became a sun porch, I used my fingertip to write in the wet concrete the date our new home was completed: "March 15, 1958."

No Notes

Even if my father had been able to get a loan from the bank to build the house, I doubt he would have done it. Just as we pooled our money to buy the land, we pooled our money on a pay-as-you-go basis to build the house. It took longer to build, but the end product was a debt-free home.

Daddy avoided debt as much as possible. One of his many practical mantras was "I don't want no notes in bed with me at night." He never took out a home loan. He never had a credit card. The only credit he used was at the grocery store in Arnco for things we could not make or grow. Even then, he would pay off the previous debt before he charged something new. And the IOU for the fifty acres? We paid that off in just five years.

As a result of his debt avoidance, my father did sleep well at night, and everything we had, we owned outright. His truck was old, but it got us from the field to the cotton gin and from home to town and back again. He was a man, very confident in himself, and too busy caring for his family to try to impress people by living beyond his means.

He also hedged his bets against the unpredictable.

In the fall, we harvested corn and stored it in stalls inside the barn to feed to the animals. We also took corn to Sewell Mill to be ground into cornmeal. Potatoes, a staple, were preserved in dirt mounds called potato hills. And Mamma canned plenty of vegetables, jams, and jellies for the winter months.

At the beginning of the first cold spell, just after Thanksgiving, came hog-killing time. For two whole days, our backyard became a festive slaughtering ground. Along with our hogs, Uncle Alfonzo and our neighbors, who included M. C. Mitchell, J. W. Kirkland, and J. C. Miller, brought their hogs for dressing as well.

After slicing up the carcasses and sorting and swapping meat parts, the community gathering would end with everyone taking home their favorite cuts for salting, smoking, grinding, and storing away for the winter months ahead. Consequently, our smokehouse out back was always stocked with country ham, pork shoulders, and sausage to see us through.

It was rare for us to slaughter a cow because we were so dependent upon them for milk and upon the bull for breeding. Mostly, we supplemented the pork with rabbits, squirrels, possums, and raccoons. We hunted to put meat on the table, but hunting was also the most fun outdoor activity of my childhood.

We were all equal in our parents' eyes, and nobody was exempt from hard work. Daddy built Mamma and my sisters a wooden quilting frame that hung on hooks from the ceiling during the day. At night, it was taken down and propped on chairs while the women sat around and stitched beautiful heirloom quilts that kept us warm at night.

There was always something for each one of us to do. For instance, we cleared the wooded areas to make way for new farmland. Using axes and a two-man crosscut saw, we cut down trees to be used for pulpwood and firewood, which we also sold.

Sugarcane stalks were harvested from the fields and hauled just a short way down the road to Daddy's syrup mill. My job was to hitch the mule to a long pole attached to the sorghum grinder and march the animal around and around in a circle. Once the mule got going on his own, Eugene and I alternated feeding the stalks of sugarcane into the grinder.

The juice was then poured into a big iron pot and cooked until it was syrupy. Daddy instinctively knew when the syrup was ready to be poured into the containers. He made the best sorghum syrup around, and he sold most of it. It was a staple of Mamma's kitchen, and it seemed like we ate syrup with every meal.

One day it rained so hard that the fields were too wet to continue plowing. Eugene and I unhitched the mules, whose names were Tom and Jim, and came in from the fields. Soon afterward, Daddy saw us goofing off, and, as though it was part of his grand plan, he quickly came up with another job for us to do: build a barn for the mules.

We started pulling nails from a pile of salvaged lumber, which we then sorted and stacked. It took us about three weeks to build Tom and Jim's barn. We must have done a good job because the shotgun-style structure is still standing in the same spot. It has been restored, but it serves as a constant reminder of the way things were back in the day.

One other early childhood incident that left an indelible mark on my character was the time I took something that did not belong to me.

Mamma and Daddy were selling chocolate bars to raise money for the church. They kept the unsold candy under their bed. When our parents were away, Thomas, Eugene, and I decided to help ourselves to a chocolate bar, figuring that one out of a whole box would not be missed. But when Daddy counted, he came up one short. It was so good that we didn't have the good sense to destroy the wrapper, which Daddy found under our bed.

He made the three of us drop our pants and bend over the old trunk in our room. He whipped us, making each of us take one bite of chocolate with every lick of his leather strap. And the whupping went something like this: *Wap!* "Take another bite!" *Wap!* "Take another bite!" *Wap!* "Take another bite!" So it went until we had devoured our second bar of candy.

I never again took anything that wasn't mine. And to this day, I don't care that much for chocolate.

7

FIND A WAY

The summer before I started my freshman year in high school, I secured two jobs on Temple Avenue in Newnan. I woke well before sunup and hitched a ride with Walter to my first job at Coweta Dairies. Starting at 4:30 A.M., I worked on a milk truck, delivering milk door-to-door to homes and small grocery stores around town.

We returned to the dairy at 7:30 A.M. and unloaded the crates of empty milk bottles so they could be put on a conveyor belt, washed, and refilled for the next morning's delivery. I was fortunate because my second job was at Jennings Supermarket, just across the street. At Jennings, I stocked the shelves, mopped the floors, and bagged groceries.

I probably made something like two dollars an hour working for the dairy and a dollar seventy-five at the grocery store. I earned enough to buy my school supplies, and I began to enjoy the great feeling of always having a little change in my pocket.

These summer jobs marked a transition from my preteen years of working on the farm to my teen years of working two jobs in the city. The days of the Ware family farming were largely behind us. After we built the new house and tried our hand at making a living from our land, my father's labor force, his strong sons and hardworking daughters, were leaving the farm to begin their own lives.

Without the extra hands to plant and reap the harvest, Daddy got a job at the William L. Bonnell Company (now Bonnell Aluminum), which had relocated to Newnan from Akron, Ohio, in the mid-1950s, when many Rust Belt companies moved to the more labor-friendly South.

My father was among the first laborers hired at the new plant, which made aluminum. It wasn't long before Daddy distinguished himself and proved his worth far beyond his labor maintenance job title.

One day, the big main furnace blew out, shutting down the plant because nobody knew how to fix it. My father and one of his closest friends, a black man named Mr. M. C. Mitchell, were the only workers with masonry skills, so the foreman asked them if they could come up with a repair solution. Meantime, the company sent for two young engineers from Akron.

When the engineers arrived the next day, they inspected the furnace, which by then was up and running again, but they could not figure out how it had been repaired. Upon request of the foreman, my father and Mr. Mitchell proudly explained the technique they had devised. It was to lap-bind the bricks so that the heat and air could not separate the masonry and cause another shutdown. Daddy learned his masonry skills building with Paul Smith.

Central High School

In the fall of 1957, I entered Central High School, leaving behind the country schools on dirt roads and going to a school in the city, where all of the streets were paved. The high school building itself was new yet still segregated.

Central must have been one of the best black high schools in the state of Georgia, given that it produced so many prominent African American businessmen and businesswomen, doctors, lawyers, and musicians, including ophthalmologist William "Hook" Hall, who worked on President Reagan following the infamous Hinckley assassination attempt, and Hamilton "Hamp" Bohannon, the famous R&B artist.

The primary reason for this distinction was that we had dedicated teachers and leaders such as professor F. A. Dodson, my high school principal.

Central High's Panthers excelled in all the three main sports, which were track and field, basketball, and football. The Panthers played their Friday night football games on Picket Field. The venue was shared with Newnan High, the white high school. To make that work, the coaches of the two institutions got together at the beginning of the year and made a schedule that allowed each school to take the field on alternating Fridays.

My favorite high school sport was basketball, and I played it with a passion. Daddy didn't mind us playing sports as long as it didn't conflict with our farm work. Fortunately, basketball season didn't begin until mid-November.

I still recall being jealous during basketball tryouts my sophomore year. We played on a dirt court in the schoolyard. As I was running through the basketball drills with the team, out of the corner of my eye, I saw my first girlfriend, Mary Francis Kelley, talking to a guy named Fred Bonner, who also liked her.

Mary Francis was the prettiest girl in the whole school. She was charming, sophisticated, well-dressed, and poised. She was my date for both the junior and senior proms, and she liked to laugh a lot and was fun to be around.

After practice was over, I asked Mary Francis what she had been discussing with Fred.

"Look, Carl," she told me firmly. "I can only drive one car at a time. And you are the car I am driving, so don't worry about it." Mary Francis was a city girl. She lived in a modest black neighborhood called Chalk Level.

After school I would walk her home, and we would sit on her front porch, with her old grandmother nearby, "nodding off to sleep"—meaning she was keeping an eye on us. Then I left for my job at the old Newnan Hospital downtown, which was for white people. The Newnan Colored Hospital was located in another black section of town called Rocky Hill.

I earned thirty-five dollars a week as an orderly and worked the night shift after school and on weekends. When my shift was over, I walked a good country mile down Temple Avenue to the William L. Bonnell Company plant, where Walter got off at 11 P.M., and then we rode home together.

The main focus of high school for me was getting a good education. The competition was fierce among my classmates, and we all had to stay on our toes. We were all striving for the highest academic honors, which would put us in the top 10 percent at graduation. There were exactly 100 students in my senior class, and I made the cut with the seventh-highest GPA.

At home, Daddy would say, "Be of good record," your grades being your record. That was the message. It was reinforced by dedicated teachers and counselors who, like Miss Sadie Allen, were disciplinarians who held us accountable and who had an unwavering commitment to preparing us for the future.

Ask any former Central High School student who's still around today to name the two most revered educators of that era, and the response will always be the same: Coach Betty McClendon, who oversaw the girls' athletic teams, and Coach Henry Seldon, who oversaw the boys. They both trained good students who excelled in sports.

Coach Seldon molded boys into men and was a no-nonsense educator on and off the field. He encouraged fun as long as we kept it clean, and he insisted that we behave as gentlemen, whether we were walking down the hall or riding on the team bus. He stressed the importance of dressing neatly and displaying strong character.

Coach Seldon's all-time record would include 120 wins and 41 losses, as well as many regional and state championships in football, basketball, and track and field.

Another teacher who was influential in my life was my English teacher, Miss Gordon. She taught old-fashioned grammar and diction. She also had us recite poetry in front of the class with clarity and conviction and then write it on the blackboard from memory. I enjoyed Emily Dickinson and Edgar Allen Poe but wasn't as wild about Shakespeare.

I gained a keen interest in math and science, which required a lot of discipline (not to mention brain power). In the process of learning how to study these subjects, I learned how to learn just about anything.

Anything but piano, that is. Determined that we would learn music, Mamma bought a used upright Whitney piano and started by teaching herself to play. She made progress quickly and soon began taking lessons from her friend Miss Katherine Strickland, a music teacher in town.

Eventually Mamma became the pianist and choir director for Oak Grove Baptist Church. She then encouraged Walter, Eugene, and me to take piano lessons. My brothers both did well and became accomplished pianists under Miss Strickland's tutelage. I went a couple of times, but my long fingers just couldn't seem to stay out of the way of each other.

The Sons of Calvary

Like Miss Strickland, Mr. Jones, my music teacher at Central, also helped me to understand that *my* instrument was my voice. I was already singing in the church choir, but then I joined the Sons of Calvary, a gospel group.

The members of the Sons of Calvary included my brother Eugene on piano and my second cousin Ernest on guitar. I sang lead and baritone in the "quartet" of five singers that featured Wilbur Cruver, Willie George Smith, Thomas Houston, and Leno Blandingburg, all guys I had known all of my life.

An older gentleman named Willie T. Hardy acted as our manager. He booked our engagements at black churches in Coweta, Carroll, Fayette, Troup, and Fulton counties. He negotiated our fees, which amounted to about two dollars and fifty cents each per engagement after he took his cut, which defied all of the math I had learned up to that point. He would always justify his agent's fee by citing extra "transportation costs" or "incidentals." In all fairness, he was a good promoter and booked us in competitive gospel concerts at city auditoriums in Carrollton, Newnan, and LaGrange. Believe me, that was a big deal back then.

Willie T. even managed to book the Sons of Calvary on a regular Sunday morning radio gospel program. We rehearsed every Thursday from 7 to 9 P.M., trying to emulate renowned gospel groups such as the Five Blind Boys of Alabama, the Soul Stirrers, and the Mighty Clouds of Joy. Two of our theme songs were "Oh, Mary, Don't You Weep" and "Look at the People Standing at the Judgement Waiting to Be Tried." We wore matching outfits. We donned blue or black suits with red neckties in the fall and winter and beige or white suits with colorful neckties in the spring and summer.

Traveling around singing the gospel became a central part of my identity.

One day, I came home after work and heard a tune I didn't recognize. Eugene was playing a smoky, irreverent piece on the piano that was definitely not gospel. So I asked him, "Man, what is that you're playing?"

"Jazz, man," Eugene responded. "Haven't you ever heard jazz before?" It turned out that our high school music teacher, Mr. Jones, had been teaching him these new chords and syncopations. I could not remember ever hearing that kind of music across the street from Central at Hines' Cafe, where the jukebox played mostly blues, R&B, and rock 'n' roll.

Eugene Steps Back

I graduated from high school in 1961, marching with Eugene, who was eighteen months older but had been held back a year in elementary school because he had an asthmatic condition that often left him too sick to attend.

We both had good grades that made us eligible for college, but our parents couldn't afford to send two of us. Eugene made a sacrifice and stepped back so that I could attend. He aspired to become a professional musician and wanted to study at a prestigious music school. "Man, you go on to college," he told me. "I'll wait until later to get my music degree."

I applied and got accepted to three colleges, and Clark College was my top choice. The tuition, room, and board, however, came to a seemingly insurmountable $975, a fortune to us. It didn't matter. My parents were dead set on finding a way for me to attend Clark, no matter what it took.

So, Daddy persuaded his brothers in the Prince Hall Masons to grant me a $100 scholarship. Mamma led the Oak Grove congregation in taking up a collection for another $100. Clark College granted me a $200 music scholarship, and I was honored to be asked by the head of the music department, the renowned Dr. J. Dekoven Killingsworth, to sing baritone in the Philharmonic Society.

Miss Martha Smith, an administrator at Newnan Hospital, liked my work, so I asked her if she and the doctors could help me get a job at Grady Memorial Hospital in Atlanta to help pay for my college education there.

The white doctors went far beyond recommending me for a job at Grady. They got together and decided they would sponsor my college education if I agreed to study premed, go on to medical school, become a doctor, and return to Newnan to practice. I was excited about their offer and couldn't wait to get home to tell Mamma and

Daddy the good news.

My father then taught me a lesson about the importance of standing on my own two feet so that I would be free to make my own decisions and direct my own destiny. A day or two later, he came home and said, "Son, I've talked to the doctors, but your family is going to find a way to send you to college. You can study whatever you want to study. You can be a doctor if you want, but with God's help, we'll figure out a way."

I wasn't disappointed in Daddy's decision. I was proud to be the son of Lois and U. B. Ware.

When it was time, both parents drove me the hour north to Clark's historic campus. Our big blue 1953 Buick was loaded down with everything I would need for my new dorm room, including a huge wooden trunk with metal straps, a family heirloom.

Once we arrived at Clark, I unloaded the car and checked into Pfeiffer Hall, the men's dormitory. That day marked the beginning of a routine of full-time work and full-time classwork that would last for the next four years.

I got settled on campus and then, on that very first day, I reported for work at Grady Hospital. I put in eight hours on the graveyard shift, from 11 P.M. to 7 A.M., which was great, because after I made my rounds, I could study and take a nap until the nurses rang my bell. When my shift was done, I caught the Fair Street trolley from downtown back to campus, grabbed my books, and went straight to my first class. And then I repeated that cycle.

8

CRADLE OF CIVIL RIGHTS

The year I entered Clark College, 1961, was the same year that Charlayne Hunter-Gault and Hamilton Holmes integrated the University of Georgia. The year before, four African American college students sat at a "whites only" Woolworth's lunch counter in Greensboro, North Carolina, and refused to leave.

The nonviolent protests ignited student activism at black college campuses across the South. Within days of the Greensboro sit-ins, a group of Atlanta University Center students met at Yates & Milton Drug Store on Hunter Street to form the Atlanta Student Movement.

Among the leaders of the student movement in Atlanta were such men and women as Danny Mitchell, Ben Brown, and sisters Wilma and Carolyn Long from Clark College, as well as Julian Bond and Lonnie King from Morehouse. Wilma would go on to become a respected educator. Carolyn, in 1980, would become the first African American woman elected to the Atlanta City Council.

Ben Brown was a scholar-politician. After the passage of the Voting Rights Act of 1965, he would be among eleven African Americans elected to the Georgia General Assembly and would later deliver the critical black electorate that helped to put Jimmy Carter in the White House. Ben would serve as deputy chair of the Democratic National Committee.

Julian would be nominated as a candidate for vice president at the 1968 Democratic National Convention. At twenty-eight, he didn't meet the constitutional age requirement of thirty-five to hold that office. It didn't matter. The nomination was a ploy to allow Julian to deliver a historic anti-Vietnam War speech during prime-time television coverage.

Those of us lucky enough to attend Atlanta's historically black colleges in the early 1960s grew up in the presence of great leaders such as Dr. Martin Luther King Jr., who frequently spoke during student rallies at the Atlanta University Center.

Like me, many of my classmates were first-generation college students, so missing even a single moment of our education was unthinkable. But through his teachings, Dr. King made us see that the causes of freedom and equality were equally important.

That historic first meeting at Yates & Milton Drug Store also gave birth to the Committee on the Appeal for Human Rights. This special body had student representatives from Clark College, Morehouse College, Morris Brown College, Spelman College, Atlanta University, and the Interdenominational Theological Center.

Before launching the Atlanta sit-in campaign, the students published their grievances in the local newspapers, both black and white:

> Today's youth will not sit by submissively while being denied all of the rights, privileges, and joys of life. We want to state clearly and unequivocally that we cannot tolerate a nation professing democracy, and among people professing democracy, and among people professing Christianity, the discriminatory conditions under which the Negro is living today in Atlanta, Georgia—supposedly one the most progressive cities in the South.

The first Atlanta sit-ins began six days later.

Everyone had a job in the civil rights movement. Some marched or made posters while others received nonviolent training to prepare them for going on freedom rides and to jail. Our professors let us make up homework assignments, rescheduled exams, and opened the science labs in the evenings and on weekends so we could catch up.

The main thing Dr. King emphasized was that we had to have the self-discipline to adhere to the philosophy of nonviolent protest. He taught that nonviolence was a powerful weapon against oppressors. I embraced Dr. King's goals without reservation until I took part in a sit-in at Grady Memorial Hospital, where I also worked as an orderly during my sophomore year.

Grady Memorial Hospital was known as "the Gradies" because there were two hospitals, one black, one white. Hugh Spalding Hospital was the black Grady, the only place black doctors were allowed to practice. The main building was the white Grady.

In my job as an orderly, I worked in all areas of both hospitals, including obstetrics, the two segregated emergency rooms, and the morgue in the basement. All of my patients were white at Newnan Hospital. Grady was a mixed bag.

The student sit-in was staged in the "whites only" reception area. We just sat quietly in chairs and on the floor in protest. The guy sitting next to me was a Morehouse College student. As we sat there, a white man stepped toward us holding a glass Coke bottle. As he swung the bottle in front of our faces, we ducked. On the second pass, he smashed the bottle over the Morehouse student's head, sending blood gushing everywhere. Luckily, it was a superficial wound, but in any event, it didn't stop the cops from loading the protestors into a police wagon and carting us off to the city jail a block and a half away on Marietta Street.

As usual, black leaders like Jesse Hill and attorney Leroy Johnson were there in no time to bail us out.

But there was something about the bloody attack in the "whites only" admission area that got to me. The idea of allowing someone to perpetrate such a cowardly act with impunity just didn't sit right. I understood the importance of nonviolent, peaceful protest, but I doubted turning the other cheek time after time. I knew that one day I could react in a way that might not only hurt the cause but endanger the lives of other people in the movement.

In 1962, my sophomore year, the Supreme Court ordered Grady to begin desegregating all of its facilities. It would not be integrated into "one" Grady until the year of my graduation, 1965.

The Civil Rights Act of 1964, which outlawed discrimination based on race, color, religion, sex, or national origin, passed into law on July 2, 1964, in the summer before my senior year. It made segregation illegal, but change did not come overnight. I remember participating in a protest march on July 3, 1964, against a restaurant called the Pickrick, near the Georgia Tech campus. It had good fried chicken at a reasonable price but was off limits to blacks.

When three of the protesters attempted to enter the restaurant to place an order, the owner, a self-avowed white racist named Lester Maddox, threatened the would-be black customers with a pickax handle. Rather than integrate, Maddox closed the restaurant. But photographs of Maddox wielding the pickax handle at peaceful demonstrators made national headlines.

The Civil Rights Act must have been a blow to Maddox, a man who had already logged two failed runs for mayor of Atlanta on a segregationist platform. The first was against William B. Hartsfield in 1957, followed by Ivan Allen Jr. in 1961.

Maddox was a smart politician who knew that his segregationist tactics in Atlanta would appeal to the broader white constituency across the state. Indeed, he was elected in 1966 as governor of Georgia on the same segregationist platform that he used in his failed runs for Atlanta mayor.

Uncle Eddie Lee's Death

In my junior year, a tragic incident occurred back home with the death of my uncle Eddie Lee Ware. It was almost a carbon copy of the murder of our neighbor Ernest "Buster" Brown.

Uncle Eddie was a house painter and a very handsome man who was popular around Newnan in the sense that he loved to have fun and people adored him, both black and white. His mangled body was found on the railroad tracks near Chalk Level, where he lived. His body reeked of alcohol, according to the Newnan police report. So the finding was that he got drunk and stumbled onto the tracks, where he was hit by a train. Uncle Eddie was no teetotaler, but he loved life.

No one believed that Uncle Eddie would put himself in a position to be killed by a train, either through suicide or by accident, no matter how drunk he got. Like other accidents of this sort in Coweta County, Uncle Eddie's death was never investigated.

Uncle Eddie Lee died on March 2, 1964. Uncle Eddie's son, Willie Ware, told me that even after fifty years, the family has yet to receive a report from law enforcement of any investigation into the cause of death. Suspiciously, the death certificate stated the cause of death as "heart attack." The family believes that Uncle Eddie's death was neither an accident nor a suicide.

9

Meeting Mary

Growing up hard on a farm, I learned early on that if I wanted to work somewhere other than the cotton field, I needed an education. My decision to attend Clark College was based on its stellar reputation as an institution of higher learning that produced successful and effective black leaders.

At the time, only five percent of the black population in the entire country completed a four-year degree. Our professors taught us that we stood on the shoulders of many other people, and they made it clear to us that we were privileged and had a moral obligation to use our degrees to make the world better for people of our race.

The professors at Clark earned their doctoral degrees from such prestigious institutions as Harvard, Berkeley, New York University, Columbia, and Northwestern, among others. Dr. James P. Brawley, who served as president of Clark College for forty years, handpicked professors who were committed to excellence in black higher education.

Some of my more notable professors included Dr. Esther Jackson, head of the speech and drama department, and Dr. Stella Brewer Brooks, chair of the English department. Dr. Pearlie Dove, another standout, put Clark College's education department on the national radar screen.

My speech and drama class was especially rewarding and sometimes taught by big-name actors such as husband-and-wife team Ossie Davis and Ruby Dee, who performed on campus and who were staunch civil rights activists.

I began my college career as a premed student, but the long lab hours did not mesh well with my long work hours at Grady, which I needed in order to stay in school. It was a catch-22, but I decided that the most important thing for me was earning a degree.

Besides, all of the upperclassmen I wanted to emulate studied the social sciences, and I was impressed by their involvement in campus life and civil rights. Those influential classmates were on the Clark debate team, which held its own with Ivy League schools in intercollegiate competitions. Some of their names included Haskell Ward, future deputy mayor of New York City; Lamond Godwin, future vice president of American Express Bank; James Felder, future US Marine and pallbearer for President John F. Kennedy; and Robert Tucker, future chairman of the New Orleans Port Authority.

In the summer following my freshman year at Clark, a high school buddy of mine, John Elder, gave me a line on a job at C&S Bank in downtown Atlanta. He had just been hired as a janitor, and there was another opening. I followed up and got the job, cleaning the offices of key executives, including C&S Bank president Mills B. Lane.

In a short time, I got promoted from janitor to mail porter. I liked the new job because it entailed trust and gave me exposure to the banking profession. I also liked it because I got to drive a three-wheeled motor scooter and wear a smart outfit that resembled a police uniform. It consisted of a gray shirt with blue necktie, blue trousers, and a police-style cap.

I did a good job shuttling mail between the Mitchell Street branch and C&S main office, so I was given more responsibility. Next, I drove a panel truck to the various C&S bank branches around the city to pick up mail pouches and bring them to Mitchell Street for sorting and redistribution.

One day, after I returned to the Mitchell Street branch and was emptying the mail pouches on the massive sorting table, several thick stacks of cash fell out of one of the pouches.

It was the most money I'd ever seen in my life. I immediately called my boss, William Perry, at his home in Southwest Atlanta.

He told me not to touch it, that he'd be right down. Once Bill arrived, he counted all $30,000 of it and locked it in a safe. I thought that was the end of the episode.

So, I was surprised when the branch manager, Wade Mitchell, who would be elected as a city alderman in 1969, came into the bank the next day to formally commend me for my integrity and the way I handled the matter.

My experiences as a mail porter fueled my interest in banking. In the summer before my senior year, I thought I saw a way to move up the ladder another rung when a group of white college kids came in to do internships. I got to know one of the interns fairly well and asked him how he had been selected. I hesitated but decided to ask the personnel director if I could apply for the American Banking Institute internship program.

The personnel director didn't hesitate to tell me that banking was not a field that I should be thinking about, and he strongly discouraged my interest in the internship program. I was very disappointed but, given the times, not surprised. There were no blacks in any professional-level jobs at C&S at that time—no tellers, no loan officers, and certainly no branch managers.

Later in my life, I would come face-to-face with this same personnel director, who by then had left C&S to join a prestigious executive search firm, so our roles were reversed. I was the chairman of the Clark Atlanta University Board of Trustees, and we were conducting a search for a new president. The former personnel director didn't recognize me, and I didn't let on that I knew who he was. I refused to allow his previous behavior toward me to cloud my judgment in selecting the best search firm for the job. We chose his firm.

Pennies, Nickels, and Dimes

Clark College gave me much more than an education. It was where Mary Alice Clark and I met. The day I met Mary was a beautiful day, the first of many over fifty-two years of marriage and counting.

A bunch of us guys were hanging out on the quadrangle behind the administration building when Mary and a bunch of her girlfriends walked past us. At the sight of pretty girls, we began whistling and tossing pennies, nickels, and dimes to rank them amongst ourselves and get their attention—truly, a schoolboy prank.

The girls, amused by our silly antics, stopped. We all got into conversations, and I spoke to Mary. As she playfully tells the story, even today, "I got a dime."

She was beautiful and petite, smart, elegant, and poised. She remembers me as a popular guy on campus who could sing and dance.

She was a freshman and I was a junior.

We came from different family backgrounds. I was a country boy and she was a city girl. But we still had some important things in common. Namely, our parents taught us the value of hard work and education, and they pushed us to achieve.

While I grew up one of eleven on the farm, Mary grew up one of six in Southwest Atlanta in a working-class black neighborhood known as Dixie Hills. Her father, Laron Clark, started his working life on a dairy farm, where her parents also met. Her mother, Doshia Blossomgame, whom we called "Miss Doshia," was a housekeeper, while Mr. Clark was a farmhand.

The dairy farm was located in a whites-only area of Southwest Atlanta. Black folks had to work in all-white neighborhoods but live in all-black neighborhoods, often far away.

Mr. Clark lived in the tiny town of Palmetto, twenty miles south of the dairy, and he needed a car to get to work. Out of necessity and through much personal sacrifice, my future father-in-law purchased an inexpensive old car and began driving it to and from his job at the dairy farm.

The very car that Mr. Clark needed to keep his job was the thing that made him lose it. When the overseer of the dairy farm saw the car, he asked to whom it belonged. Mr. Clark claimed ownership, to which the white boss replied, "Well, you need to find you another job." No other explanation was given, leaving Mr. Clark stunned after a few years of being a conscientious and, he thought, valuable farmhand.

Mr. Clark did not allow this misfortune to become a setback in his life. He met Mr. Harold Andrews, later a deacon at Oak Grove Baptist Church, who was working at Atlanta Gas Light Company. Mr. Andrews helped Daddy Clark (as we all called him later) get a job at the gas company, where he worked until his retirement, more than forty years later.

Like my mother, Miss Doshia was utterly devoted to her children and their education. In fact, all six of her children attended college, the first generation in the Clark-Blossomgame lineage to do so.

Our courtship took some maneuvering because of my busy schedules for class and work. We might catch a movie once in a while or spend time together at the home of my sister Louise or that of Mary's parents.

I completed all of my course requirements for graduation by the end of the first semester of my senior year. That meant I finally had time to enjoy college life a little more on the party side.

I continued to work full time for C&S as a mail porter but also picked up odd jobs on the weekend. They ranged from washing cars to janitorial work and preparing the set of the WSB-TV newsroom at White Columns on Peachtree.

During my senior year I lived with my sister Mildred and her four children on Penny Lane in Eagan Homes, a public housing project in Vine City. Mildred had a car, a bluish-gray four-door Dodge. It was so old that one day, as I was driving along Hunter Street, now Martin Luther King Jr. Drive, the hood blew off! The incident caught me completely off guard, because it was my role to keep the car road-worthy and its tank full of gas. Fortunately, no injuries resulted, and I had enough money to get it fixed. And I never told Mildred.

During my senior year I joined Kappa Alpha Psi fraternity. To be a part of this distinctive group was a real opportunity. Apart from the popularity of the Kappas on campus, I was intellectually attracted to the fundamental purpose of Kappa Alpha Psi, which was achievement. Years later, I was honored when my close friend and fellow Clark-ite Sam Hamilton, the fraternity's Grand Polemarch, presented me with the Laurel Wreath, our highest award.

Dr. Wiley S. Bolden

It may be true that some of the most auspicious chance meetings in life take place in the produce section at the grocery store. While I was working on this book, I was picking up something for Mary at the Kroger near our home when I ran into Dr. Wiley S. Bolden. My old professor, friend, and former dean of students was easily recognizable to me, even at age ninety-eight.

I spoke with him and, after a little squinting, he recognized me, too, and he introduced the lovely young woman at his side: his great-granddaughter, a freshman at Clark Atlanta University. After we exchanged quick pleasantries, I asked if he might have a few minutes at some point to rehash old times, given that I was writing my memoirs.

56

A couple of weeks later, he made time to sit down and talk. He reminded me that until the 1960s, segregation was so widespread that there was no place you could go in the South to get a master's degree except Atlanta University. If, somehow, you got the money and managed to get accepted to one of the white Ivy Leagues outside the South, like Princeton, you could go, but they could not house you in the dorms because they had no facilities for black students.

By 1965, the world outside the South had begun to open up, as white schools offered opportunities to black students. Because the South continued to ignore the Civil Rights Act of 1957 and would not allow black students into Southern universities, the states had to pay the difference between what it would cost you to go out of state for school and what it cost if you stayed in your home state for your education.

Oddly, Dr. Bolden said, those circumstances turned out to be an advantage for some students, including me. As dean of students, part of his job was to match graduating seniors who wanted to pursue postgraduate studies. He got to know all of his students, and he knew me as a conscientious young man from his psychology class.

One day, as I was walking across campus with Dr. Bolden, he asked me about my plans for the future. There I was, on the cusp of graduation, and uncertain about my next steps. Teaching was an option. But I wanted to go on to graduate school or perhaps to law school.

"If I don't go to grad school, I think I'll probably get a job teaching and may go back to my hometown," I responded with uncertainty.

"Come to my office," Dr. Bolden said. "I want to show you some information about a fellowship that you should apply for."

What Dr. Bolden had earmarked for me was an Office of Economic Opportunity internship at Carnegie Institute of Technology, now Carnegie Mellon University, in Pittsburgh. It was open to students from historically black colleges in the South who had at least a B average. The family income had to fall below the poverty line, around $3,000 a year back then. My parents' income fell well below that figure.

"They said, 'We do not necessarily want the valedictorian of the class, but we want a person who will work well with disadvantaged young teenagers and is just an all-around good person,'" Dr. Bolden recalled at his beautiful home in Southwest Atlanta.

Dr. Bolden chose me because of my leadership potential, which he recognized when I successfully ran for president of the Clark College Men's Association. The goal of that group was to get Clark men actively participating in the low-income neighborhoods surrounding the campus as well as assuming leadership roles on campus.

At Dr. Bolden's urging, I applied to Carnegie, in competition with students from historically black colleges and universities across the South.

I was one of twenty who got in.

10

BECOMING AN URBANOLOGIST

Mary and a small crowd of well-wishing friends walked me onto the tarmac as I boarded United Airlines to Pittsburgh, Pennsylvania, in mid-September 1965, my first flight anywhere. I felt both excited and apprehensive. As the plane approached the city, two hours later, I was perplexed by the golden-yellow haze that turned out to be pollution from steel mills. I had never seen anything like that before.

From the airport, I grabbed a taxi to Squirrel Hill, a wealthy, predominantly Jewish neighborhood, where I would move into an old red brick house on Beechwood Boulevard that had been subdivided into apartments. Eight of Carnegie's historically black college and university scholars from the South would call this place home for the next year.

My new roommate was a Morehouse man named Art Davis, whose hometown was Raleigh, North Carolina. We dropped our luggage and immediately went in search of rags to wipe down the windows, which were thick with yellow grime. Art was smart and a genuinely good guy. I quickly learned that he had his own nuances about food, meaning he didn't share it willingly. But being the only Atlanta guys, the two of us had a lot in common, and we genuinely liked each other.

The next morning, Miss Millie Wolf, our group coordinator, assembled all of us on campus at the Margaret Morrison College of Carnegie Tech for orientation. As we went around the room to introduce ourselves, I learned that we all had a lot in common, from our experiences growing up in the South to HBCU sororities and fraternities.

The Office of Economic Opportunity internship was a work-study program that required us to spend twenty hours a week in class and another thirty hours a week working with agencies that focused on community development in Pittsburgh neighborhoods.

My work assignment was with the Allegheny Council to Improve Our Neighborhoods, called ACTION Housing and established in 1957 by then-mayor David Lawrence and philanthropist Richard King Mellon to address the city's most pressing housing issues. I was thrilled to learn that Art Davis and I had both been selected to work at this prestigious agency, one of the leading community development corporations in urban America.

ACTION Housing assigned Art and me to help organize block clubs and tenant associations. We were the staff for the neighborhood leaders, who tended to be strong black men and women. They performed these roles on a volunteer basis and represented their neighborhoods in meetings with the Pittsburgh power structure.

The leader I would learn the most from was a woman named Mrs. Dorothy Mae Richardson. Art and I were assigned to help Mrs. Richardson organize her Central Northside neighborhood through an organization called Citizens Against Slum Housing, or CASH.

Mrs. Richardson was a housewife and Pittsburgh native who grew up in the Central Northside neighborhood, where she attended school and started her family. She owned her own home on Charles Street and took pride in making it the showcase of the neighborhood. In our first meeting with her, Mrs. Richardson told Art and me that she simply wanted her surrounding neighborhood to have the same qualities. The solution was not to tear down the whole neighborhood, she said. The solution was to have the slumlords repair and maintain their properties and to organize the residents in cleaning up and beautifying the neighborhood.

As staff to Mrs. Richardson and CASH, Art and I passed out flyers in the neighborhood, going door-to-door to encourage residents to attend meetings. We also kept meeting minutes, organized cleanup campaigns and community garden projects, and taught people the meaning of sweat-equity housing rehabilitation projects. One of the most rewarding aspects of our job was getting kids involved in the community around the creation of parks and playgrounds.

Mrs. Richardson reminded me of my mother. She was a heavyset woman with a medium-brown complexion who looked you straight in the eye when she spoke to you. She treated Art and me like we were her children. She would invite us into her home, where she conducted CASH meetings with tenants and homeowners, often with such guests as Jim Cain, ACTION Housing's rehabilitation specialist, and the City of Pittsburgh housing-code-enforcement officials. The Carnegie program would position me to learn firsthand the intricacies of urban community development.

Because the majority of blacks in Pittsburgh were more likely to live in the city's segregated and dilapidated housing, they were more likely to be forced out of their homes than whites. City code inspectors went to blighted areas such as Northside, the Hill District, and Homewood-Brushton to inspect homes for code violations. When houses were declared unfit for human habitation, the owners were given a reasonable amount of time, usually thirty to forty-five days, to correct the violations. Otherwise the house was condemned and the occupants were evicted.

Northside housing, like that in other blighted neighborhoods, was substandard and egregiously below code. The physical condition of the homes—often with leaking roofs, faulty electric wiring, unsanitary plumbing, and broken windows—made these structures unfit for human habitation. As bad as the structural problems were, the sanitation was even worse. There was hardly any semblance of extermination for rodents or roaches, and garbage piled up uncollected on the streets for weeks at a time. The place was a slum.

The tenants who were evicted were relegated to public housing projects that further exacerbated the urban housing crisis.

One of the ways CASH fought back was by organizing tenants to withhold their rents and pressure the landlords to make improvements. The rent-withholding strategy was an effective tool in some cases. In others, powerful landlords evicted tenants for nonpayment, violating court orders. I vividly recall black families being evicted from their homes and forced into even worse slum areas because they dared to join a rent strike.

Mrs. Richardson became a powerful voice for change. When she spoke her mind about cleaning up her neighborhood and saving the community, people listened. City Hall listened. Business leaders listened. And some slumlords listened. My bosses at ACTION Housing not only listened but partnered with CASH in the effort to realize this articulate and powerful Pittsburgh woman's dream.

I listened, too. I learned so much from her strong leadership. I began, in my professional career, to convince people to do the right thing. Mrs. Richardson would listen, and she would make demands only when people refused to do the right thing.

The CASH community action model was closely monitored by the US Department of Housing and Urban Development, headed by Robert C. Weaver. In 1966, under President Lyndon Johnson, he became the first secretary of HUD and the first African American to be appointed to a US Cabinet-level position. After his appointment, federal funding began to flow to cities in earnest to address the urban blight that was choking major American cities and spurring unrest nationwide.

Eventually, sixteen financial institutions would join CASH's efforts by creating a revolving low-interest-rate loan fund to rehabilitate rundown houses.

Although I was just a student there to organize, such an education was priceless. It was not uncommon to come into work on a Thursday morning at ACTION Housing and see Mrs. Richardson preparing for a press conference. It intrigued me to see how she wielded the raw power bestowed upon her by her neighborhood to force change.

In 1968, the year the Fair Housing Act passed into law, Mrs. Richardson's efforts led to an entirely new field of community-based development with the founding of Neighborhood Housing Services of Pittsburgh. Its nonprofit model quickly became an important resource for community leaders across the country. A decade later, Congress institutionalized it with the Neighborhood Reinvestment Corporation, today called NeighborWorks America, a nonprofit network of more than 240 community development organizations working in urban, suburban, and rural communities.

Learning How to Eat Spaghetti

The Carnegie internship proved to be a powerful experience for me in so many ways. It was a good education for me because I've always been a constant observer of people, especially people I think I can learn from. In fact, that's how I learned to eat spaghetti Bolognese the correct way, Italian style.

Because we were so closely aligned with Mellon and Carnegie in-stitutions, we were exposed to virtually every art and cultural museum experience in the city. They even helped us to open up bank accounts at Mellon National Bank. Because Pittsburgh is predominantly a Catholic city, one of our most memorable visits was a dinner for the HBCU group hosted at the Oakland home of a prominent Catholic parishioner.

We all sat down at a formal dining table. I took one look at all of the knives and forks and spoons and immediately knew I had no idea what to do at all. Clark College had taught us many things to prepare us for the world, like how to eat a salad.

But never did anyone there broach the subject of spaghetti.

Unlike some of my classmates, I didn't touch the perfectly dis-played food on my plate. I waited and watched others, nibbling on a piece of bread until I had figured it out. The proper way to eat spa-ghetti entails gouging the spaghetti with your fork and then twisting it around on the largest spoon from the place setting until you have a manageable, rolled-up bite of pasta.

11

Praying for Guidance

Over my Christmas break, I returned home from Pittsburgh to marry Mary. We were expecting our son, Timothy, a fact that we had managed to keep a secret.

Surrounded by family and friends, we were married on January 1, 1966, in a small but lovely ceremony in Mary's parents' home.

As our families came together, we learned we had even more in common than we had realized. Amid all the laughter and happiness, we learned that our fathers had known each other as teenagers and had great stories to tell about working in the fields, and about hunting and fishing together.

The wedding was followed by a one-night honeymoon at the Walahaja Hotel & Ballroom on Chapel Road in Southwest Atlanta. It's closed now, but its elegant accommodations at the time made the Walahaja the Ritz-Carlton of black hotels. It was the place where, if you had attended an affair there, you had made it.

After the short honeymoon, on January 3, I once again left Atlanta and drove back to school in my 1964 Mustang, my first car. I had purchased it with a down payment of $500 and financed the $2,000 balance. It was cheaper than buying a plane ticket and saved me from the two-way, sixteen-hour Trailways bus ride.

The Mustang was only two years old, but it was already an American classic because of its smart design, sleek styling, and affordability. My car was burgundy with bucket seats and four-on-the-floor.

My fascination with Mustangs began in college. If I needed a car for the prom or the Kappa Dawn Dance, or if my buddies and I went to a Clark-Tuskegee football game, we always rented a Mustang. I drove that Mustang throughout my Pittsburgh years. In fact, I liked it so much that I drove it for a few years after returning to Atlanta. Finally, I gave it to my father, who proudly drove it around Newnan until it died.

After our marriage in January, Mary put her studies on hold so she could join me in Pittsburgh that March. I rented another apartment for us and the baby, just a few blocks away on Dalzell Place in Squirrel Hill. Soon after Mary arrived, our son, Timothy Alexander Ware, was born at Magee-Womens Hospital on April 9, 1966.

I embraced fatherhood with enthusiasm, and I focused on my education and work as I had never done before. After all, what was at stake was the future of my family, not merely my career. That meant I was almost always working or in class. I wasn't sleeping much, and the rigid schedule frequently left Mary home alone with our infant son.

We found a capable and cheerful sixteen-year-old to help Mary after school. The girl also kept Mary and the baby company until I returned home in the evenings. At twenty, Mary was almost a child herself. And it was her first time living away from the comfortable surroundings of her family and friends in Atlanta. There was nothing to be done about the icy, cold Pittsburgh winters, which she never adjusted to.

We put forth our best effort to make it work, even though our finances were extremely tight. We discussed how to handle the situation and decided that Mary and the baby would be better off in Atlanta, where we already had a solid family support system in place. The decision to be separated from my wife and child was not an easy one, but it was the right thing to do.

So, in early August, we packed up the Mustang and drove back to Atlanta. Then I returned to Pittsburgh to prepare for graduate school. The Carnegie program had ended, and I received a graduate fellowship in the master's degree program at the University of Pittsburgh Graduate School of Public & International Affairs, or GSPIA.

Although separated by almost 700 miles, Mary and I talked on the phone every day for as long as we could afford in an era when long-distance calls were paid for by the minute. I always drove back home for holidays. We learned a valuable lesson during those early days of our marriage that would continue to serve us well throughout our lives together: we didn't need to be in each other's presence all the time to build a lasting relationship. We nurtured every moment we were blessed to have together.

Almost a year later, the Detroit riots broke out—first, as an immediate response to police brutality, but also heavily fueled by anger over segregated housing and schools, and over rising black unemployment. This weeklong uprising would become one of the most violent and deadliest urban revolts in the history of our nation. More than 7,000 people were arrested, most of them black. Of the forty-three people left dead, all but ten were African Americans.

In a sense, the crises in American cities inspired me to pursue studies in urban affairs with even more determination to help shape policy and programs that would address the root causes of urban rioting.

What made the eighteen months at GSPIA so exciting was that Pittsburgh, already dubbed an "urban laboratory," was on the cutting edge of urban planning. Between my GSPIA and Carnegie experiences, I was getting a comprehensive understanding of urban planning and public policy. I studied physical planning elements such as street engineering, design, and construction; city management; economic development; and housing and social planning.

I earned a full graduate fellowship that allowed me to attend GSPIA as a full-time student. I continued to work at ACTION Housing twenty hours a week to supplement my income. Graduate school was about figuring out how to keep up with the academic rigor, making ends meet, and taking care of my family obligations.

Grad school was exciting and offered the potential for a fulfilling career. In the mid- to late sixties, there were very few African American urban planners with master's degrees in public administration in the country. GSPIA was among the top graduate schools in this field of study. I would be able to count myself among the few professionally trained black urbanologists in the nation.

Our professors were the people who had written the book on urban planning. One of my professors, Dr. Clifford Ham, coauthored a book titled *The Resurgent Neighborhood*. His research detailed how Chicago, under the twenty-one-year regime of Mayor Richard Daley, was transformed from an old Midwestern city with dying infrastructure into a vibrant metropolis.

I was fascinated to learn how neighborhoods were organized

around ward politics to get citizen groups working with City Hall to revitalize communities.

My favorite professor at GSPIA, Dr. Cliff Hendricks, was gruff and wore a white handlebar mustache and a goatee. He received his PhD from Berkeley. Dr. Hendricks was popular because he made learning fun. His city planning class gave me my first encounter with a computer, the kind that filled an entire room and was programmed with keypunch cards.

To gather data for the computer, teams of students were assigned to conduct traffic counts at intersections. A team would post itself at a busy corner to count cars, pedestrians, and the frequency of traffic light changes by using a handheld counter.

We would then return to the computer room and enter the raw data by using a keyboard to produce punch cards. The punch cards were inserted into the computer, which then spat out the results of our traffic survey. I was thrilled to learn that the timing of traffic light intervals wasn't random guesswork. It was an exact science.

The knowledge we gained in grad school was as broad as it was deep. We learned the density required of the various materials used to construct a street, such as gravel, sand, concrete, and asphalt. We then compared Pittsburgh street engineering codes with the codes in other cities, including Atlanta, San Francisco, New Haven, and Washington, DC, and we conducted analyses of different standards.

I was fortunate to have dedicated professors such as Earle Onque, who taught city planning at GSPIA and was distinguished as one of the first minorities in the country to be both a registered architect and a certified city planner. He was my faculty advisor, and he took a personal interest in my success, encouraging and guiding me throughout the process of completing my master's thesis.

"Black is beautiful"

I was home in Atlanta for Easter in March 1967, and I remember walking with Mary and Timothy through Mozley Park, one of our favorite places, set in a shady, old residential neighborhood in Southwest Atlanta. Mary had dressed Timothy in his first little Easter outfit, and together they made a perfect picture of everything I wanted in the world. In fact, at that moment, I didn't want to go back to Pittsburgh.

Then, of course, reality set in. I had an incredible opportunity in GSPIA. Mary was also on a tight schedule because she had returned to Clark to complete her bachelor's degree in education and was busy juggling school with a baby.

Even though we lived apart, we were very much together, constantly on the phone to the point where I'd call home with things like what I would cook for Sunday dinner or just to say I'd grab a burger and beer with the boys.

I made friends with a fellow who lived in the apartment across the hall. His name was Chuck Hart, and he worked at US Steel. We took turns cooking dinner, and we enjoyed hanging out at our favorite jazz clubs in the Hill District. The district was a jazz mecca. Places such as Crawford Grill and Mason's Bar & Grill featured such jazz greats as guitarist Wes Montgomery; guitarist and vocalist George Benson; drummer Art Blakey; and Rahsaan Roland Kirk, a blind saxophonist who could play three horns simultaneously. Best of all, for us, for a two-dollar cover charge, we could catch a matinee, sit and listen as long as we wanted, and enjoy an inexpensive but scrumptious meal and Iron City Beer. Often, my other Pittsburgh buddies, Lester "Mitch" Mitchell and Hiawatha Fountain, joined me and Chuck to round out the rowdy group.

I introduced Chuck to his future wife, Barbara, a GSPIA classmate of mine. Chuck, Mitch, and I were all in Hiawatha's wedding party in 1966, and we remain close friends to this day.

During this period, I started doing a lot of soul-searching around our struggle against police brutality, racism, and discrimination. Just before Christmas 1967, the film *Malcolm X: Struggle for Freedom* opened. It had a profound impact on my way of thinking. It fueled the struggle between my felt need to assert a degree of militancy and the necessity to continue my education and professional development.

I made friends with a couple whom I came to admire, a black man and a white woman whose names escape me now. They were extremely militant and very open about it. Both were from West Virginia. I latched on to them and started listening to their ideas about Malcolm X and author/civil rights activist Eldridge Cleaver, one of the early leaders of the Black Panther Party. As these new ideas began to emerge in my consciousness, I struggled with my own identity.

I wore a dashiki, grew a beard, and wore my hair in a big Afro. I wore a T-shirt religiously that read, "Black is beautiful, and it's beautiful to be black."

The Urban League of Pittsburgh

As graduation from GSPIA approached, I was being recruited by HUD in Washington, DC, a few municipalities, and the Urban League of Pittsburgh. I chose the Urban League because it offered me the opportunity of a lifetime.

The Urban League setting gave me hands-on management experience and the ability to practice what I had been trained to do. My new title would be director of housing. I would run my own department, recruit my own staff, and administer large budgets and new programs. Equally important to me, the Urban League offered sanctuary for the black consciousness I needed to express. I started my new job in August 1968.

The Urban League was an interracial, private-sector-driven agency focusing on economic self-reliance, parity, power, and civil rights. Founded in 1918, the Urban League of Pittsburgh focused on education, job training, and economic development as well as human, housing, and legal services.

As the director of housing, I was one of four department heads who reported to Leon Haley, the deputy director of the Urban League of Pittsburgh, who reported to Art Edmunds, the executive director. The other department heads were also young black professionals starting their careers.

I was twenty-six years old, had a staff of thirteen, and headed up a brand-new department. I was no longer organizing block clubs and neighborhood projects. I was administering a major Ford Foundation-funded program called Operation Equality, the goal of which was advocating equal housing opportunity for blacks in Pittsburgh. The objective of the program was to integrate Pittsburgh's segregated white neighborhoods, where blacks were being systematically discriminated against and denied access to housing of their choice.

To say that I never had self-doubt or that I was never concerned about my readiness to lead this effort would be false. But I would have been ineffective as a leader if any self-doubt was discernible to my team. What I had on my side was the confidence that comes from being prepared. But I also believed that I could rely on my faith in God to help my own mission.

Most of my sleepless nights were not sleepless because I didn't think I could do the work. They were sleepless because I was awake figuring out how to get the job done.

I learned a lot about attention to detail. I learned about the importance of facts in analyzing and understanding specific tasks. Even more important was learning how to communicate with people and to motivate them to execute tasks successfully.

I had to come to grips with the fact that I simply did not know all I needed to know and that I was learning while leading. On the evenings I was not attending meetings, I studied how to implement our mandate to break the segregationist patterns of Pittsburgh housing. That meant, among other things, learning the geography and demographics of the city, especially all-white enclaves that were unfamiliar, such as Mount Lebanon and Sewickley.

We recruited mostly white volunteers to become testers. They were unpaid, and most of them were students and housewives. We set up training workshops to teach them the techniques of fair-housing testing and gain their buy-in on the tenets of Operation Equality. I'll always be in awe of the volunteers and their altruistic zeal to change the pattern of discrimination in Pittsburgh neighborhoods.

If we heard of a case with a black family rejected in a rental or mortgage housing application in an all-white neighborhood, we would send a white tester to determine whether the house or apartment was available.

Most of the time, our surveys revealed that when we sent a white tester to make an application, the housing suddenly became available. Once we documented discrimination, we would take the realtor and landlord to court and place as many black families as we could in previously all-white neighborhoods.

Just as the Black Panthers had challenged me to define my wider beliefs, at the Urban League, Art Edmunds challenged me to expand my worldview by showing me how to work within the system. Art was just as agitated over the black condition as I was.

For the Love of Golf

Art played more golf than anybody I'd ever seen. Art not only played golf regularly, but he also talked about golf incessantly. He talked about how important it was for him to play the game well and how his love for the game connected him with the wealthy white folks and corporations that contributed money to the Urban League. Art helped me to understand that playing golf was a vital tool in gaining access to powerful and influential people.

I took the insights Art shared with me about golf as a strong hint. I had been exposed to golf by Jimmy Porter, a classmate at Clark who was on the golf team. He taught me the fundamentals of the golf swing with an eight iron on the recreation field behind University Homes, next to the campus.

In Pittsburgh, I found an old set of clubs in the attic of my apartment on Dalzell Place and began regular practice at a driving range on the outskirts of the city. It was the start of a lifelong passion for a game that also gave me exposure to people and places most folks could only dream about.

The Death of Dr. Martin Luther King Jr.

My work life was beginning to take shape, and I could envision a long career with the Urban League. But all that changed on April 4, 1968.

I was sitting in my office in downtown Pittsburgh when my assistant, Sandra Mitchell, walked in and gave me the news of Dr. King's assassination at the Lorraine Motel in Memphis.

"No," I said in disbelief. "That cannot be."

I turned on the radio and heard the news of his death. They didn't call it an assassination at first. They just reported that he had been shot after leading a march of Memphis sanitation workers who were on strike for higher wages. As he famously told the workers, "We've got to give ourselves to this struggle until the end. Nothing would be more tragic than to stop at this point in Memphis." Dr. King believed the strike would expose the need for economic justice and equality.

Dr. King's death was the saddest day in my life until that moment. Art called the entire staff into the conference room, led us in prayer, and stated that it would be understandable if we wanted to leave work that afternoon to be with our families.

With no family in Pittsburgh, I returned to my apartment and sat at the window alone and cried. Later, I watched television news coverage of the assassination. Riots broke out in 110 cities across the country, including Pittsburgh, where whole commercial districts were set ablaze, and countless people were arrested. I stayed awake, praying for guidance. As morning broke, I had made a decision.

The next day, I walked into Leon Haley's office and told him that my place was back in the South, where I could make the greatest contribution to fulfilling Dr. King's dream. Leon selected my deputy, Jim Frazier, to replace me. Thus, true to its equal opportunity mission, the Urban League of Pittsburgh hired its first white department head.

12

"Carl Cares"

Driving back to Atlanta from Pittsburgh, I turned my future over and over in my mind. For starters, I had no job. I had sent out a few feelers expressing my desire to work at City Hall or the Atlanta Housing Authority. One of the letters I sent was to Dr. Vivian Henderson, president of Clark College, who had succeeded my old mentor, Dr. James P. Brawley.

Vivian was confidant and well-connected in business and political circles locally and nationally. An economist by training, he was also engaging and outgoing, a perfect public relations man for Clark College, who backed it up with a sharp intelligence and quick wit.

At the time I came back to Atlanta, Vivian had just founded the Southern Center for Studies in Public Policy, a think tank headquartered on Clark's campus. Part of its work was to produce an annual assessment of the state of black politics in Georgia. Vivian hired me as a consultant to work with the Southern Center.

Vivian launched two other big projects at Clark, the WCLK radio station and a mass communications program that has trained outstanding media personalities such as Spike Lee, CBS Atlanta anchorwoman Amanda Davis, NBC New York anchorwoman Jacque Reid, and Broadway's African American maestro Kenny Leon.

Vivian asked if I had ever thought of going on my own in the housing industry. He then told me about a friend of his, an enterprising attorney named James Robinson, who had just started an exciting new housing consulting firm called Urban East.

When Vivian introduced me to Jim, he and I liked each other instantly. My enthusiasm grew as Jim painted a picture of all of the affordable housing developments he was trying to get built across the Southeast. But my enthusiasm waned a little as he revealed that the position was also commission based. Remuneration was tied to our success in packaging low- and moderate-income multifamily housing developments under the HUD-sponsored Section 221(d)(3) and Section 236 housing programs.

The four principals in the office, including myself, were Jim, attorney Pickens Andrew Patterson, and attorney Ted Smith. I was the only one who was not a lawyer.

At Urban East, we introduced the sponsorship concept to leading pastors, including Rev. Martin Luther King Sr. of Ebenezer Baptist Church; Dr. William Holmes Borders, pastor of Wheat Street Baptist Church; and Rev. Joseph E. Lowery, pastor of Central United Methodist Church. We explained how they could use their churches' strong economic base and community stature to build low- and moderate-income housing for qualifying members of their congregations and the public at large.

Using the Federal Housing Administration financing structure, we packaged noteworthy housing developments in Atlanta, including Martin Luther King Jr. Village, sponsored by Ebenezer Baptist Church; Wheat Street Gardens, a seniors-housing project sponsored by Wheat Street Baptist Church; and Central Methodist Gardens, sponsored by Central United Methodist Church.

Because we were among a handful of firms pursuing such initiatives, we had a steady stream of these projects in Atlanta and packaged similar housing deals in other Southern cities, including Houston and Beaumont, Texas; New Orleans and Baton Rouge, Louisiana; Columbia, South Carolina; Daytona, Florida; and Birmingham, Alabama. The Prince Hall Masons, under the leadership of Grand Master John G. Lewis, became the principal sponsor of the majority of Urban East developments. I was proud to work with the organization that had meant so much to my father and had granted me my first college scholarship—a hundred dollars, which had been a tenth of one year's tuition, room, and board.

For me, one of the most memorable John G. Lewis phrases was, "Gentlemen, I'm your consultant. My fee is zero, and it doubles every day."

Through my training at GSPIA and my experiences at ACTION Housing and the Urban League of Pittsburgh, I had become a bona fide planning and redevelopment expert. As such, I convinced my partners Jim Robinson and Andy Patterson that we should pursue a consulting relationship with the Atlanta Model Cities program. This federal program, which Atlanta took part in, was a bold initiative of the Lyndon B. Johnson presidential administration to apply comprehensive physical, economic, and social strategies to revitalize blighted urban neighborhoods.

After I got their buy-in, we began discussions with Model Cities director Johnny Johnson, a prominent Atlanta real estate broker, who was appointed by Mayor Sam Massell. We won a bid to provide housing consulting services for the Model Cities neighborhoods of Grant Park, Mechanicsville, and Summerhill. Our contract with Model Cities encompassed consulting services in the areas of housing rehabilitation, new housing construction, and housing counseling services to residents.

This contract broadened Urban East's capabilities beyond packaging HUD multifamily development. We became a comprehensive housing consulting company. Shortly after the success of the Atlanta contract, we secured a similar deal with the Savannah Model Cities program.

The Urban East offices were located at the corner of Peachtree and 8th streets, inside 900 Peachtree Street in Midtown. At the time, it was the only black consulting firm of its kind and probably one of the first black businesses to be located in the city's white business district.

Practically no black architectural firms existed at that time, so we gave a young architect named Joe Robinson his first big break in designing major housing developments. Before that, he had done a handful of single-family residential and church projects and was teaching industrial art at Washington High School.

We partnered Joe with our lead architectural firm, Muldawer & Patterson, which was located in our building on Peachtree Street. The principals, Jim Patterson and Paul Muldawer, both white men, were not only great architects, they were wonderful human beings who were good friends to all of us at Urban East. They embraced Joe and helped him to learn multifamily design.

Buying Our First Home

I was able to secure an advance commission, which Mary and I used to rent and furnish our first apartment on Gordon Road in Adamsville. We became virtually inseparable, working together to manage our new household. She had graduated from Clark and was teaching elementary school full time.

With both of us working, Timmy spent a lot of time with his Atlanta grandmother, Miss Doshia, who lived a short three miles from our apartment. It worked out nicely because Mary's youngest brother, John Paul, was only a few years older than Tim, and they became bosom buddies.

The money at Urban East turned out to be good, and it allowed us to live comfortably. By 1970, we were able to save enough to buy our first home, located at the corner of Willis Mill Road and Mill Acres Lane in the Cascade Heights neighborhood. In addition to its charming French provincial architecture, the house was especially attractive to me because it was within walking distance of the first hole at the Adams Park golf course.

Just eight years earlier, Atlanta mayor Ivan Allen and the Atlanta Board of Aldermen had approved legislation to erect concrete barriers across two streets in Cascade Heights to discourage blacks from buying homes in Peyton Forest, an upscale subdivision there. Black voters had elected Allen to office, and they were livid at the betrayal.

Civil rights leaders called for boycotts of local white businesses on the west side, and protesters marched in front of City Hall and carried signs that read: "ATLANTA'S BERLIN WALL." The barricades were removed seventy-two days later, after a judge ruled them unconstitutional, but people who lived through it could never erase the embarrassing and insulting event from their minds.

Mary and I were certainly aware of this history, but by the time we moved in, Cascade Heights was integrated, and we felt comfortable and welcomed by our white neighbors.

In the evenings, after work, I would walk through the woods to the Adams Park golf course to work on my short game, chipping and putting and practicing my swing and occasionally squeezing in a couple of holes before dark.

Until 1955, I would not have been allowed to play Adams Park golf course. Alfred "Tup" Holmes had been denied access there and filed a lawsuit against the City of Atlanta that ended in the US Supreme Court, which struck down Atlanta's "separate but equal" ordinance as it related to public golf courses.

As I worked to establish Urban East with Jim, I got involved in two local political campaigns—Ben Brown's run for Georgia state representative, and that of another Clark alum, Ira Jackson, who became one of the first blacks to get elected to the City of Atlanta Board of Aldermen.

One day, Maynard Holbrook Jackson, a young African American legal aid lawyer, came to Urban East to discuss his plan to run for United States Senate. Maynard was outgoing, outspoken, and exuded the kind of confidence, communication skills, cockiness, and wit that just made you believe he was a winner.

It was 1968, and he was running against incumbent US Senator Herman Talmadge. I remember thinking Maynard couldn't possibly win, given that no black person had run a statewide race and won in Georgia since Reconstruction. And then there was the fact that even though blacks made up 35 percent of Georgia's eligible voting population, fewer than 20 percent of them were registered to vote.

Maynard believed the urban vote in Atlanta and the black vote statewide would be enough to get him into a runoff with Talmadge in the Democratic primary. In the end Maynard didn't win, but he made tremendous inroads into Talmadge's territory, winning almost a third of the statewide vote and carrying Atlanta.

With that base of support, in 1969, Maynard was elected vice mayor of Atlanta. He served with Mayor Sam Massell, the city's newly elected first Jewish mayor.

Maynard's election showed how the Voting Rights Act of 1965 was changing the face of politics in the South. White politicians began to see that they had to pay attention to black voters, and black politicians began to see that they really did have a chance to win elections.

I was enormously impressed with Maynard. Some of his political talent and knowledge was probably inherited from his grandfather Rev. John Wesley Dobbs, whose civil rights activism included overturning white primaries in Georgia.

That first meeting with Maynard at Urban East proved to be fortunate and would mark the beginning of a strong relationship between the two of us.

My First Foray into Politics

In October 1970, I got a call from Lester Purcell, the executive director of the Atlanta Housing Authority, who asked if I'd be interested in coming on board as the deputy director of urban redevelopment.

The position was ideal at that stage of my career. It provided good income and security for my family. It would also give me prestige and influence in the community and provide the exposure I needed to achieve my ultimate goal of running for public office.

In less than eighteen months at AHA, I was promoted from deputy director of urban redevelopment to director of family and community services, and that marked the true beginning of my career in politics.

At AHA I had come to know just about every grassroots leader across the city. And in my new role as director of family and community services, I came to know all of the tenant association presidents on a first-name basis.

The low-income housing projects were scattered throughout the city, including such well-known locations as East Lake Meadows in East Atlanta, Perry Homes in northwest Atlanta, Jonesboro Heights near the federal penitentiary in Southeast Atlanta, University-John Hope Homes, Grady Homes, Carver Homes, and Herndon Homes near downtown Atlanta.

That was important because, in 1972, roughly 50,000 people lived in public housing in Atlanta. Fewer than 20 percent of those people who were eligible to vote were actually registered to vote.

At AHA, we studied the federal guidelines to determine whether there were any rules that would prohibit us from using AHA staff and other resources to conduct voter education and registration in the housing projects. There were none.

And so, with the approval of the AHA board of directors, we began a voter education and registration campaign throughout Atlanta's public housing communities. It was a citywide effort championed by business, religious, and political leaders.

My staff of roughly 200 social workers and community service aides, many of whom lived in the public housing projects, served as the ground forces who actually conducted the voter registration efforts.

Until we began these voter registration efforts in Atlanta, public housing residents were marginalized and isolated in geographic locations where they were all but ignored by politicians.

The impact of this newly established political force was first felt during Andrew Young's second bid for Congress in 1972. In 1970, he'd run against Congressman Fletcher Thompson for the same post and lost. But this time around, the outcome would be different. The main reason Andy won in 1972 was the heavy turnout of newly registered voters from the Atlanta housing projects.

It was an honor to work with enlightened grassroots leaders such as Ms. Susie LaBord, head of the citywide tenant association, who lived in Grady Homes; Mrs. Louise Whatley, who lived in Carver Homes; and Mrs. Mary Sandford, president of the Perry Homes tenant association. Perry Homes, with more than a thousand residents, was the largest of the Atlanta public housing projects.

The mission at AHA, however, was not politics. It was about transforming federally funded housing projects into livable communities where mothers on welfare had a safe environment for their children while pursuing jobs or job training. And, of course, public housing was intended as a vehicle for people to become self-reliant and even buy their own homes. It was not intended to be a permanent solution, with generation after generation of families finding themselves trapped and stigmatized by the lifestyle of "the projects."

At AHA we took full advantage of the programs funded by HUD and the federal Department of Health, Education, and Welfare, a forerunner of the Department of Health and Human Services, to establish early childhood development centers in every single Atlanta housing project serving more than 3,000 children.

We recruited licensed social workers to train community service aides whom we recruited from the housing projects. This formal training was designed by the dean of the Atlanta University School of Social Work, Dr. Genevieve Hill. This project allowed housing residents to earn certifications and develop skills that were transferable outside of the public housing environment.

We then used another federally funded program called Title 16 to establish senior citizen centers for the elderly living in the housing projects. Again, we trained community service aides to provide support to these senior centers.

$\approx$

In May 1973, I told AHA executive director Lester Purcell of my intention to run for Atlanta City Council.

"I would encourage you to do that," Lester said, "but you may have to resign."

The question was whether an executive of AHA could also hold elected office. The attorneys said, "No," and I resigned.

By then, Mary had gone to work as a manager for JCPenney. The fact that I was able to run for political office at all was because of the unfailing support from Mary and both our families.

In the summer of 1973, I announced my candidacy for the city council to represent District 11. Maynard Jackson had already declared his candidacy for mayor earlier that same year.

There was much talk of a changing of the guard that would give black Atlantans their turn at running the city. The Atlanta Charter Commission dramatically altered the political landscape by creating twelve council district seats and six at-large council seats to replace the old citywide aldermanic election process.

Oddly enough, despite Atlanta's reputation for racial harmony, incumbent Mayor Sam Massell, who previously won office with a majority of the black vote, attempted to scare white voters by using a racial slogan: "Atlanta's Too Young to Die." It was supposed to imply that electing a black mayor would somehow be lethal for the city.

Whereas the mayor's race between Maynard and Sam was a bitter battle, my own campaign was run a little more modestly. Having the endorsement of neighborhood leaders gave me a tremendous amount of grassroots support, although Atlanta's prominent black business and civil rights leaders supported my opponents.

One candidate, Willie Bolden—one of the unsung civil rights

lieutenants of Dr. King's—naturally had the civil rights leaders in his camp. My other opponent, Jim Maddox, was an executive at aerospace giant Lockheed. He had most of the black business leaders in his camp.

My campaign boasted more than fifty regular volunteers who canvassed almost every street, knocked on doors, and talked to voters about my candidacy. We also put to use my experience in voter registration and population demographics.

Even though the newly created 11th Council District had transitioned from majority white to a majority black population by 1973, it remained split roughly 50-50 among registered voters. Many of the registered white voters lived outside the city, and they had friends and relatives who still lived in the city.

That proved especially important in two senior citizens' high-rise buildings in District 11 that housed more than 300 registered voters, most of them white. My opponents ignored these voters, but I believed they were the key to carrying the district. I visited them often and paid attention to their concerns.

These voters became my loyal supporters and put out a brochure that said "Carl cares about us and our neighborhoods." Word spread rapidly, and "Carl Cares" became my campaign slogan.

In the general election, I garnered 90 percent of the white vote and split the black vote evenly with my opponents. That ended with me in a runoff election against Jim Maddox, which I handily won using the same campaign strategy as I had in the general election.

My opponents had the perceived advantage of endorsements from black leaders. However, I cannot take full credit for the "white voters" strategy. Kudos to my white Adams Park neighbor and at-large councilman Jack Summers, who gave me the tip about voter registration demographics in the 11th Council District.

I also had my whole family in my corner. Timothy, who had just started grade school, often came along with me as I canvassed neighborhoods. Mary and Timothy frequently accompanied me to campaign events such as picnics, barbecues, baseball games, and other neighborhood functions.

It also didn't hurt that I had three big sisters. My sister Mildred was working for the United States Postal Service. And, unbeknownst to me until recently, in true big-sister fashion, she used her position at USPS to help get me elected.

This episode came about after my family decided to put on a barbecue fundraiser for the campaign, the idea being to raise money by selling tickets. The campaign rented a horseback riding stable on Cascade Road, where we could hold the event.

Mamma and Daddy invited the entire Oak Grove Baptist Church congregation up to Atlanta and took care of the food and catering.

What I didn't know was that Mildred convinced some of her drivers to sell tickets. She had postmen campaigning! If it was a crime, it's too late to prosecute.

In the end, we had a huge crowd, and the event raised about $2,500, which pretty much covered the expenses for the entire campaign.

I also had my big sister Louise working behind the scenes on my behalf. She was still employed by J. Paul Austin, chairman of the Coca-Cola Company. I guess you could say she used her position, too, since she managed to get campaign contributions from a few of Austin's friends, including former mayor Ivan Allen.

On election day, Mildred arose at 6 A.M. to put flyers on cars, and she talked to every passing pedestrian about her little brother's campaign for city council. At the end, she was so tired that she didn't even attend the victory celebration. She fell asleep in her clothes. Just as in my childhood, my siblings supported me in fulfilling my dreams. I was determined to do well, and I was blessed to have so many people likewise determined on my behalf.

The results on November 6, 1973: Maynard, at age thirty-five, became the first African American mayor of Atlanta, defeating the city's first Jewish mayor. Wyche Fowler defeated Rev. Hosea Williams in a runoff election for president of the city council. I was among five new African American council members elected to the body, which split the council down the middle with nine black members and nine white ones. At the same time, two black women were elected to the Atlanta Board of Education, giving it a 5–4 black majority. It was the pivotal year in the changing of the guard in Atlanta politics.

᠕

One of my earliest acts as a public servant and member of the transportation committee was to be a passenger on Delta Airlines' inaugural flight, which went from Atlanta to Denver. I joined other members of the Atlanta City Council, members of both the Georgia General Assembly and the Fulton County Board of Commissioners, and city business leaders. I was seated next to Georgia Senator Crawford Ware from Troup County, forty-five minutes southwest of Coweta County.

I did not know Crawford Ware, but it quickly became clear that he knew me, as he immediately started talking about my family background, my grandfather, and my father—and he even knew my ancestors.

"I knew your Grandpa Pete and where he was born, and I know all of your ancestors," he said. "They lived with us on the plantation down there."

I was honestly surprised, shocked, and speechless. It was clear he was simply trying to make a connection but also that he really couldn't understand the weight of his words for me. Despite the shock, it didn't elicit any particular feelings of hatred—my parents just wouldn't allow us to hate or react to such comments in that way.

And why would I? I was Carl Ware, a member of the city council, going about the business of Atlanta and overseeing the billion-dollar expansion of Hartsfield International Airport.

13

THE 25-PERCENT POLICY

It was a busy time in my life, and I was making decisions that would set the course for my future on many fronts. Not only had I been elected to the Atlanta City Council, but on January 3, 1974, I went to work for the Coca-Cola Company as a government affairs specialist. I was recruited by J. Paul Austin, and I reported to Ovid Davis, head of government affairs.

At a press conference around that time, WXIA television reporter Marc Pickard asked me if it was a conflict of interest to serve on the city council and work for the Coca-Cola Company at the same time.

I didn't hesitate to reply: "Everyone needs a real job." By design, the elected office I held was a part-time civic responsibility.

I was working for the Coca-Cola Company on issues at the state and federal levels but not on issues at the local government level. And I figured Marc's question came as a result of heightened media scrutiny of politics thanks to the Watergate scandal that started in the summer of 1973.

Things were done differently back then. And Coca-Cola had a long history of civic leadership in Atlanta that included allowing employees the freedom to serve in public office. In fact, Mayor William Hartsfield, one of Atlanta's most revered mayors, also worked for the company. I was following in some pretty big footsteps.

The government affairs group consisted of Ovid Davis and five other seasoned lobbyists. Ovid's incredibly smart and capable administrative assistant, Norma McDonald, kept the team running as a well-oiled government-relations machine. We had an office in DC, and our people knew their way around Capitol Hill and the White House. I was the newest member of the staff and the first African American to be hired in this highly sensitive area of the company.

My orientation for the job took into account several different aspects of the business. I rode route trucks, visited restaurant customers, and toured the syrup concentrate plant in Hapeville, Georgia, as well as some bottling plants around the state. I attended countless staff meetings and briefings, where I listened to public relations, sales, and marketing presentations. I also saw how Coca-Cola lab technicians went about their work, creating new products.

In the next phase of my orientation, Ovid took me on my first trip to Washington, DC, as a Coca-Cola executive. Walking the halls of Congress with him for the first time was an awe-inspiring experience. He introduced me to key members of Georgia's congressional delegation. In addition to my general assignments in Washington, I was thrilled to have the opportunity to forge business relationships with members of the Congressional Black Caucus and, nationwide, with state legislative black caucuses.

In addition to my government-relations responsibilities, J. Paul Austin asked me to represent him as staff facilitator with the Opportunities Industrialization Centers of America founded by Rev. Leon Sullivan, then also a director at General Motors. Austin was a member of the board of directors of OIC, which was created in an effort to get American corporations to invest in its training centers in cities across the country. These centers trained workers in various fields that industry needed.

Chairing the Public Safety Committee

Meantime, my work on the Atlanta City Council started with a bang when city council president Wyche Fowler appointed me chairman of the public safety committee, which oversaw police, the fire department, and civil defense.

As background, the Atlanta Police Department was officially desegregated in 1948. Yet more than twenty years later, in the 1970s, a perception lingered that the APD was as unfair to its black officers as it was brutal and insensitive to the city's black citizens. For example, black officers were denied the opportunity to compete for promotions within the department, and the APD had one of the highest homicide rates against African American men when compared with police departments nationwide.

On APD police chief John Inman's watch, a young, unarmed black man was fatally shot by police when he got out of his car in downtown Atlanta. Inman's white officers collectively decided to plant a knife on the dead man. The investigating officer who responded to the shooting determined the knife did not belong to the victim but was instead planted by the APD. After filing his report, Officer Lewis Graham, who was white, was demoted.

As chairman of the public safety committee, I initiated an investigation independent of the mayor's office to determine the extent to which the APD was unlawfully profiling and targeting black males for nonexistent crimes. We also wanted to find out whether the allegation of police planting weapons on crime suspects was true or false.

We conducted public hearings to get the facts. We heard from members of the APD itself, granting police officers who came forward immunity from reprisal for their testimony about unlawful activities in the department. Two black officers did come forward. The men were reprimanded by their superiors but not fired. We also had citizens come before the committee with stories of police brutality and what was perceived as unlawful conduct by police officers.

The public safety committee found sufficient cause to support the firing of Police Chief John Inman. There were many bizarre elements to this case, and coverage of it dominated headlines and the nightly news for months.

Maynard fired Inman and appointed a man named Clinton Chafin in his place. The problem was that Inman, who refused to be supervised by a black mayor, refused also to be fired by one. Instead of packing up his desk and leaving quietly, Inman locked himself inside his office.

My old friend Larry Dingle was an eyewitness to one of the bizarre incidents. At the time he was working as a police officer on the same floor as Inman in the APD's old Decatur Street building. Larry had worked his way up from beat cop after graduating from Morehouse and held a planning and research role.

Larry was headed toward the police chief's office when he saw newly appointed police chief Clint Chafin and Lieutenant C. J. Strickland standing outside a swinging door and gripping their pistols. Inman and Junior Spence, who headed up the APD's SWAT team, were on the other side of the door, similarly positioned with their weapons at the ready.

Inman had been given an unusually long eight-year employment contract as Sam Massell was leaving office. As a result, Inman filed a lawsuit for wrongful termination, so the ability to fire him was tied up in the courts for a long time.

"It was clear that there was essentially a war, and there was enormous tension between certain members of the newly installed city council and the Inman administration," Larry recalls. In one instance, a young black officer was given a promotion for planting lottery slips in a gas station owned by former alderman and newly elected black city council member Ira Jackson.

Ira wasn't at the gas station when the police came. Charges were lodged against his brother but later dropped. Nevertheless, the episode made clear that some people were willing to go to extreme lengths that could become a threat to life and safety.

Because of my support for removing Inman and overhauling the APD, many people believed my life was in danger. I received threatening telephone calls from anonymous callers claiming to represent the Fraternal Order of Police, which, at the time, was reputed to be an all-white police organization. The mayor assigned two police officers from his own detail to provide twenty-four-hour security for my family and me.

I took the threats seriously, but I had no intention of backing down. To render Inman harmless, we reorganized city government and created the Department of Public Safety. Instead of reporting directly to the mayor, under this restructuring, the heads of the police, fire, and public defense departments would report directly to the commissioner of public safety.

We also transferred the day-to-day duties of the police chief to the commissioner of public safety, effectively preventing Inman from causing further damage to the city. The long court battle ended with the Georgia Supreme Court allowing Inman to keep his title and draw a salary for the length of his contract. He stayed, but we made sure that his new office was far removed from the APD—ten blocks away, in the Atlanta Civic Center.

Sunday Night Meetings

Much like the Atlanta Police Department's having been mired in discrimination and racism before my election to the city council, there were also virtually no black or female contractors, suppliers, or vendors participating in the city's massive public works bidding process, which amounted to more than $600 million between 1974 and 1981.

The black city council members knew we could not allow this condition to continue in a city where the majority of the population was African American. We also knew that it was incumbent upon us to use our political power and public policy to get economic justice. Its pursuit was why I had so desperately wanted to get back to Atlanta from Pittsburgh after Dr. King's assassination. It was the work that I knew I could and must do.

We, the newly elected black mayor and newly elected black city council members, did our most important work on Sunday nights, far removed from the public eye. After a long Sunday of church and family obligations, we met in one another's homes, a private room at Pascal's, or a café (that was technically closed on Sunday evenings) located on Martin Luther King Jr. Boulevard. We knew the owner, and she made it comfortable for us to meet privately in her obscure little restaurant without fear of being discovered by the press.

Maynard and the black council members were well aware that Georgia's Sunshine Law prohibited us from forming policy out of the public eye, but doing so was the only way to keep the critics at bay until we got it right. We came out of those meetings in agreement, in lockstep with the mayor, including on areas outside city hall's policy jurisdiction, such as the Atlanta Board of Education, Metropolitan Atlanta Rapid Transit Authority, the Atlanta Regional Commission, and the Georgia General Assembly.

Those private Sunday meetings provided a way to come to agreement on issues that should be raised at the Atlanta Action Forum, the city's black/white business coalition, a modern version of decision-maker politics. Instead of the cigar smoke-filled rooms of the past, the Atlanta Action Forum was a group of twelve business leaders, split 50-50 black and white. The group specifically excluded religious and civil rights leaders.

In the Action Forum meetings, nonbinding community decisions were made on such issues as school board elections, economic power-sharing, and advancement of black business professionals in key decision-making roles. Action Forum members were the CEOs of such companies as Delta Airlines, Georgia-Pacific, Atlanta Life Insurance, Georgia Power, Coca-Cola, Citizens Trust Bank, and the major white-run banks and leading real estate developers. They were men including John Portman, Roberto Goizueta, Jesse Hill, Herman Russell, Harold Dawson, and John Cox. Eventually Roberto asked me to represent him at the Action Forum meetings.

The most important legislative policy initiative of that era evolved from the Sunday night meetings. That was where we came up with the 25-percent minority participation strategy. The city ordinance remains in place today and requires that at least 25 percent of all city contracts for goods and services be granted to minority- and female-owned businesses.

But when it was passed, the 25-percent law shook the foundations of Atlanta's most venerable and powerful institutions, including banks, as well as law, accounting, construction, architectural, and engineering firms. The law affected all companies doing business with the City of Atlanta.

Maynard and those of us who stood with him on affirmative action and minority participation in city contracts were vilified as devils incarnate. Some business leaders even predicted that we would drag the city's all-important bond rating to the bottom of the barrel among American cities.

In the midst of this barrage of criticism and antagonism from the business community, I first met legendary Atlanta business leader Robert W. Woodruff, chairman and CEO emeritus of the Coca-Cola Company. I was sitting with Ovid Davis in his office on Plum Street, our world headquarters, a modest, four-story, red brick building.

Out of nowhere, the unmistakable aroma of a fine cigar wafted into the room. Ovid stood up. I could smell the cigar but had no idea why it made Ovid jump the way he did until he told me: "The boss is coming."

I rose to my feet in time to see Mr. Woodruff, who had stepped down as chairman of the company but was still known as the biggest "mule"—meaning someone who pulled the weight of the community in Atlanta business. I had never met him, but I strongly appreciated his reputation for bringing together leaders, black and white, in common cause. In 1964, Mr. Woodruff held a dinner in honor of Dr. Martin Luther King Jr.'s winning the Nobel Peace Prize. Woodruff was determined that Atlanta would celebrate this great achievement of a native son. The invitation of the city's white leaders to the black-tie affair was a summons, not a request.

As Mr. Woodruff walked into the office that day, Ovid said, "Boss, this is Carl Ware. He's a city councilman, and he works here at the company."

"I know who he is," Mr. Woodruff said. "Sit down. Sit down, both of you." Then he asked me, "How's my city today?"

"Mr. Woodruff, your city is doing well," I replied.

He continued, "How's Maynard doing?"

"Maynard is doing just great," I told him. "You know we've got our challenges."

"Yes, I know," he agreed, puffing his Cuban. "But you all just keep up the good work. The city is in good hands."

It was a very big deal for me to know that Robert W. Woodruff approved of the direction in which we were leading the city. I also knew that had it not been the case, he would have made it known in no uncertain terms.

I delivered Mr. Woodruff's sentiment to Maynard, who was ecstatic about his support.

The Jackson administration was embarking upon the largest public works project in the city's history: the $1 billion expansion of Hartsfield International Airport. It would become the first test of how the 25-percent policy would work. Implementation of the economic power-sharing strategy required putting operating standards and procedures in place that would treat every contract and bidder the same.

To that end, the city council passed a resolution that stated the city's preference for majority-white general contractors to form joint ventures with minority contractors. The general contractors would be required to subcontract at least 20 to 25 percent of their projects to minority firms.

In Atlanta, city contracts awarded to women and minorities increased from 1 percent in 1974 to 24 percent in 1981. It is estimated that $2.5 billion in contracts were awarded to women and minorities through 2012. These businesses were viable ones that had previously been locked out of the process because of historically discriminatory policies and practices.

One of the broader impacts of the Atlanta empowerment model was that previously all-white accounting and law firms began hiring minorities and women, and Atlanta became a mecca for minority contractors. The 25-percent joint-venture policy created an endless and steady stream of new professionals and economic opportunities, and it literally changed how business was done, not just in the public sector but in the private sector as well.

For instance, when Coca-Cola embarked upon the construction of its new world headquarters on North Avenue, we used the joint-venture model and teamed majority company Holder Construction with minority company H. J. Russell & Company. Several minority- and female-owned subcontractors were also engaged in this private sector development.

Atlanta's procurement process became the model for other cities, states, and federal agencies and is still widely in practice today.

The smartest move Maynard made in executing the airport expansion was to appoint George Berry, the city's most adept public administrator, as commissioner of aviation. George managed Hartsfield International so well, even during construction, that we didn't miss a beat in becoming the world's busiest airport.

George kept the Atlanta business community informed and engaged throughout the process and all the major players on the same page, including Delta Airlines, the Atlanta financial institutions, and New York investment banks, not to mention the bond-rating agencies. George's expert leadership ensured the success of the joint-venture process and ultimately the Hartsfield expansion.

The implementation of the 25-percent joint-venture requirement dispelled the myth that economic inclusion meant sacrificing quality. Quite the contrary: the billion-dollar Hartsfield International expansion project did not bankrupt the city or lower its bond rating. Hartsfield was completed ahead of schedule and well within budget.

Following Maynard's death, his monumental contribution to the city and the nation was recognized in 2003 with the renaming of the transportation hub to Hartsfield-Jackson Atlanta International Airport.

14

BRINGING DR. KING'S DREAM TO LIFE

When newly elected president Jimmy Carter appointed US Congressman Andy Young to serve as US ambassador to the United Nations in 1977, it created a cascade of political vacancies. Andy's seat in Congress was filled by then-Atlanta City Council president Wyche Fowler, who won it in a special election. And I was unanimously elected by the eighteen-member Atlanta City Council to fill Wyche's unexpired term.

The new city charter mandated the city council elect the next president from its members if the vacancy occurred during the last two years of the outgoing city council president's four-year term.

In the city elections of that same year, I ran for president of the city council in my own right. My campaign headquarters were located downtown on Spring Street, next door to the Civic Center MARTA station and in the shadow of the Atlanta Apparel Mart. A longtime friend of mine, attorney Bill Ide, agreed to chair my campaign and head the fundraising effort. I first met Bill at the Atlanta Housing Authority when I was the deputy director of housing and he was our legal counsel, working for law firm King & Spalding.

Others aspired to the office, including Richard Guthman, chairman of the city council's finance committee. Eventually Guthman threw his support behind me.

Effectively, I ran unopposed in the general election except for one candidate whose name was Johnny B. Good. Johnny B. was a nice fellow, and that was his real name. The only other potential competition was Hosea Williams, who initially let it be known that he was interested in running for city council president but ultimately decided against it.

As I campaigned for city council president, I was getting strong encouragement from business leaders, neighborhood associations, and religious leaders throughout the city to run for mayor after Maynard's second term ended in 1981.

I considered my campaign for city council president a dry run for the mayor's office. The mere fact amped up my adrenaline as I canvassed every corner of the city.

My experience driving the mail truck for C&S Bank finally paid off. I could make a speech at the Buckhead Business Association on the north side of town at six o'clock and still drive to Carver Homes in Southeast Atlanta for a 7:30 P.M. political rally. There wasn't a neighborhood that I didn't go to at least once.

In addition to speaking at such business and civic forums as Rotary, Kiwanis, and the Atlanta Business League, I met personally with key Atlanta business leaders, listened to their concerns, and asked for their support.

The one-on-one sessions were a way to get to know people better. One of my most memorable meetings was with media mogul Ted Turner, whom I met in 1976, the year he bought the Atlanta Hawks. He frequently invited me to his suite to watch the games.

This time, however, we met in his old office at Turner Communications Group, near the Georgia Tech campus. I owned stock in the company, which I bought when I worked at the Atlanta Housing Authority. It had been a profitable investment, and I thanked Ted for that. I also thanked him for his support of my campaign for city council president and told him I was getting strong encouragement to run for mayor—and that I would need his continued support.

"Well, Carl, I wanna run for mayor, too," he said in his signature Southern drawl.

I said, "Are you serious, Ted?"

"I don't know," he said. "I might be. Four years is a long way off."

We laughed, talked a little more baseball and basketball, and that was the end of the meeting.

I won the city council election, garnering 90 percent of the vote.

The city council presidency opened up a world of leadership opportunities outside Atlanta. I was elected president of the Georgia Association of Black Elected Officials, GABEO, whose membership included city, county, state, and federal elected officials. Consistent with the GABEO agenda, we invited the governor, the labor commissioner, the state school superintendent, and the commissioner of public safety to address our annual conferences. Then we lobbied these officials to get things done on behalf of black Georgians.

My personal escort for GABEO meetings throughout the state was a man named Lucius Sullivan, one of the first black Georgia state troopers. I was on a perpetually tight schedule, and so we would tear up I-75 to get to my appointments. Lucius and I are still friends to this day. Early in his career, he was part of the civil disorders unit of the Georgia State Patrol. Whenever there was a race riot or uprising anywhere in the state, the Georgia State Patrol sent the brothers in first. Lucius could talk the skin off a grape and defuse the situation so there was no need for the troopers to engage the public.

GABEO's membership never met without discussing the fundamental issues of voter education, voter registration, and getting out the vote. Wherever we met for the annual conference, whether Savannah, Columbus, Atlanta, or Albany, we conducted a voter-registration drive. One year, for example, while meeting in Brunswick for the annual conference, we mobilized the entire conference to attend a one-day voter-registration campaign in nearby St. Mary's in Camden County.

St. Mary's, a gateway to Georgia's barrier islands, had no black elected officials despite the fact that it was also one of the oldest black communities in the state. None of us wanted that record to stand. Following the drive, the community elected blacks to its school board and to the Camden County Board of Commissioners.

Also during this time, I was elected vice president of the National League of Cities. Through it, I met one of the most progressive mayors in the country, Richard "Dick" Lugar, who was nearing the end of his terms as mayor of Indianapolis and president of the National League of Cities. I admired Dick greatly because he was such a strong champion of the urban agenda who lobbied Washington passionately on behalf of American cities. My good friend Senator Sam Nunn, a Democrat, often praises Senator Lugar, a Republican, for his bipartisanship, demonstrated in his cosponsorship of the Nunn-Lugar Act to reduce the Soviet nuclear threat.

I was soon on a first-name basis with the mayors of most major

American cities, and I lobbied Congress, the White House, and all of the federal agencies affecting cities—the departments of Labor, Commerce, Transportation, and Housing and Urban Development.

The confluence of the positions I held as president of the Atlanta City Council, vice president of the National League of Cities, and as an executive of the Coca-Cola Company catapulted my name onto the national stage.

Ingrid Saunders Jones

In 1977, during my second year as city council president, Maynard and I created the Urban Fellows Program, an initiative patterned after the White House Fellows program. From a pool of twelve candidates, we selected four outstanding young executives: a black woman, a white woman, a white man, and a black man. All would be assigned to positions in city government, three in the Office of the Mayor and one in the Council President's Office.

Among the four selected was a young woman from Detroit named Ingrid Saunders Jones. She was executive director of the Wayne County Detroit Child Care Coordinating Council and the only fellow who wasn't a lawyer, MBA, or PhD. Her decision to leave such a prestigious position and relocate to Atlanta and the uncharted waters of a brand new program must have been difficult.

She was my top pick...and she was Maynard's top pick. And we fought over her. The Council President's Office got Ingrid, and the other three candidates went to work in the Office of the Mayor.

With Ingrid, there would be three in the Council President's Office, including my secretary, Pinky Rutledge. We were in the process of modernizing the administrative and legislative policies and procedures of the city council. Until that time, legislation was recorded by hand, typed, and manually filed in the City Clerk's Office. Looking anything up was tedious and time-consuming. The modernization of the council took us from all-handwritten documents to microfiche, which sounds ancient now but was revolutionary then. Ingrid took charge of this seemingly daunting task.

She also dug into all of the old binders filled with newspaper clippings about Atlanta from the beginning of time. She studied binder after binder to learn the Atlanta power structure and who the movers and shakers were. As she stated, "I immediately came to understand that Coca-Cola was at the top of the pyramid."

Coca-Cola was far and away at the top of the pecking order in Atlanta. Next came the banks. Then there were the Chamber of Commerce, Central Atlanta Progress, and the Atlanta Business League.

Ingrid quickly learned that, in city government, the movers were Maynard Jackson, mayor; myself, city council president; and councilman Q. V. Williamson, chairman of the powerful finance committee.

Our work was complemented by able individuals, including Lyndon Wade, who headed up the Atlanta Urban League; attorney Donald L. Hollowell; and John Cox, VP of Delta Airlines and former head of the legendary Butler Street YMCA. Indisputably, the three most powerful black business leaders were Herman Russell, Jesse Hill, and attorney Felker Ward. Black bankers on the list included Mutual Federal Savings & Loan CEO Fletcher Coombs and Citizens Trust Bank CEO Owen Funderburg. Of course, these men wouldn't have been able to get anything done without such legislators as Georgia State Representative Grace Towns Hamilton and Georgia State Senator Leroy Johnson.

Ingrid was indispensable. She installed business routines that kept the city council running smoothly. That allowed me to develop my own routines, balance my job responsibilities at Coca-Cola, and fulfill my duty as president of the city council.

Ingrid's very first job for me, however, would be propitious: she set up a search system to vet candidates for a newly created position, clerk of council. Among the top ten resumes was one belonging to Larry Dingle, the young officer who had witnessed the armed standoff between the two Atlanta police chiefs.

I hired Larry as clerk of council, the administrator and designated custodian of the council's legislative actions and records.

Larry Dingle and Ingrid Saunders Jones were a formidable team who became my "kitchen cabinet" in running the affairs of the legislative branch of city government, including the orchestration of city council meetings, drafting of legislation, and staffing of councilmanic committees.

Larry would go on to study law at night and earn his law degree from Georgia State University. Eventually, he would attract big-name clients such as the Coca-Cola Company, Equitable Real Estate Investment, and Tyler Perry Studios. Ingrid would retire from Coke as senior vice president for global engagement and chair of the Coca-Cola Foundation.

But back then, what I saw most in Larry and Ingrid were two hardworking professionals with unimpeachable character and integrity, high potential, and the drive to succeed. This triangular friendship would take us through more than forty years of business and civic duty.

Bringing Atlanta's Banks into Balance

Changing the way the city's procurement and contracting processes worked was only half the battle in leveling the playing field so that African Americans could have a fair chance to participate in Atlanta's thriving economy. Maynard, Q. V. Williamson, and I brainstormed on ways to use the city's financial leverage with Atlanta banks to get them to adopt and implement their own policies of inclusion.

There were just six banks in downtown Atlanta handling about $600 million in tax funds that flowed through the city's coffers. That currency represented all of the hard-earned dollars of all the city taxpayers, yet none of these banks had African Americans in their management structures, nor were there any African Americans on the boards of these six banks. Of the 120 vice presidents across all of the banks in the city, not a single VP was black.

We met with the bank presidents behind the scenes, without holding a single press conference or initiating any public attack on the lending institutions. Despite our best efforts to talk our way into an equitable solution, we were getting no response.

Eventually, Maynard quietly gave the banks a thirty-day ultimatum: comply with the city's affirmative action guidelines or face losing the city's accounts. On day twenty-nine, the smallest bank, First Georgia, said it would comply. Another larger bank, which I'll leave unnamed, continued to be defiant. So on day thirty-one, Maynard instructed city finance commissioner Charlie Davis to close the city's smallest account with the larger bank, just $500,000, and transfer the funds to First Georgia.

Once the banks complied, a search for qualified African American candidates followed, and our offices at City Hall were flooded with resumes. Atlanta became one of the few cities in America where the traditional downtown banks had integrated boards of directors and high-ranking African American vice presidents and senior officers.

15

COCA-COLA UNIVERSITY

Historically, the two highest-ranking elected officials in city government, the mayor and city council president, were at loggerheads on public policy and administrative issues, often thanks to differing political agendas.

But with Maynard and me, things were different. We were both African Americans who had been mightily influenced by the teachings of Dr. Martin Luther King Jr. In fact, Maynard and I often shared personal stories about how Dr. King's assassination affected our respective decisions to enter politics.

In our five-plus years of working together in city government, Maynard and I used our political power to bring about economic justice. We put into practice the slogan that labeled Atlanta "the city too busy to hate," elevating the city into a progressive international marketplace. We accomplished these things because we always put the city's best interests ahead of our individual political interests.

I had looked forward to succeeding Maynard as the city's next mayor and building on the strong legacy we created together. So it was with great difficulty in August 1979 that I resigned as president of the Atlanta City Council and abandoned my political ambitions to accept one of the top marketing positions at the Coca-Cola Company.

The offer, however, was bittersweet. Charlie Boone, vice president of special markets for Coca-Cola USA, died of a heart attack at age forty-seven. It happened unexpectedly one Saturday morning while he was at work in his office on North Avenue.

Charlie was a pioneer of ethnic marketing, a genuine rubber-meets-the-road marketing guy. He built a formidable national team of black marketing executives who increased Coca-Cola market share in every major American city. Charlie was one of my heroes.

Charlie joined the company in 1958 as a special market representative for the Columbia, South Carolina, bottling franchise. From there, Charlie was recruited to head a new position at Coca-Cola USA where he would oversee the special markets program nationwide. His job was to persuade bottlers to hire special market representatives to develop the black consumer market in their bottling territories.

Charlie's responsibilities also entailed creating marketing and advertising programs aimed at increasing sales of brand Coca-Cola and allied products in the black consumer market. In this capacity, Charlie became known as "Mr. Coca-Cola."

More than anyone else, Charlie helped to define the role of Coca-Cola in urban America, and he did it at a time when American companies were beginning to recognize the tremendous purchasing power of black consumers. Food, tobacco, automobile, beer and liquor, and, of course, soft drink companies all had marketing plans aimed at capitalizing on this emerging buying power.

When I transitioned from the governmental affairs role in the company to the marketing role, I knew I needed to augment my skill set with more marketing and operational knowledge. I was determined to demonstrate to the naysayers that I could do as good a job as Charlie and also take the special markets team to the next level.

But first I needed credibility, and so I embarked on a four-month learning tour of the business. In New York City, I rode route trucks selling and merchandising Coca-Cola products in small mom-and-pops, bodegas, Manhattan high-rise office buildings, restaurants in Harlem and Brooklyn, and supermarkets on Long Island.

Next, I traveled to Montana for yet another view of how race plays out in America. Montana is interesting for a black person because it is the least black state in the nation, with an African American population of less than 1 percent. I never had a racial encounter there, but I did have a case of mistaken identity one day as I was working in a small supermarket. The store owner, a friendly white woman, came up to me, gushing, "I didn't know you were working for Coca-Cola now! You were my favorite football player at the University of Montana."

This woman thought I was the Grizzlies' running back because they had only one black on the team at the University of Montana—the running back. She thought I was that athlete.

"Oh, I wish that was me," I said with a smile. "I am just a hardworking Coke salesman who came in here to learn what I can about servicing your store." I didn't let her get embarrassed by her assumption that, because I was black, I must have been that one black football player. Instead, I complimented her lovely store and made one last pitch to her to purchase more cases of Coca-Cola.

In Helena and Bozeman, Montana, I gained even greater insight through hands-on experience. I worked on the production line inside a bottling plant and learned the intricate network of delivery scheduling and how it related to what was loaded onto the trucks. Also in that Montana environment I learned about long-haul deliveries. The economics intrigued me—how you could drive a load of Coke products sixty miles, drop it off in just two or three locations, and still make a profit.

After Montana, my learning tour continued to Phoenix, Arizona, and San Antonio, Texas, where I got involved in the introduction of a new Coca-Cola project called Mellow Yellow. Mellow Yellow was to be Coca-Cola's answer to Mountain Dew, a highly caffeinated, citrus-flavored, carbonated soft drink that catered to rural Americans, especially blue-collar workers and teens.

Mellow Yellow was a fascinating introduction, and a difficult one, because Mountain Dew had such a big head start. What I learned from this experience was that our customers liked trying new ideas to draw consumers into their stores. Brand Coca-Cola would always get our foot in the door to tell the profit story of new products. In the end, Mellow Yellow, which had ample marketing investment, did not overtake Mountain Dew's lead.

Those months of training between September and January were like attending a Coca-Cola university, which today has been institutionalized as part of the Coca-Cola learning system. There was one other thing I did to get myself better prepared for the job. I went back to school.

Feeling the need for more quantitative skills, I embarked upon the executive MBA program at Georgia State University, where I focused on finance and economics, marketing and advertising, and communication technology. The program was designed for busy executives like me, with all its classes happening evenings and early on Saturday mornings. Some of my classmates were top execs from such companies as Georgia Power, Delta Airlines, Atlanta Gas Light, Equifax, and major Atlanta financial institutions.

I chuckle when I think back. When I left to do my field training, I had no idea what my salary was going to be in my new job. It turned out that it exceeded my expectations, quadrupling what I earned as a government affairs specialist. And then it hit me that I had reached an entirely different income bracket, a position that made me eligible for annual bonuses and long-term incentive payouts.

I hit the ground running when I took charge of the special markets team. Rather than having my geographically dispersed staff come to Atlanta to meet me, I decided to meet each local marketing manager on his home turf. That meant traveling to the District of Columbia, Boston, New York, New Orleans, Raleigh, Columbia, Miami, Chicago, Pittsburgh, Memphis, Philadelphia, Cleveland, Houston, Dallas, Los Angeles, and Birmingham, all of which I accomplished in short order.

All of my special market managers in the field were black men. At headquarters, three black women managed our market research, planning, and budgeting functions. What impressed me most about my team was that they were an incredibly talented group of executives. I wondered where these people had been hiding in the company and why they were not being given opportunities to excel in areas outside of special markets. Once they got to know me better, they voiced their frustrations about being isolated.

What made me different from most black Coca-Cola employees was that I entered the company at a level where I had direct access to the top players—CEO J. Paul Austin, COO Don Keough, and VP Ovid Davis, who were my mentors. I attended meetings where big decisions were made that affected budgets, people, markets, and the global business as a whole.

In special markets, I managed the relationship with Chicago-based Burrell Advertising, led by the legendary Tom Burrell.

All advertising at Coke USA came under the domain of another black executive named Bill Sharp, who was the first African American to head advertising for a major consumer goods company in the nation. After Bill left Coca-Cola, he started Sharp Advertising in Atlanta, which specialized in black marketing and advertising. Our paths would cross yet again at the Georgia Power Company, where, upon my recommendation as a board member, management hired Bill to hone the energy provider's message to black consumers across the state.

Together, Bill Sharp and Tom Burrell created the famous "Coke adds life" advertising campaign. One commercial depicted a bunch of black kids sitting on the steps of a brownstone in Harlem and singing, "Coke adds life, Coca-Cola." The characters in the ad were doing what kids liked to do in those days: doo-wop and imitating their favorite R&B icons, like the Temptations. The commercial was effective because it captured kids' best moment and gave it back to them. The commercial turned out to be a blockbuster for brand Coca-Cola among youth throughout urban America.

My strategy was to bring a more holistic approach to the task of ethnic marketing. I knew that market leadership was dependent upon how well a company engages its consumers and communities. Furthermore, I knew that it was important to recognize the intrinsic value created in those relationships beyond mere transactions.

We aimed to create messages that struck the proper balance between product placement and community values. We did it by capturing wholesome images of families enjoying Coke while they were grilling in the backyard or celebrating special events like holidays and weddings.

An Unusual Bequest

Just as we were depicting wholesome American moments in our marketing at Coke, I had my own personal American moment one clear, crisp fall day in 1980. I was sitting in my office at the Coca-Cola Company's headquarters when my mother called with news from Newnan: "Mister Angelo wants to talk to you about buying the land."

"Mister Angelo" was Angelo Grenga. My mother, of course, was of the generation for whom it was customary to place a "Miss" or "Mister" in front of the first name of white folks. The practice created a mixture of formality and familiarity that typified the subtleties of social interaction between blacks and whites in the South for much of my mother's life.

Mister Angelo's father was the owner of part of the land that my family had once sharecropped. He had stopped by my parents' house that morning and told Mamma he was putting 106.2 acres of his family land up for sale. He also told her that, before his father passed away, the elder "Mister Angelo" made his wishes clear: if the land was ever sold, he wanted my father to have the first chance to buy it. If my father couldn't buy it, he wanted the land to be offered to my father's children. It was an unusual "bequest" for a white, Southern landowner.

I had been thinking about buying land in Coweta County for a long time anyway and was in the midst of negotiating the purchase of a 25-acre plot closer to Newnan.

But this piece of land was different, something far beyond a business investment. For me, it was almost a spiritual thing. Buying 106 acres that were contiguous to my parents' fifty acres would allow me to expand and solidify the homestead my father had started.

I didn't have to think about whether I wanted to buy the 106 acres from Angelo Grenga. I asked myself just one question: "Can I afford it?" It didn't take much figuring to know that I could. I cleared my calendar for the afternoon and headed to Newnan.

As I drove, I couldn't help thinking about how what was happening was like the forming of a circle when a line folds back on itself. The linear part of history was shifting for this event. I was a black man going to see a white man about buying some land. By 1980, I wouldn't be expected to call Angelo Grenga "Mister Angelo." But I did.

I would eventually buy other contiguous tracts of land until the farm was about a thousand acres, with fields and lakes and hardwood and pine forests, and an abundance of deer, wild turkeys, coyotes, and rabbits. What started as an addition to the old farm became a small plantation that we now call Lucky Feather. It overlooks the old lake, which we cleaned up, expanded, and renamed Lois Ware Lake.

"Did you beat him?"

Things just kept falling into place for me, many that were a result of planning and hard work and others that appeared to come out of the blue.

I remember driving down Northside Drive with Herman Russell in his light-brown Mercedes-Benz. We were headed to Coca-Cola headquarters for a meeting with Bob Holder and Roberto Goizueta to discuss their involvement in the expansion of the new corporate campus. Herman casually remarked, "Carl, you serve on every nonprofit board in the city. But none of these boards pays."

I thought nothing of it. And then one day, I was playing golf with Bob Scherer, the CEO of Georgia Power, whom I knew through my work on the Atlanta City Council. We were playing at Snapfinger Woods Golf Club, and we sat down to lunch after the match. We talked about a number of things—our golf scores, city politics, and our families. In fact, we talked about everything but Georgia Power.

No sooner had I returned to the office and sat down at my desk than my phone rang. It was Roberto calling. "How did your golf outing go?" he asked.

"Bob Scherer was a gracious host, and it was good getting to know him better," I replied.

"Did you beat him?"

"I think so," I said.

"Maybe you shouldn't have," Roberto said, laughing. "He was interviewing you to come on the board of directors of Georgia Power. And if you are happy with it, he wants to come by and formally extend the invitation. You'll be the first Coke executive to serve on that board. I hope you'll serve."

"Of course, I will serve," I said. "It's a great honor."

The next day, Bob came to my office to make the formal offer. A few months later, I extended an invitation to Bob to serve on the board of trustees of Clark Atlanta University. Bob graciously accepted. It would mark the beginning of a long-standing tradition of Georgia Power executives serving on the CAU board. In fact Bill Dahlberg, who succeeded Scherer, and Allen Franklin, who succeeded Dahlberg, both served on the CAU board. I would serve on the Georgia Power board for twenty-two years.

16

A BETTER COMPANY

At Coca-Cola USA, our efforts to penetrate the fast-growing Hispanic market intensified. I initiated a search for the special markets department (later called the Black and Hispanic Marketing Department) to find someone whose job would be to market Coke within various Latin American communities.

A prerequisite was that this marketing executive would possess the skill set to understand the segmented nature of the Hispanic markets—Cuban Americans, Mexican Americans, Puerto Ricans, and other Latin American groups. After interviewing several candidates, I hired Coca-Cola USA's first Hispanic marketing manager, a beer-industry marketing and advertising executive named Tony Flores.

As I was building the black and Hispanic marketing teams, the company was confronting a potential boycott of its products, led by Rev. Jesse Jackson.

Jesse Jackson—one of Dr. King's lieutenants who was standing on the balcony of the Lorraine Motel when King was assassinated—was taking the battle for economic justice from the streets to the executive suites of corporate America. His clarion call was, "The black community needs economic reciprocity, not just social generosity."

Jesse founded Operation PUSH (People United to Save Humanity) in 1971 and based the organization in Chicago. It would pursue social justice, civil rights, and political activism.

Jesse said if black consumers represent 10 percent of a company's sales, then 10 percent of its bottling ownership, distributors, senior-level positions, vendors, and suppliers must be black. The companies he called out publicly included Kentucky Fried Chicken; Burger King Corporation; Anheuser-Busch; the parent company of 7-Eleven; and, of course, Coca-Cola.

Coke was an easy target, and we were vulnerable because there was a lot of truth in what Jesse said. Despite the fact that 19 percent of Coke's product sales were to black consumers, there were no black bottlers, no black distributors, and very few black suppliers of significant inputs such as bottles, crates, or trucks. There were no black contractors building Coke bottling plants and no black architects or interior designers who had ever done any work for Coke. We had no outside black accounting firms, and there were certainly no black banks with any Coca-Cola accounts.

At the time corporate America was digging in its heels and opposing any formula that could be construed as a race quota. Ultraconservative president Ronald Reagan had just been elected to the White House, and many white Americans were tired of hearing about civil rights and affirmative action. Jesse's demands for economic inclusion of blacks in the American marketplace prompted even more resistance throughout corporate America.

In 1981, big changes came to Coke. J. Paul Austin retired as chairman. Roberto Goizueta replaced him. Roberto, an exiled Cuban aristocrat, started with the company in 1954 as a chemical engineer in Havana and worked his way up the ranks.

That same year marked the start of an unprecedented period of growth for Coca-Cola. Don Keough, an Irish American who began working with the company in 1950, became president. As the global expansion began, he would come to be known as one of Coke's most powerful bosses. Under Roberto's leadership, Coke's stock value would skyrocket from $4.3 billion to more than $152 billion.

Despite the fact that Roberto shunned the notion of being identified as a minority himself, I remember him making the point in a meeting with senior Coca-Cola executives that our business system ought to fairly reflect our consumer base. That's all he said. People listened and started to rethink their opposition to what Jesse was saying. Roberto wasn't outwardly agreeing with Jesse, but he was saying, "We've got to do better."

At the stage I was brought in, there had been a breakdown in the negotiations between Coke and Operation PUSH. The two Coke negotiators, one black and one white, struck a defensive tone that was insulting to Jesse. The negotiations came to an abrupt halt, and Jesse threatened a boycott of our products.

Don Keough took me aside one day and asked me to find out

what Jesse was really after. He asked me to analyze our vulnerabilities and make a business-based recommendation. Don and I both knew that the potential adverse impact of a product boycott over racial disparities in the company would damage our reputation. If we got out ahead of the issue and got it right, though, we would be a better company.

Before I reopened negotiations with Jesse, I sought the advice and counsel of African American business leaders including Herman Russell and publisher John Johnson, as well as such civil rights leaders as National Urban League president Vernon Jordan, NAACP CEO Dr. Benjamin Hooks, and SCLC president Rev. Joseph E. Lowery. I also took the pulse of black political leaders, among them the mayors of such major cities as Chicago, Los Angeles, and, of course, Atlanta, as well as members of the Congressional Black Caucus. Amid these discussions, which were ongoing, I felt I was in a stronger position to negotiate a win-win for the company and for Jesse and Operation PUSH.

Figuring out what Jesse wanted took several personal visits to his home in Chicago, trips that I made at his invitation. We were comfortable with each other from the start because he knew me from my days as president of the Atlanta City Council and my work in civil rights. It also didn't hurt that Jim Felder—a South Carolina legislator at the same time that I was president of the Atlanta City Council, and also a Clark College alum—was Jesse's lead negotiator.

Some of the conversations between Jesse and me took place at his home on the South Side of Chicago. A couple of times I even enjoyed shooting a few hoops with Jesse and his kids, including his namesake, Jesse junior, a precocious teenager who later became a US congressman. Jesse's wife, Jackie, made me so welcome that I felt as if I were walking into my sister Louise's living room. Most of our talks took place at the Operation PUSH offices in an old community center, a large building with bare, utilitarian furniture.

But we also welcomed Jesse at Coca-Cola's headquarters on North Avenue for a meeting in the company's executive conference room on the 12th floor. The building was very modern with the exception of several life-size, full-length, full-regalia portraits of Confederate generals. I always felt uncomfortable as an African American doing business under the gaze of those portraits, especially when we had international guests who didn't criticize us openly so as not to offend.

The situation was made even more uncomfortable for me by the fact that the interior decorating had been done when the building was built in 1978 after I was recruited by the Coca-Cola Company. Even though our families had been close, there was this incomprehensible yet complete insensitivity, as if anything like these paintings could ever be okay. I was certainly used to it. Black businessmen, clergy, and community leaders were forced to move about the city with such constant and clawing reminders of a claim to hold onto the traditional Old South.

Early in my career, I could do nothing about the situation. I was just a minnow then. I had tried to get traction on redecorating to no avail. But I had grown into a shark, and in anticipation of Jesse Jackson's visit, I insisted that the portraits be removed. And they were.

Retiring long-dead Confederate generals should have been the least of my worries. My job was to figure out how to get Coke out of a major national embarrassment. For starters, we were less concerned about a boycott than we were about its potential damage to our reputation and brand image.

Jesse saw the threat of a boycott as an opportunity to demonstrate his power to pressure companies to change their behavior toward a significant segment of their market. Somewhere along the way, Jesse learned that there were legal ramifications to declaring a boycott unless the product offended a specific class of people. So he reworded his campaign from boycott to "selective withdrawal of enthusiasm."

Jesse was smart, did his homework, and surrounded himself with advisors who included public relations professionals, lawyers, bankers, and economists. He had a unique style. Jesse built his arguments using market research and business logic and then delivered his message as an old-fashioned Baptist preacher would do. From our talks, I surmised that he wanted an agreement based on specific goals and measurable economic impact.

I worked with my team to quantify in dollars and human resources what the agreement would look like. In other words, the agreement would cover our senior-level management and board of directors, procurement, distribution, and franchise ownership. This was what Don meant when he asked me to come up with a business-based solution. My recommendations would be good for the Coca-Cola system and good for our shareholders.

Once we had all the facts, I discussed our plan with Don as we were flying from Atlanta to Chicago on the company jet. As we reviewed my report, he told me my numbers were too low, and we needed to raise the total value of the proposed PUSH agreement. He even said to me, "Carl, I'm blacker than you!" We kept working on our plan until we arrived at the meeting with Jesse at PUSH headquarters. Don and Jesse shook hands on the tenets of the agreement, then we invited Jesse to Atlanta for a press conference to announce the now famous Coca-Cola/Operation PUSH agreement at our North Avenue headquarters on August 10, 1981.

The company agreed to invest millions of dollars in black-owned businesses and to increase the number of blacks in senior management and on our board of directors. The agreement covered the appointment of black distributors and suppliers. The company would establish meaningful relationships with black banks, including deposits and loan accounts. Advertisement in black-owned newspapers and magazines would quadruple, as would the outlay with black-owned advertising agencies. We also pledged significantly more financial support for historically black colleges and universities and to increase the number of black internships.

The creation of the first black-owned bottling franchise was well underway when the PUSH agreement was signed.

Looking back, I still don't think Jesse knew what he wanted in concrete economic terms. I think he just wanted what we all wanted: to fulfill Dr. King's promise to advance the civil rights movement from protests to politics and economics. Jesse was the catalyst who made our internal efforts more effective. He would say, "There are the true shakers, and there are the jelly makers."

I came to realize what Roberto meant when he said we had to do better. It was a personal victory for me to see the Coca-Cola/PUSH agreement signed. The Coca-Cola Company became the first American corporation to sign the PUSH agreement.

I brought on Ingrid Saunders Jones and consultant Bill Clement to help devise a plan to implement the Coke/PUSH agreement. Ingrid had been working as Maynard's executive assistant at City Hall as he approached the end of his second term in 1982. Bill was then a future CEO of Atlanta Life Insurance Company and among the many successful grandsons of civil rights stalwart Rev. John Wesley Dobbs.

Ingrid and Bill worked with the PUSH consultants: Alexis Herman, who would become secretary of labor in the Clinton administration, and Ernie Green, former assistant secretary of labor under Jimmy Carter. Ernie had also been one of the Little Rock Nine in his youth. Together, the two teams developed detailed tracking and reporting systems that would serve to brief Rev. Jackson and Don Keough on progress as the agreement was being implemented.

One of the key institutional changes that came from the PUSH agreement was the establishment of Coke's minority supplier development program, created to identify and make opportunities available to qualified minority- and woman-owned businesses. It became a part of the Coca-Cola business routine.

As we were repairing our US operations, even more disturbing issues loomed in South Africa, where the Coca-Cola business operated under the system of apartheid. Because of my track record, I was tapped to head a new corporate group and promoted to senior vice president of the Coca-Cola Company to provide leadership for these highly sensitive initiatives.

Identifying Coca-Cola's First Black Bottler

The decision to recruit the first black Coca-Cola bottling franchisee was such a fundamental shift in the company's hundred-year-old franchise bottler system that it had to be handled at the highest level of the company.

Finding Coca-Cola's first black bottler was no easy task. Our challenge was to identify and recruit someone who had the financial strength to invest in a bottling franchise and who was in a position to own and operate it as a lifelong interest.

Until that time, US bottlers were successful in large part because they had been franchised by families who ran them as family businesses, handing down ownership through the generations.

I conducted exploratory conversations with many wealthy black entrepreneurs across the country. In Chicago, I met with John Johnson to explain what we were trying to accomplish. John founded Johnson Publishing Company, publisher of *Ebony* and *Jet* magazines. He was the first black millionaire to make the *Forbes* 400 list. John was interested in the investment, but only as a passive investor. His passion was publishing and media.

A similar story came from my meeting with boxing promoter extraordinaire Don King, whose net worth at one point was estimated by *Forbes* to be near $350 million. I met with Don in his New York office to discuss the proposition. Again, he stated his willingness to invest, but we'd have to find somebody else to operate the business.

In Atlanta, I discussed the franchise opportunity with Herman Russell. My pitch to Herman was that if he acquired a Coke franchise, we would train one of his sons to become the bottler. Like others I'd already approached, he saw it as a good passive investment.

We had a steady stream of interest from well-intentioned professional athletes who did not have the ability and willingness to invest, own, and operate a franchise.

We weren't looking to put together a conglomerate investor group. We wanted a businessman, an entrepreneur who would give the franchise the time and attention it required to be successful.

After an extensive search, we found J. Bruce Llewellyn, who was recommended to me by attorney Bill Coleman, transportation secretary in the George H. W. Bush administration. Bill would become the second African American to serve in the Cabinet of the United States. He heard from my Atlanta friend Jesse Hill that we were looking for a candidate and called to recommend that I talk with Bruce Llewellyn.

Bruce was the owner of Fedco Foods Corporation, a chain of nine supermarkets in the Bronx and Harlem that he had purchased in 1969 through a leveraged buyout before such tactics were commonplace. Pepsi had already approached Bruce about acquiring one of its franchises in upstate New York, but the negotiations fizzled. He and I talked on the phone, and then I flew to New York with my colleague Richard Hiller, Coca-Cola VP of business development, to meet

Bruce in person.

Richard and I spent a whole day visiting Bruce's stores and getting to know him better. Bruce had an impressive background in banking and finance. He had served as chairman of Freedom National Bank, the largest black-owned bank in New York, where he succeeded American baseball hero Jackie Robinson. His wife, Shahara Ahmad-Llewellyn, was a consummate businesswoman in her own right and well regarded for her civic work in New York City.

Not only did Shahara and Bruce have impressive credentials, but we could see clearly from our first meeting that he was a leader. As we toured his stores that day, Richard and I watched how Bruce greeted his managers and customers. He was a hands-on operator, efficient yet very much with a human touch. Over lunch at an Italian restaurant in Brooklyn, we learned that Bruce would need to sell Fedco (which he did, ultimately) to purchase a franchise.

We left the meal in high hopes and, on the way back to the airport, Richard and I agreed that we had finally found Coke's first black bottler. We knew the company would find a way to make the deal work with the right operator.

The Coca-Cola Company owned just over a one-third interest in the Philadelphia Coca-Cola Bottling Company and substantial interest in the publicly traded Coca-Cola bottling company of New York. The synergy between the two franchises would be a critical factor in the creation of the first black-owned franchise.

The next day, we reported to Don Keough how impressed we were with Bruce and told Don that we wanted to explore a deal structure that would bring in other investors to support Bruce as the operator.

Our recommendation pleased Don. He then told us that he'd been working quietly behind the scenes and that Bill Cosby, a Philadelphia native, might want to invest in the deal. "Carl, why don't you go out to Los Angeles and see if you can get him involved?" Don suggested. Coca-Cola owned Columbia Pictures, and Don had struck up friendships with many of the studio's movie stars, including Bill Cosby.

I flew to Hollywood to meet with Bill. When I walked into the Columbia Pictures studio, he greeted me playfully: "How much money is this gonna cost me?" He added, "Don Keough is always digging in my pocket for something."

In principle, Bill liked the idea of being a part of a bottling deal in his hometown and agreed to invest. But we still needed to introduce Bill to Bruce to make sure the chemistry worked.

In the meantime, the Coke marketing people had been courting Julius "Dr. J" Erving to become a Coke spokesperson. Julius was, of course, the NBA player whose artistry and style popularized the "slam dunk" in the 1970s. He was a Philadelphia icon, and he was the undisputed superstar of the NBA. In my discussions with the marketing folks, the thought of Julius the owner and Julius the spokesperson was simply irresistible.

After vetting the thought with Don and Bruce and getting their approval, I reached out to Julius to gauge his interest in becoming a partner in the bottling deal.

Fortunately, we spoke a common language, golf. When I invited him to Atlanta to discuss the deal, I also invited him to play a round of golf with me at the Capital City Club, where I had recently become a member.

Founded in 1883, the Capital City Club was one of the most exclusive private clubs in Atlanta. But there was another golf club in town that outranked them all, and that was where Julius wanted to play.

"I'd love to play at Capital City," he said, then paused. "But do you think we can get a round in at Peachtree?" The Peachtree Golf Club is among the top 100 in the world and so exclusive that I knew only one executive in the entire Coca-Cola Company who had a membership there: Chairman Roberto Goizueta.

I told Julius I'd try. At first I didn't ask Roberto. I thought I'd tap one other contact who had a membership at Peachtree to see if he could get us in. My Peachtree connection put forth the request, but it was rejected. I knew that didn't bode well for Coke's budding relationship with Dr. J, so I confided in Roberto what had happened.

Roberto just said he'd handle it. A couple of days went by, and the day before Julius was to arrive, Roberto called me up to his office and said, "I got you and Julius a tee time."

I thanked him, then I asked how he'd pulled it off.

"I just told them that if the two of you couldn't play...the Coca-Cola Company would never have another executive play at Peachtree Club," he said. "That was it." Suffice it to say, I was thrilled that Roberto had also asked former Atlanta mayor Ivan Allen Jr., a political ally of mine who was also a member of Peachtree, to play the round of golf with us.

With Julius on board, we were ready to do business.

The first leg of the deal involved Bruce, Bill, and Julius acquiring Coke's interest in the Coca-Cola bottling company of New York. Bruce then spent the next year shadowing CEO Charlie Millard, a veteran operator, to learn the ins and outs of running a bottling business. As an owner, Bruce served on the board of the New York bottling company and as chairman of the Philadelphia Coca-Cola Bottling Company while the last details of the Philadelphia deal were being finalized.

In December 1985, Bruce and Shahara, along with Bill Cosby and Julius Erving as passive investors, acquired a majority share of the Philadelphia Coca-Cola Bottling Company, making it the fourth-largest black-owned business in America.

The Coca-Cola Foundation

As the man in charge of all aspects of Coca-Cola's external relations, I was constantly reevaluating our corporate community engagement strategy. We were also concluding the Philadelphia deal, so I had to focus my attention on the need to restructure our approach to corporate philanthropy.

At the time, all of the company's major gift requests were being channeled through the Woodruff Foundation. That loosely structured corporate giving group, which reported to me, made small contributions to local charities, sometimes matched by local bottlers. Our corporate philanthropy was further fragmented by the practice of some senior executives making contributions from their own budgets. And so there was no central core giving strategy to support the community or the brand.

We conducted thorough research on the subject of corporate philanthropy and consulted several experts in the field. One invaluable expert was Dr. James Joseph, former president of the Cummins

Foundation, who was then president and CEO of the Council on Foundations. Dr. Joseph visited me and my team in Atlanta to help us kick-start the Coca-Cola Foundation in 1984.

I served as its first chairman. With Roberto's approval, we targeted giving away 1 percent of the previous year's operating income. The Coca-Cola Foundation would operate solely in the United States, focus on education, and leverage bottlers' local community contributions in a variety of areas. The foundation gave us a vehicle that would align our corporate philanthropy with our business strategy.

One of the early requests for foundation support came from Percy Sutton, the black pioneer politician and media trailblazer. Percy had been the longest-serving borough president of Manhattan, from 1966 to 1977. In 1970, he led a group of black investors to found Inner City Broadcasting Corporation, one of the first broadcasting companies to be wholly owned by African Americans.

Chuck Andrews, a housing consultant and former business associate of mine from San Antonio, Texas, introduced me to Percy.

Percy acquired Harlem's then-derelict Apollo Theater in a bankruptcy sale for $220,000 with the idea of restoring it and revitalizing the surrounding neighborhood. Part of his vision was to open the theater to area residents and to keep ticket prices affordable. Pouring millions of dollars into the renovation, coupled with the high cost of bringing in billboard talent, made pricing tickets within reach of residents impossible, however.

The Apollo Theater was a national treasure and was protected on the US National Register of Historic Places. I agreed to sponsor some of the performances, which was neither a good marketing investment nor a fit with the Coca-Cola Foundation's mission.

I called Percy to let him know that we could not continue to support the Apollo through foundation contributions and recommended he restructure the Apollo project as a not-for-profit foundation.

After a few heartfelt conversations with Percy, who started and owned "Showtime at the Apollo," he agreed. Soon after that, the Apollo Theater Foundation was born. Today, this living landmark of African American heritage, culture, entertainment, and history is operated as a service to the community.

I passed the torch of leading the Coca-Cola Foundation to Ingrid Saunders Jones. Ingrid later handed that torch off to Helen Smith Price, current president of the Coca-Cola Foundation. It was an honor for me to read Helen's recent announcement that the foundation has contributed more than $909 million and expanded beyond its original focus on education to include such areas as clean water and women's economic empowerment.

17

"Leave no stone unturned"

Less than eighteen months after the signing of the Coca-Cola/Operation PUSH agreement, Don Keough and Roberto Goizueta invited me to lunch with them in Roberto's private dining room for an even bigger assignment.

"Carl, we want you to go to South Africa," Roberto said gravely. "I want you to find out what our posture should be in South Africa."

Don added, "Leave no stone unturned."

The Coca-Cola brand and our reputation as a welcomed corporate citizen around the world, not just in the US, were at stake. In addition, the personal reputation of the much-hailed leadership duo of Roberto Goizueta and Don Keough, who steered the Coca-Cola Company's stock price from mediocre growth to meteoric highs in the 1980s, was on the line.

Both men had traveled to South Africa to assess the situation in Coke's tenth-largest market for themselves. The market was an important one for the Coca-Cola Company. South African consumers alone represented 10 percent of the company's worldwide sales. South Africa, under the oppressive yoke of apartheid, was on the brink of civil war. Everyone feared the situation would end in a bloodbath.

Until that time, the company had been placated by the profits streaming in from South Africa and the rosy pictures painted by the white South African managers who flew into Atlanta to deliver their quarterly updates. These managers could not explain away such things as the plantation-style working conditions at two of Coca-Cola's most visible operations, the Minute Maid juice plant in Durban and the Amalgamated Beverage Canners plant in Johannesburg.

In the eyes of the world, however, the entire Coca-Cola system was coming to be seen as complicit through its presence in South Africa and its payment of taxes that directly benefitted the apartheid regime. P. W. Botha, the tyrannical South African prime minister, was known for his use of state security and military personnel to direct violence against black South Africans.

More and more Americans were becoming angered by the images of brutality and poverty in South Africa that came into their living rooms via the nightly news. Students at campuses across the country protested the US corporate presence in South Africa and called on university pension funds to divest. States including New York, whose pension funds reached into the billions of dollars, threatened to divest in US companies doing business in South Africa.

Coca-Cola, the largest beverage company and the most recognizable brand in the world, came under pressure from human and civil rights organizations, the US Congress, the exiled African National Congress and such organizations as TransAfrica, the oldest African American foreign policy group in the US.

As the largest private-sector employer on the continent of Africa, we knew we would have to demonstrate our abhorrence of the system of apartheid. Whatever actions we took would have to be seen by the ANC, black South African consumers, and US critics as the gold standard for US corporate responsibility in South Africa.

The tipping point for the company to deploy me to South Africa was probably a report called "The Plantation Experience." The Coca-Cola Company had commissioned a market research firm, Consumer Behavior, to conduct an assessment of its bottling and canning operations against the backdrop of our compliance with the Sullivan Principles. Consumer Behavior was founded by Eric Mafuna, a black South African who had launched his market research firm after a distinguished career at internationally renowned advertising agency J. Walter Thompson.

Rev. Leon Sullivan developed the Sullivan Principles in the 1970s. He was founder of Opportunities Industrialization Centers of America and a board member of General Motors, one of the largest employers of blacks in South Africa. Most US companies doing business in South Africa had signed the Sullivan Principles by that time.

The tenets of the Sullivan Principles included (1) nonsegregation of the races in the workplace; (2) equal pay for equal work; (3) development of training programs to prepare nonwhites for supervisory, administrative, clerical, managerial, and technical jobs; (4) increasing the number of nonwhites in management and supervisory positions; (5) improving the quality of life for nonwhites in housing, transportation, school, recreation, and health facilities; and (6) working to eliminate laws and customs that impeded social, economic, and political justice.

What Coke's top Atlanta executives saw in "The Plantation Experience" report was something ugly that struck an old and tender nerve. They associated the plantation-style management and slave-labor conditions at Coke's Minute Maid plant in the Northern Transvaal region (now the Limpopo Province) with the American system of plantation slavery.

At the time of my first visit, much of sub-Saharan Africa was reeling from the vestiges of colonialism and civil war. However, South Africa was the only African nation in which the colonizers were homegrown. The Dutch arrived in 1647 and claimed the land, where their descendants developed a new language, Afrikaans, meaning "African Dutch."

People often draw comparisons between the struggle of blacks under apartheid and the struggle of African Americans during slavery and Jim Crow. The difference in South Africa was the sheer scale and impact of the apartheid laws called the Group Areas Act and the Bantu Homeland Citizenship Act. As these laws were put into effect, starting in 1948, millions of blacks were relegated to nominally independent homelands and separate residential and business sections in urban areas.

Nelson Mandela wrote in his autobiography *Long Walk to Freedom* that the key difference between the two nations' struggles was that the "United States was a democracy with constitutional guarantees of equal rights that protected non-violent protest; South Africa was a police state with a constitution that enshrined inequality with an army that responded to non-violence with force."

I could easily relate to the indignity of the racially based pass laws, which were a part of the American system of slavery. What was not on display for an African American Coca-Cola Company executive was the trauma and stress that the black South African population endured on a daily basis.

Rev. Frank Chikane, who became director of the presidency of South Africa under Thabo Mbeki, describes it succinctly in volume four of the *Truth and Reconciliation Commission of South Africa Report*: "A world made up of teargas, bullets, whippings, detention, and death on the streets. It is an experience of military operations and night raids, of roadblocks and body searches. It is a world where parents and friends get carried away in the night to be interrogated. It is a world where people simply disappear, where parents are assassinated, and homes are petrol bombed."

In the cities, the Group Areas Act resulted in sprawling urban ghettos called townships. One of the best known was Soweto, almost fifty-eight square miles where more than a million black workers were forced to live in shantytowns governed by oppressive pass laws. The Group Areas Act not only had the effect of keeping blacks out of white areas, it also forced black South Africans to commute long distances to work.

The Population Registration Act of 1950 required people to be classified according to race. Black South Africans had the fewest rights. Next came the coloureds, people we would call "mixed-race" or "biracial" in the States. Then came the Indians, or South Asians from former British India. At the top, with full rights, were white South Africans.

Against this backdrop, on March 4, 1983, I embarked on a twenty-two-day journey that would take me to Nigeria, Ethiopia, Kenya, Zimbabwe, and finally South Africa.

I have been asked many times why I chose those four countries to visit first. Apart from the fact that I wanted to gauge the attitudes of some key sub-Saharan countries toward South Africa, the simple and most direct answer is that they are all English-speaking countries.

What's more, Nigeria, Ethiopia, and Kenya were the largest countries in sub-Saharan Africa. And Kenya and Nigeria had vibrant Coke operations, as did Zimbabwe, which was undergoing a political transition from colonial Rhodesian rule to African rule.

After a month of briefings, which included country-specific business overviews, organizational structures, bottler ownership and distribution, plus ethnic, tribal, political, and governmental structures, I felt well prepared for my first trip to Africa.

But I knew that I could never in a donkey's years prepare myself for the emotions I would feel on my first trip to the motherland.

As I boarded British Airways in Atlanta for the eight-hour flight to London's Heathrow Airport, I felt an extraordinary sense of excitement, as if somehow this trip would mark a turning point in my life.

It dawned on me, as the plane took off, just how far I had come. I thought about my father and his courage to cast that first ballot in Coweta County. About my mother taking in laundry from white folks. About rising before the crack of dawn to slop the hogs and then working as an orderly at Newnan Hospital after school until late at night. I thought about all the people at Oak Grove Baptist and the Prince Hall Masons who had pitched in so that I could attend Clark College.

It was no small distance to cover. I was born with a seemingly bleak future but had become a senior vice president of the Coca-Cola Company who was flying first class on a critical mission to solve a perplexing business problem and perhaps change the course of history. I said a silent prayer thanking God for this calling, with a complete understanding of just how blessed I was. As I considered my journey to that point, I felt a stronger purpose to use my position to help my brothers in South Africa.

I was aware of the fact that I wasn't traveling as the average American business executive. I carried with me the power and authority of the Coca-Cola Company. I knew that Don Keough had already phoned ahead with explicit instructions on this point. Don and Roberto wanted to hear the truth about our South African operations, not the glossy reports from the white South African managers.

My first stop would be Lagos, Nigeria. The Nigerian Bottling Company (NBC), originally franchised in 1951 under colonial rule, had thrived through a bloody civil war in the late sixties, as well as through several military coups. The country was then a democracy headed by President Shehu Usman Aliyu Shagari.

Nigeria had enjoyed a degree of prosperity as the second-largest oil-producing country in the world behind Saudi Arabia but was, at the time, suffering from the effects of a world oil glut that drove down prices, cramping its development and causing political unrest. Later that year, in fact, President Shagari would leave office when Major General Muhammadu Buhari seized his government in a military coup. At the base of all of this political upheaval was corruption.

A Coca-Cola Nigeria Bottling Company representative named Laolu Ikekube met me at the Murtala Muhammed International Airport in Lagos. Laolu impressed me as we drove with our security escort through a traffic maze that would make a Manhattan rush hour seem like a Sunday cruise through rural Coweta County.

It appeared that there were no traffic lights or laws. To get anywhere in Lagos required an armed escort, which meant another vehicle drove in front of us, sirens blaring and blue lights flashing. The lead vehicle carried two armed security guards, one driving while the other hung out the window, brandishing a machine gun and blowing a whistle to get the cars and the masses of human traffic to clear a path for us.

At first, I thought the security people were local policemen but soon learned that everybody who was considered important had private security, an arrangement sanctioned by law enforcement to get you where you needed to go—if necessary, by force and intimidation. It was the most bizarre thing I've ever seen in my life.

At the Sheraton Hotel, I showered and changed clothes and then set out for my first meeting at the Nigerian Bottling Company's Ikeja plant, a few miles away.

My first lasting impression of Lagos was of its people. The faces were so familiar, and I could identify aunts, uncles, sisters, brothers, college classmates, and church members at Oak Grove in nearly every face I saw. I was intrigued by the sheer mass of human activity and voices in the crowded streets. What I came to learn later was that the boisterous mannerisms I witnessed at every kiosk along the way to our destination were simply the Nigerian way of negotiating.

At the Ikeja Coca-Cola bottling plant, I was greeted by Chief Bashorun Adesanya, a tall, distinguished Nigerian wearing traditional robes. He was the chairman of the Nigerian Bottling Company.

At a lunch he hosted for me, he introduced me to the plant supervisors and employees. The meal featured local dishes including curried fish and chicken and an array of delicious Nigerian vegetables and desserts. I was ready for the plant tour after that. I thanked the employees and the managers for their hospitality, and then Bashorun took me on a tour of the five-year-old bottling plant. Coca-Cola, Sprite, and Fanta were produced there and then distributed throughout Lagos. The plant had no air-conditioning, but the building was spotless.

As was my habit on plant visits, I stopped to speak to the janitor, a lab tech, and the workers on the plant floor. All bottling plants had a similar layout. The administrative offices were just behind the main lobby. Next came the sales department, product labs, and finally the production hall. I'd walk up to a worker who had a free hand, shake it, and say something like, "Thank you for working for Coca-Cola. You're doing a great job. We appreciate you."

These people occupied what were some of the best jobs for blacks in the country at that time. Even so, the simple thanks was intended to make each worker feel that his individual contribution was valuable. I was the first African American Coca-Cola executive who had ever visited the Lagos plant from Atlanta. As far as they were concerned, I ran the Coca-Cola Company.

Back then, for a Coke executive, nothing pleased the ear more than the sound of a bottling line in production. The clinking of glass against glass, the swishing of the product as bottles were filled made a distinct *cha-ching cha-ching* noise. When I randomly pulled a freshly filled bottle of Coke off the line and took a big sip with an *ahhh*, it always elicited a wide smile from the production workers. Then and always, I enjoyed touring bottling plants because of the people who actually produce Coca-Cola.

But I was on a different mission in Nigeria. After leaving the plant floor, Bashorun and Laolu led me to a conference room for a discussion about why I was there. I opened the meeting with the big question: "What is your impression of what's going on in South Africa?"

To a person, the response was that South Africa was headed toward civil war and that it was going to be a bloodbath.

I followed that question with the next most important one: "What should the Coca-Cola Company be doing in South Africa on both the business and political fronts?"

The Nigerians said the company must be on the right side of political change, meaning supporting the black South Africans in their struggle. This theme was one I heard echoed later in Ethiopia, Kenya, and Zimbabwe.

That evening we were joined by the Coca-Cola Nigeria region manager from London. Although Coke was bottled and distributed locally, Coca-Cola's region manager for Nigeria lived in England and worked out of our London office in Windsor. The finance manager, the sales manager, and even the technical engineers lived in England and commuted to Nigeria.

After dinner Bashorun and Laolu privately shared their concerns over the brutal apartheid regime's police state and the military excursions meant to destabilize neighboring black-ruled Botswana, Zambia, Zimbabwe, Angola, and Mozambique.

On my second day in Nigeria, I departed the Sheraton Hotel around 5 A.M. to catch a flight 500 miles north to Kano, the second-largest city in Nigeria. On my way to the airport, as the sun came up, I was amazed at the body-to-body, bumper-to-bumper automobile and moped traffic already on the streets, all going somewhere but nowhere fast.

On the flight, I reviewed my notes and was excited to have the opportunity to learn more about the people and culture of the Islamic city of Kano. The official language was English, but the Hausa people who made up the largest ethnic group in West Africa spoke their own language on the streets.

I arrived ninety minutes later at the Mallam Aminu Kano International Airport, where I was met by an Irish gentleman whose name escapes me. His job was to drive me to NBC's Challawa plant, some twelve miles away from the airport.

Despite Kano's having an international airport, I saw no tourists and few signs of Western influence. In fact, visiting Kano felt very much like taking a trip in a time machine. The ancient city walls date back to 1095, the time of its first king. I wondered just how much had changed since its precolonial days, when the city served as the gateway to the trans-Sahara trade route, where caravans of camels and men transported gold from western and central Sudan to the Mediterranean Sea economies in exchange for salt.

I wish I had seen more of Kano. As it turned out, my visit coincided with the arrival of the Harmattan, an annual sandstorm that blows in from the Sahara Desert. No sooner had I checked in at the hotel where all the expats stayed than this wonder of nature rolled in like a giant rogue wave.

I am certain it was not intentional, but my hosts omitted telling me to cover my face as we toured the plant and made a few rounds in the market on foot. As a result, I inhaled so much of the tiny, glass-like shards of sand that I spent most of the night awake in the hotel with a massive nosebleed. I went to the front desk to see if I could get some medical help, but the phones were down.

I returned to my room and bathed my bleeding nostrils in the bathroom sink, hoping that would stop the flow of blood. The tepid water provided some relief before the electricity went out, leaving me in complete darkness. I half nodded off to sleep. At some point in the middle of the night, I was jolted awake by the sound of loud music coming from downstairs.

Once again, I went to the front desk to inquire. Was the power back on? It turned out that the hotel had one generator, which they used for the bar, where a group of expats was enjoying an all-night party.

I was relieved to be out of the Harmattan but disappointed that I wasn't able to talk to more people before my NBC guide dropped me at the airport the next morning to catch my flight back to Lagos. That same evening, in Lagos, I was driven to the airport by Laolu. At the check-in counter, I learned that my flight to Addis Ababa, Ethiopia, had been canceled. Still physically weak, I found myself stranded. I couldn't reach Laolu by phone, so the Ethiopian Air flight attendants helped me find a small hotel nearby.

In my room, I tried to turn on the bedside lamp, but it didn't have a bulb. The front desk clerk said if I wanted a light bulb for my lamp, it would cost more "dash," which is another word for rip-off. I had already traded in my naira, the Nigerian currency, and told them so. But he gladly accepted my US dollars. And a light bulb was delivered to my door.

The victory was short-lived. Once I had light, I could see there were no sheets on the bed, and in the bathroom there were no towels or soap. I called the desk again. "How much is it going to cost me, all-inclusive, to spend the night here?" I asked incredulously.

I should have put two and two together. The truth was that the few dollars I spent on necessities were a minor windfall in a country where the average monthly income is something like $123 US.

The next morning I was finally able to reach Laolu, who picked me up from the hotel and took me to lunch before we made our way back to the airport. This time Laolu did not leave until he saw my plane take off.

18

Temperature Rising

The first-class service on Ethiopian Air Lines, the best in sub-Saharan Africa, was a welcome relief. I enjoyed a pleasant meal with a glass of decent cabernet. I drank a silent toast to my friend Sam Ayoub, an Egyptian who was also the Coca-Cola Company's chief financial officer at the time. Sam had helped to launch Ethiopian Air Lines, modeling it after some of the best airlines in Europe. It pleased me to finally experience what I had heard Sam and Roberto talk about many times back in Atlanta.

En route to Addis Ababa, Ethiopia, I thought about the purpose of my visit there while at the same time realizing that I was making the most direct West Africa to East Africa connection by plane. I also knew from my briefing that our Coke franchise was a parastatal, owned and operated by the Ethiopian government. The bottling plant was not in production because the country was in the midst of a civil war.

The Ethiopian Civil War began in 1974. It started when Emperor Haile Selassie I—the last ruler of the House of Solomon, descendants of King Solomon of Israel and the Queen of Sheba—was removed from office in a coup d'etat. The usurpers were the Marxist Derg, a military committee of enlisted men and low-ranking officers. After repelling the Italians in 1936, Ethiopia could lay claim to being the only sub-Saharan African country that had successfully resisted colonization. This victory was an immense source of national pride for the Ethiopian people.

By the time I arrived in 1983, hundreds of thousands of Ethiopians were fleeing the violent political and economic repression that would eventually leave more than a million dead. That same year the country was hit by a drought and subsequent famine that would kill an estimated 400,000 more people in just twenty-four months.

I knew from a business perspective that even in the best of times the Ethiopian market of 55 million consumers was very difficult to penetrate. Its mountainous geography made it a production and distribution nightmare.

When I stepped off the plane, I was moved by the red-carpet welcome that had been prepared for me, despite the fact that I didn't consider myself a dignitary. The welcoming party included a troupe of little girls dressed in beautiful floral costumes. Each child presented me a bouquet of flowers until my arms were as full as my heart.

The local Coca-Cola PR man, an Ethiopian with a small security detail of two, escorted me to the Hilton, the only international hotel in the city. Despite my briefing and everything I had read and thought I understood, I have to admit I was startled to see, in the center of Addis Ababa, military tanks crewed by Cuban soldiers armed with machine guns.

After I checked into the hotel, showered, and ate a little breakfast, I was taken to the Addis Ababa bottling plant, which initially opened in 1959. As we approached the plant, I saw that it was surrounded by armored tanks, and my stomach sank again.

Inside the plant there were no sounds of clinking bottles on the production line. The plant was staffed by a skeleton crew that was helpless to produce Coke without concentrate and sugar, which were impossible to import because of the war. I listened to the general manager's concerns and made a mental note to revisit his issues with Claus Halle, president of Coca-Cola International.

I departed Addis Ababa the next day for Nairobi, Kenya, my ultimate East Africa destination. My flight touched down midday at Jomo Kenyatta International Airport, which is named for revolutionary leader and statesman Jomo Kenyatta, who led the country as prime minister upon independence in 1963, after forty-three years of colonial rule.

My reception was a relatively quiet one. I was met by Paul Makurro, head of external affairs and the highest-ranking black Coke executive. I was booked into the Nairobi Serena Hotel, which is renowned for its fine dining and well-appointed rooms, all of which came with light bulbs and towels.

Coca-Cola had started operations in Kenya in 1948 with Nairobi

Bottlers. The upper management of the Coca-Cola Company East Africa consisted primarily of expatriates. The region manager was an Italian named Eddie Ferrari. The general counsel, Stuart Eastwood, was a Brit who would become a division manager on my staff when I took over as president of the Coca-Cola Africa Group.

I connected easily with the vice president of operations, an Indian named Prittipal Singh, or "Pritt" for short. We played a round of golf at the exclusive Muthaiga Golf Club, where he shared his thoughts about the Indians who lived in the Phoenix township of Durban, South Africa.

Once we finished the 18th hole and sat down for drinks in the clubhouse lounge, I had a chance first meeting with a man named Philip Ndegwa, an economist and governor of the Central Bank of Kenya, who later became chairman of Kenya Airways in 1991. When Ndegwa learned about my mission, he expressed his ardent support for Nelson Mandela and other imprisoned ANC leaders in their efforts to overthrow the apartheid regime.

Unlike Nigeria, where the region office was based in London, Kenya's Coca-Cola executives all lived in Nairobi. Another important detail that differentiated Nigeria from Kenya was that the Coke business in Kenya was completely dependent on the South Africa sugar cartel.

Back at the Serena Hotel that evening, Eddie hosted a dinner for me to have an open discussion with his senior managers on the subject of Coca-Cola in South Africa. I posed the same two questions I had raised with the Coke executives in Nigeria.

The Kenya team was nervous about the continuity of the supply of sugar from South Africa and its impact on the business in East Africa. They were less forthcoming on the issue of black ownership in the South Africa bottling system. This reticence was not surprising to me because there were no black bottling owners in Kenya. They were clearly indignant about the treatment of blacks by the apartheid regime and voiced their fears about the implications for other African nations of a racial war in South Africa.

The following day, I caught a three-hour-long British Airways flight to Harare, Zimbabwe's largest city and its capital. Over Tanzania we flew past the snow-covered peaks of Mount Kilimanjaro, one of the seven natural wonders of the world and the tallest mountain on the continent. I was awed by its majestic beauty and splendor.

Zimbabwe would be my last stop before South Africa, and I could feel the political climate warming along with the temperature as I made my way south.

On the flight, I read a story about a massacre in which sixty-two young men and women were gunned down on the banks of the Cewale River in the Lupane district, less than 300 miles west of the capital city.

These killings would become known as the Gukurahundi massacres. Many sources suggest they were ordered by the country's future president, Robert Mugabe, and carried out by his elite North Korea-trained soldiers, known as the Fifth Brigade. The death toll would reach 21,000 civilians by the time the killings ended in 1987.

I had read about such atrocities from a much safer distance. They were becoming commonplace in other parts of the continent, and the African National Congress's armed struggle with the South African oppressors was also heating up. In May of that year, the ANC would carry out one of its deadliest attacks when it targeted the South Africa Air Force headquarters with a bomb set to go off during rush-hour traffic. The blast injured some 200 people and killed more than a dozen.

Zimbabwe had gained its independence only three years earlier from Great Britain. The white Rhodesians were the British who colonized Zimbabwe in the late 1800s and under whose rule the country was called Southern Rhodesia until its independence in 1980. Zambia, colonized in 1924, was called Northern Rhodesia until it gained independence in 1964.

When I arrived, the country was still in the midst of a power struggle between Joshua Nkomo and Robert Mugabe. Nkomo led the Ndebele people, who made up about 20 percent of the population, while Mugabe led the majority Shona people, who constituted 70 percent of the population.

Mugabe finally prevailed in 1987. But on my first visit, I knew him only from newspaper accounts. I could have never guessed that in the years ahead I would become a regular guest of Mugabe and his wife, Sally.

Charles Rukwava, Coke's community and government affairs manager in Zimbabwe, greeted me at the airport and expedited my clearance through customs.

As we drove through the outskirts of town into downtown Harare, it reminded me of Atlanta thirty years earlier.

At the company's Harare office, I met the staff, 99 percent of whom were Rhodesian. It appeared that the roughly 100,000 white Rhodesians still living there were all working for the Coca-Cola Company. The system was completely and unapologetically managed by white Rhodesians.

After a few exchanges on the matter of South Africa, it was clear to me that the white Rhodesian managers had misread the tea leaves. They were too confident in their responses to me as they said they had solved "their problem" in Zimbabwe. The time had come for South African managers to get *their* act together.

It seemed that the Rhodesian managers harbored the notion that Zimbabwean employees should be subservient and that they were not smart enough to do the top jobs. For the white managers, their position at the top of the food chain was because it was a birthright, and the end of colonialism did not mean the end of their sense of privilege. I knew then that we had to change the old colonial system in the Coca-Cola Africa business to reflect the values I helped to shape in Atlanta.

Following the initial discussions at the Harare office, I took a tour of the local bottling plant that was franchised to Delta Beverages, a company that dated back to 1946, when it was founded as Rhodesian Breweries Limited. At Delta Beverages, I was met by a black Zimbabwean named Joe Mutizwa.

Joe attended the University of Rhodesia but left with other students to fight for independence. He was captured and jailed for three years before he finished his degree at the London School of Business. Joe had previously been an economist with the Reserve Bank of Zimbabwe and had recently joined Delta as a personnel officer. He would eventually rise to become CEO and chairman of the board. To me, Joe Mutizwa epitomized the determination, spirit, and incredible resilience of the African people.

As I met more people at the plant, it became clear that Joe was an example of Delta's business practices and not a product of the usual window-dressing strategy. The picture was odd. The bottler proved to be more advanced in its development and placement of black Zimbabweans than the Coca-Cola Company. In the meeting with Joe and CEO Patrick Rooney, someone pointed out to me that Delta had a deliberate plan to recruit and develop black Zimbabweans who would eventually earn leadership roles in every aspect of Delta's operation. I remember saying to myself, "Wow, this is a good example of what needs to happen in South Africa—indeed, throughout the continent."

This impression was a decidedly positive one—and one of the legacies of the Rhodesian regime. Despite their racism and brutality, the British here had invested more in the educational development of the black population than any other country I had studied. This educational infrastructure made stories like Joe Mutizwa's possible.

19

SOUTH AFRICA, AT LAST

On the flight from Harare to Johannesburg I found it nearly impossible to relax and enjoy any of the amenities of the first-class cabin on South African Airways. I was the only black person among a group of white Zimbabwean and South African businessmen who were speaking Afrikaans, presumably carrying on business as usual. The situation on the plane lent a thin veneer of normalcy that in no way reflected the dangerous conditions on the ground in South Africa.

A few months earlier, the South African Defense Forces had conducted military raids on the neighboring states of Zimbabwe, Zambia, and Botswana, which harbored ANC activists and ANC bases. The military raids in Lesotho alone resulted in the deaths of forty-two people—thirty of whom were said to be African National Congress members, the others women and children.

It was an atmosphere of close and imminent danger. Executions of people who opposed the state were commonplace. A famous example was the public hanging of Marcus Motaung, Jerry Mosololi, and Simon Mogoerane, known as the Moroka Three. These men were accused of engineering attacks on a police station. International protests to save them were ignored by the apartheid regime.

The ANC fought back with its own military actions, which included bombing the Supreme Court building in Pietermaritzburg and setting off four bombs that damaged the Koeberg Nuclear Power Plant near Cape Town.

When people of color who were considered important or influential visited South Africa, the government granted them the same rights as whites during their stay, and they received the official status of "honorary white."

The practice was absurd, of course, but I thought it might be the apartheid enforcers' way of saying they weren't such bad guys after all. They were, in fact, good hosts. This practice was explained to me before I left Atlanta, and I was interested to see how such a policy could be implemented, given that I am as dark-skinned as most black Africans.

I was met by an Afrikaner at Jan Smuts International Airport in Johannesburg. The airport was then named for a past Boer prime minister but would later be renamed for ANC president Oliver Tambo.

Hennie Viljoen was the head of government relations for Coca-Cola in South Africa. I enjoyed Hennie's forthright manner, and he let it be known that he was among many white South Africans who were leading conflicted lives. On one hand, they were ashamed of their government. On the other, they enjoyed the privileges of being white. It created a moral dilemma for Hennie.

Hennie's job on this trip was to show me the physical manifestation of apartheid as it played out in our business and in the lives of the people who consumed our product. He broke it down into what he called "structures," which he pronounced with a thick Afrikaans accent as "struktuur."

But first he took me to a Holiday Inn near the airport, where I checked in for a good night's sleep. The next day we drove to the airport, where we boarded a sixty-minute flight south to Durban, which boasts the largest Indian population anywhere in the world outside India and is renowned for its miles of sandy beaches and the warm waters of the Indian Ocean.

From Durban we drove four hours to KwaZulu, home of the Zulu people. It was one of the ten nominal homelands, or Bantustans, created under the Bantu Homeland Citizenship Act of 1970. This legislation served to denaturalize blacks as South African citizens, force them to leave their homes, and resettle them in areas including KwaZulu, which had no natural boundaries or heritage. The Zulu Bantustan was cobbled together from many disconnected stretches of land.

The Zulus' chief minister, appointed and controlled by the apartheid government, was Mangosuthu Gatsha Buthelezi. Chief Buthelezi was of royal Zulu blood and was the son of Chief Mathole

Buthelezi and Princess Magogo kaDinuzulu, the sister of King Solomon kaDinuzulu. He was against foreign corporate disinvestment, and his Inkatha Freedom Party was a political rival of the ANC's.

The other homelands were Transkei and Ciskei, home of the Xhosa people; Bophuthatswana, home of the Tswana people; Venda, home of the Venda people; Lebowa, home of the Pedi people; Kangwane, home of the Swazi people; QwaQwa, home of the Sotho people; Gazankulu, home of the Tsonga people; and kwaNdebele, home of the Ndebele and given self-government status in 1984.

We drove for three hours through miles of Zululand countryside, where the Zulus were held captive in their territory by pass laws, something I was exempt from as an "honorary white." By law, blacks were required to carry passbooks whenever they were outside their homelands or other designated areas.

It was Sunday, so we stopped at a Zulu Methodist church that was holding services and slipped into the back pew. The men wore Western clothes while the women wore colorful dresses of Zulu fabrics. When they sang "What a Friend We Have in Jesus," I imagined myself in my mother's childhood church, Jones Hill United Methodist.

At the end of our journey through KwaZulu, we stopped at an Indian restaurant near Durban. It was not a random food stop, as I first thought, but a part of Hennie's planned orientation for me. When he asked for service, the proprietors said that Hennie could be seated, but I could not. The law said that a black South African could not be seated in a restaurant next to a white person.

The Indian owner of the restaurant was just enforcing the law, albeit one humanly degrading to me. Once Hennie told them that I was an African American and not a South African, it was okay for me to sit at any table next to any patron in the entire restaurant. Hennie knew what the response would be before we entered the restaurant, but he wanted me to experience the race law firsthand.

"Now, Carl, you see the struktuur of apartheid, of this crazy madness," he said, expressing disgust and shame. Hennie did his job well. It was my first personal encounter with the harsh reality of apartheid. But it was not unfamiliar to me, having grown up in Coweta County under Jim Crow.

More Strange "Struktuurs"

On Monday morning we boarded a two-hour flight to Cape Town, which Hennie described as another struktuur unto itself. He pointed out that Cape Town was the bastion of the Boer apartheid system. He took me to the Western Cape, where the majority of people categorized as coloured lived. We then toured Khayelitsha, a sprawling township where Africans from desolate rural homelands were migrating in search of a better life. I saw little children playing barefoot in open sewage and houses fabricated from scraps of tin.

Khayelitsha seemed out of place against the backdrop of Table Mountain's indescribable beauty and the luxurious high-rises and modern tourist attractions stretching along the Atlantic Ocean.

In the Western Cape, I met and spoke with several South African people categorized as coloured who resented the racial classification law and saw themselves as pawns of the apartheid regime. They resented the government even more because of the brutal forced removal of 60,000 coloured residents from their homes in District Six near the Cape Town central business district. District Six was bulldozed and declared a whites-only area.

On Tuesday morning, Hennie drove me along the Atlantic coast and stopped at an old lighthouse. We got out of the car, and he pointed across Table Bay to an island, which I recognized as Robben Island, where Nelson Mandela was imprisoned until he was moved to Pollsmoor Prison in 1982, a year before my first visit. I stood there, gazing tearfully at this desolate symbol of evil that would become a monument to courage.

Our next stop was Peninsula Beverages, the Cape Town Coca-Cola bottler, where I was introduced to the managing director, Dave Lewis. We had a brief discussion about the purpose of my visit, and Dave assured me of his commitment to equality and fairness in the workplace, citing his efforts to recruit and develop coloured supervisors and managers. As we were touring the facility, he proudly introduced me to a savvy young sales manager named Corey Julius, who grew up in the Western Cape and whose family members had been victims of the forced removal.

Dave would become one of my closest confidants as I went about developing the Coca-Cola strategy for South Africa. I also came to know Corey quite well. Whenever I visited Cape Town, I enjoyed spending time with him on his routes, where I got acquainted with his customers in the informal market of Khayelitsha, the fastest-growing township in South Africa.

We made our way back to Johannesburg, where the bulk of my luggage still hadn't arrived from Nairobi. I had picked up a couple of shirts in Cape Town, but for the most part, I had been living out of my carry-on bag, and I had no more clean shirts, let alone suits that I would need for my business meetings.

Hennie took me to an upscale men's haberdashery, Gray's men's store, at the Carlton Center in downtown Johannesburg, the first super-regional shopping center in the city. Hennie introduced me to the owner, an Indian man named Yusuf Surtee, as someone in desperate need of his services.

As I stood before the full-length mirror and Yusuf expertly took my measurements, I quickly found that not only did Yusuf know everything about men's clothing, he seemed to know everyone who was anyone in South Africa.

Yusuf was the personal clothier and comrade of the leaders of the struggle against apartheid. That circle included Bishop Desmond Tutu, the Anglican bishop of Johannesburg. I didn't know it then, but Yusuf would escort me to my first meeting with the spiritual leader in Soweto two years later.

I bought a couple of suits, one of which I wore to Coca-Cola's South Africa division headquarters in downtown Johannesburg that afternoon. The office was located in a modern office park with exquisite landscaping.

I looked forward to finally meeting Fred Meyer, division manager for South Africa. Fred's most enduring legacy would be that he ran a very profitable operation. He planned a "state of the business" presentation for me in the executive conference room that adjoined his well-appointed office suite.

Hennie joined us, as did Ernest Mchunu, the highest-ranking black executive and first black manager at Coca-Cola in South Africa. He headed community relations and reported directly to Fred.

I was eager to hear what Fred had to say about the company's relationships with the black community. But I was disappointed when I realized that Fred was listening just as intently as I was to Eric Mafuna, the author of "The Plantation Experience" report. Fred brought Eric in to deliver the presentation and answer my questions.

Having made an in-depth study of our business in South Africa, Eric spoke expertly about the company's plans to invest in microbusinesses in the townships, healthcare clinics, education programs, and other social investments. His talk was very interesting but struck me as a rehashing of the company's compliance with the Sullivan Principles, which I already knew by heart.

I made a mental note of how Fred's "overview" neglected to make any reference to how he planned to address the matter of black equity participation in the system and black management development.

As much as I cared about the corporate social-responsibility programs and understood their value, I knew these efforts would be meaningless if the company did not address the fundamental issue of black economic inclusion within the Coke system.

After I asked questions about the business, it was explained to me that we had contractual distributorship agreements with a few black South African businesspeople including Richard and Marina Maponya, who were our distributors in Bophuthatswana. Fred also mentioned briefly the Kunene family, another black Coca-Cola distributor in the township of Vosloorus.

In 1983, there were several Coca-Cola bottling franchises in South Africa. None were black-owned.

Don Keough's instruction to me to "leave no stone unturned" prompted me to probe the matter of ownership a bit deeper with Fred Meyer and his management team.

Fred didn't say much about our corporate social-responsibility programs, but he had quick answers and arguments against the idea of black ownership: there were no black South Africans with the kind of money it took to purchase a bottling franchise, he said. He also noted that the entire country was already franchised, and besides, none of the existing franchises were for sale.

After the meeting, the four of us drove to the Devland bottling plant, which served our consumers living in Soweto. They showcased the lunchroom. It had been integrated during the J. Paul Austin era, despite South African law, which required plants, factories, and other work facilities to be segregated.

After the plant tour, I was finally able to see Soweto, a name derived from "South Western Townships." As we approached the main entrance for Soweto, I saw plumes of dark smoke billowing into the sky and smelled the foul odor of burning garbage. Once there, I saw huge mountains of smoldering refuse, incineration being the usual Soweto method for disposing of its tons of waste.

Soweto had started as a squatters' camp of improvised huts built from whatever materials were available, a place laid out in a haphazard way that created a confusing warren of streets. Apartheid laws prohibited black South Africans from living in the area, but the government looked the other way so that black domestics and manual workers could live close to their low-paying jobs in the Johannesburg mines and the homes of white South Africans who lived in luxury. Soweto had grown over the years until it became a city of 1.5 million black people, with the poorest of the poor living in government-built hostels and thrown-together shacks. The township's relatively well-off people lived in solid and substantial homes.

Ernest, for example, lived in a beautiful and meticulously landscaped modern home, which he proudly showed me, as he had shown Roberto Goizueta and Don Keough when they visited Soweto.

I was taken past a school to see Coke's "good works" and to Baragwanath Hospital, the largest hospital in the Southern Hemisphere. And I came away with a working knowledge of the challenges we faced in South Africa. We were in compliance with the Sullivan Principles, just like most US companies doing business there. But mere compliance was not enough. And our business system needed a radical overhaul.

The last thing I remember about my first journey to Africa and to South Africa is getting home. In those days you couldn't fly directly from South Africa to Atlanta. I had to fly up the coast of West Africa to the Cape Verde islands for refueling and, from there, to New York. I had a close connection at Kennedy, so I made a mad dash for my connecting flight. In that pre-cell phone era, I had to wait until I landed in Atlanta to call Mary to pick me up at Hartsfield.

As a result, Mary wasn't waiting for me at our pickup spot. I hadn't seen my wife and son for twenty-two days, and I did not want to ride home in a cab. I phoned her to pick me up. When Mary arrived, she found me outside Delta baggage claim, sound asleep on top of my luggage.

My parents, Lois Wimberly Ware and Ulas B. Ware, on their 50th wedding anniversary.

Our wedding photo at Mary's parents' home in southwest Atlanta, January 1, 1966. We would have a one-night honeymoon at the Walahaja Hotel & Ballroom in southwest Atlanta before I returned for graduate school in Pittsburgh.

With my son Timothy and his two lovely children, Renita and Aaron, 2016.

Daddy U. B. with his six lovely daughters: Louise, Joyce, Julia, Mildred, Evelyn, and Barbara, on his 90th birthday. At 90, my father was lauded by the Coweta County Board of Commissioners and cited in the *Newnan Times-Herald* for his courageous vote in 1949.

My brother, Sergeant Major Thomas Ware, served 28 years in the U.S. Army, including two tours of duty during the Vietnam War. Like all military families, the Wares are proud of Thomas's outstanding service to our nation.

Me with my brothers Walter and Thomas during our family reunion celebration, 2015.

This family photo captured the theme of my first campaign for the Atlanta City Council in 1973. My mother and father, Mary, and our son, Timothy, had my back. The slogan: "Carl Ware Cares." I was 26 years old.

This photo of me as president of the Atlanta City Council and Mayor
Maynard Jackson is a snapshot of how closely Maynard and I worked
together on many groundbreaking initiatives such as the expansion
of Hartsfield International Airport, the ordinance requiring minority
participation in all procurement contracts, and the restructuring of the
Atlanta Police Department.

Atlanta Mayor-elect Shirley Franklin joins me, at that time executive vice president of The Coca-Cola Company, at the Atlanta USA Olympics Community Celebration.

This photo was taken the day I was named Africa Group president in
January 1993. I would spend the next seven years restructuring and
"Africanizing" the Coca-Cola system throughout the continent.

This quality standard was issued to all Coca-Cola employees and bottlers throughout the continent of Africa dated November 1, 1991. "Any job worth doing is a job worth doing right the first time" was a lesson I learned from my father.

One of my favorite photographs—Ingrid Saunders Jones and my executive assistant Linda Wight share a warm embrace that was symbolic of our team spirit and support.

Pictured from left to right: Ingrid Saunders Jones, Coca-Cola Company chairman and CEO Roberto Goizueta, National Urban League president John Jacob, and me during a reception for John at our home in Atlanta on July 19, 1991.

Visiting Equatorial Africa during my time as group president of the
Coca-Cola Company. I very much enjoyed visiting customers but
more importantly, listening to their experiences with Coca-Cola.

Visiting with a customer in the Niger marketplace. Coca-Cola's business relationship with African customers and consumers underscores the importance competitive advantage of Coca-Cola throughout the African continent.

A group president of Africa touring a bottling plant in Ghana with a production supervisor.

Inspecting empty bottles for defects before they are loaded onto the filling line, an inspiring moment for me and the workers.

Lab technicians demonstrate how carbonation is tested in the Ghana bottling plant lab.

Coca-Cola president Don Keough, Coca-Cola Company chairman and CEO Roberto Goizueta, and I welcome Archbishop Desmond Tutu to Coca-Cola headquarters, ushering in a new era of business relationships in South Africa.

Pictured from left to right: SCLC president Rev. Joseph E. Lowery, Archbishop Desmond Tutu, Coca-Cola Company chairman and CEO Roberto Goizueta, Leah Tutu, Mary, and me. We were honored to welcome the Tutus to Atlanta to celebrate Coke's disinvestment from South Africa. Desomond and Leah Tutu were guests in our Atlanta home during this visit.

I met with South Africa President F. W. De Klerk in the Cape Town
Government Administration Building in June 1989. A few months
later De Klerk announced the unbanning of the ANC and the release
of Nelson Mandela. De Klerk was honored alongside Mandela with
the Nobel Peace Prize in 1993.

I joined Nelson Mandela for a fundraising dinner hosted by Peter Guber, chairman and CEO of Sony Entertainment, and attended by the Who's Who in motion pictures, entertainment, athletics, and politics in Los Angeles, July 1993.

This photo appeared in newspapers around the world, taken during the 1994 convocation honoring Mandela at Atlanta's High Museum. I proudly joined with Mandela in a clenched fist, the traditional salute, as we sang the ANC National anthem, Nkosi Sikelel.

The day after his inauguration as president of South Africa, Nelson Mandela gave me a warm welcome and private audience in the Union Buildings presidential chambers in Pretoria, May 10, 1994.

Celebrating newly elected president of Nigeria in 1999. Pictured from left to right: former U.N. Ambassador Andrew Young, Alex Cummings (who succeeded me as group president of Coca-Cola Africa), former U.S. Ambassador Don McHenry and member of The Coca-Cola Board of Directors, Nigeria President Olusegun Obasanjo, and myself.

One of the proudest moments in my career was receiving the Junior Achievement Award and being inducted into the Atlanta Business Hall of Fame, March 30, 2003.

As a member of Kappa Alpha Psi fraternity, I was privileged to receive the fraternity's highest honor. My former classmate and Grand Polemarch of Kappa Alpha Psi Sam Hamilton pins me with the Laurel Wreath in August 2003.

As Executive Vice President (January 2000 to February 1, 2003) my job was to serve as Coca-Cola ambassador across the globe. In the photograph above, I am congratulating a Coca-Cola Vietnam executive and a technical school principal at a ceremony donating funds for a community computer training school in Ho Chi Minh City.

Bill Clinton and I were co-recipients of the UNCF Presidents Award for Service and Philanthropy to UNCF Colleges and Universities. Pictured from left to right: Me, Bill Clinton, Mary, and Michael Lomax, president of the United Negro College Fund, March 9, 2007.

An Encounter with a Spiritual Icon

Back in Atlanta, I made my report to Don and Roberto, as well as to Claus Halle, president of Coca-Cola International. I began by telling them that we had no way to gauge how black South African community leaders perceived the company. And the only connections between the company and the community were one black South African manager and a consultant. The white managers relied solely on Ernest Mchunu and Eric Mafuna for these relationships.

I made several recommendations, including that we commission Consumer Behavior, headed by Eric, to closely monitor the volatile situation in South Africa and introduce us to the black business and political leaders we would need to work with as we devised a new strategy for the Coca-Cola Company.

Eric was uniquely qualified for this assignment. Among other professional affiliations, he founded the Black Management Forum, a powerful think tank that championed black economic empowerment. Eric's research reports would be sent directly to me in Atlanta to avoid the Coca-Cola South Africa division management filter.

I expressed my concerns to Atlanta management about the risk of merely continuing along the lines of constructive engagement vis-à-vis the Sullivan Principles. I also recommended that we explore the implications of partial or total disinvestment.

I told Roberto, Don, and Claus that we could not know the answer until we understood the thinking and positions of such anti-apartheid clerics as Bishop Desmond Tutu, Rev. Beyers Naude, and Rev. Allan Boesak. We needed to know the opinions of business leaders including Gibson Thula; Richard Maponya; Dr. Nthato Motlana, head of the Soweto Committee of Ten; and Sam Motsuenyane, head of the National African Federated Chamber of Commerce. But most importantly, we needed to establish relationships with exiled

African National Congress leaders such as Oliver Tambo, Thabo Mbeki, Johnny Makhathini, and Barbara Masekela.

Claus became my ally. And he imparted sage advice to me on how to handle my relationship with the South African managers: "Carl, you make compelling arguments for change in our business strategy, and I agree with you. But you have to work with Fred and his team to get them on board with us. We can't be two Coca-Cola companies. We must be one."

Based on my experience in building consensus around difficult business and political issues, I couldn't have agreed with Claus more. Even so, I told him that I would need his help to get buy-in from the white South African division managers and bottlers.

I also knew I needed Claus in my corner because the white managers would be outraged at even the notion of me meeting with the exiled ANC leaders, which I fully planned to do.

Soon after I made my report to senior management in Atlanta, and following many long conference calls with Eric, Ernest, and Hennie in South Africa, I decided to take a long-overdue vacation.

I felt honored to be entrusted with the South Africa strategy. But it was also a high-pressure assignment that I would have to balance with my already significant responsibilities as Coca-Cola's senior vice president of external affairs.

I needed a few days to recalibrate and check on my parents. Mamma had just been diagnosed with terminal cancer and was undergoing treatment, which meant many doctor visits and some overnight stays at Newnan Hospital.

While back at home, I hung out at the old fishing cabin at the lake, which was more like a swamp when I bought the land five years earlier. But I organized weekend work crews that included Daddy, brothers Eugene and Walter, Timothy, and my nephew Derwin Ware. We labored vigorously to clear the kudzu around the cabin and made the whole place livable.

The cabin became our family retreat. We made it country cozy, with a pot-bellied stove for winter, a ceiling fan for summer, and a tin roof for relaxing rain sounds that made me want to sleep anytime, day or night. It was where I taught Timmy to hunt and where he spent holidays and summers on his dirt bike and trailing behind my father around the farm.

As a family, we shared the hope that Mamma was going to be all right. Even if she wasn't going to be all right on Earth, she certainly would be in heaven. We cherished every moment we had with her. Instead of wringing our hands and making Mamma nervous, Mary and I spent those bright spring afternoons doing ordinary things like sharing family meals with my brothers and sisters.

Mamma and Daddy by then were well into their second parenthood, and at ages sixty-eight and seventy-two, they seemed to have a lot of living left to do. Just as the last of us had left home, my sister Evelyn's son Derwin came to live with them full time.

Derwin and Timmy kept each other occupied while Mary and I visited with my parents. As was my habit, I brought them trinkets from Africa—little things like a wood carving of a giraffe for Daddy and a pretty Zulu necklace for Mamma. We always had fun unpacking and marveling over the souvenirs that I brought back from my travels.

"What's it like over there in Africa?" my father asked, referring to the continent of Africa as one big country rather than fifty-two separate nations. I did my best to explain and to paint a vivid picture of the different countries, cultures, and tribes. I described the densely populated cities, the shantytowns, remote villages, and abject poverty, the Harmattan in Kano, the big-game animals in Kenya, flying by Mount Kilimanjaro, and the vast sugarcane plantations of South Africa.

Daddy would always get a chuckle out of my saying, "I saw Grandpa Pete" or "I saw Deacon Rowe!" In other words, in Africa, I saw people who looked just like us.

"I wish you all could go," I told them fervently. "I wish you could see the land of our forefathers. You would be amazed." Even as the words escaped my lips, I knew they never would.

Mamma and Daddy might never see our African motherland, I remember thinking, but they had carved out their own little piece of paradise for themselves and their twelve children. The house was still alive with constant visits from grown children and their spouses, scores of grandchildren, and even more neighbors and friends than ever before. My brother Eugene and his family lived across the road.

Walter, by then a successful contractor in Newnan, lived in nearby Welcome, Georgia, with his wife, Catherine, and their six children.

My parents never made a big deal about wedding anniversaries, but Mamma and Daddy decided to celebrate their fiftieth anniversary with a ceremony at Oak Grove. They wore white and kissed at the end of the ceremony, surprising their grandchildren with such a public display of affection. When I mentioned it to my sister Mildred, she pointed out that one of her distinct early memories was of our parents holding hands on their evening walks together as a young couple. Fifty years later, my parents fell asleep beside each other in their easy chairs, their Bibles at hand and the TV blaring in the background, and they awoke every morning at the crack of dawn to cook breakfast together, always the same, like clockwork.

As we drove away, Mary noted that Mamma had lost weight, though we agreed she had not lost her desire to make sure her family was well fed. In the trunk of our car were two shopping bags packed with plastic containers of frozen okra, tomatoes, black-eyed peas, and squash from the garden. Mamma always put away enough vegetables to feed an army.

Once we got back to Atlanta, I packed again for a long weekend with the Road Dogs and left for Hilton Head to play golf. We never had trouble filling out the eight-foursome, thirty-two-golfer roster. My fellow Road Dogs were educators, doctors, lawyers, judges, business owners, corporate executives, politicians, ministers, and engineers. We'd meet at 6 A.M. outside Greenbriar Mall in Southwest Atlanta, fill two large vans (more like buses), and take off for Jekyll Island, Myrtle Beach, Hilton Head, Orlando, or the like for a long weekend of golf and camaraderie.

In the evenings, we'd hang out at the golf villas and have fun playing cards, eating, drinking, telling jokes, and jonesing the guys who lost. Among my closest friends in the group were Roland Blanding and Bill McClure. We played golf all day Thursday, Friday, and Saturday, then capped off the tournament with an awards dinner to pass out trophies to the winners of the first, second, and third flights. We had a very special flight we called the "moon flight" for golf scores that were too high to count. Sunday morning, we'd squeeze in nine holes and head back to Atlanta.

146

❧

In the months that followed my first trip to South Africa, I commuted between Atlanta and Johannesburg to travel throughout the country and visit other nations in Southern Africa, yet another broad listening tour.

Don McHenry, ambassador to the United Nations during the Jimmy Carter administration and a member of the Coca-Cola board of directors, traveled with me on some of my visits to South Africa. Don opened up his closely held ambassadorial contact list to me and imparted his knowledge about international diplomacy and the interaction between the apartheid regime and Washington, DC.

Don introduced me to people, including South African author and political activist Nadine Gordimer, winner of the Nobel Prize for literature. I developed relationships with important thought leaders. Among them were Rev. Beyers Naude, the leading anti-apartheid Afrikaner cleric, as well as attorney Arthur Chaskalson, future president of the Constitutional Court in South Africa under Mandela. Chaskalson had successfully challenged the legality of apartheid legislation, thereby crippling the government's ability to enforce influx control laws, which dictated the movements of blacks from rural to urban areas. I also met liberal, anti-apartheid South African parliament member Helen Suzman through Don.

Eric introduced both Don and me to many people, including Dr. Nthato Motlana, leader of the Committee of Ten, which organized Soweto residents against apartheid following the 1976 uprising. After apartheid fell, Motlana formed New African Investments Limited, which purchased previously white-run corporations. For this reason, Motlana is called the Father of Black Economic Empowerment.

I established relationships with exiled ANC leaders outside South Africa. I met Johnny Makhathini for the first time in Zambia, where he lived in exile. Johnny eventually became the ANC's unofficial representative to the UN. Because of his work, the image of the ANC changed from terrorist organization to legitimate government in exile. At UN sessions in New York I spent many hours talking with Johnny about the future of South Africa.

Meanwhile, back in the US, I stayed in close contact with leaders of the Congressional Black Caucus, the National Conference of Black Mayors, and the National Conference of Black State Legislators. I conferred with Randall Robinson of TransAfrica, C. Payne Lucas of Africare, and served as a board member of the African American Institute. I was a frequent guest at the embassies of African ambassadors in Washington, DC.

I gave speeches on university campuses to explain the Coca-Cola Company's position, but more importantly I got to hear what people were thinking. At Smith College in Northampton, Massachusetts, I barely got out of a session with my suit jacket on because students were so adamant about Coke getting out of South Africa, but I escaped unharmed. At Emory University in Atlanta, I participated in a forum where former president Jimmy Carter was present. When I finished my remarks, Carter asked, "Carl, why doesn't Coke just leave South Africa? Just get out tomorrow?" The former president's questions greatly influenced my thinking, and all of these interactions on college campuses added a sense of urgency to my work.

In the spring of 1984, we assembled a task force of some of the best minds in the Coca-Cola Company from the legal, finance, public affairs, and business development departments to conduct a more in-depth analysis of the South Africa situation. We assessed the effectiveness of our social-responsibility programs—how much money we were investing and what impact these programs were making in the areas of education, health, and black youth development.

I asked Eric Mafuna to gauge the attitudes and opinions of labor unions and community leaders as we began to restructure our efforts in the black community. Their feedback to the company was: "Don't develop programs for us. Develop programs with us." We then focused on the Coca-Cola business relationship with black customers in the townships.

My team was a conscientious, hardworking group of Coca-Cola executives. It included Brant Davis, who was then working in the corporate communications group; Peter Rosen from corporate human resources; and attorney David Snyder, general counsel of the South Africa division, who had spent time in Atlanta and was disgusted with the apartheid system. Hennie and Ernest were invaluable on the ground, navigating our efforts internally with division management

148

and externally in government circles.

By then, Ernest had hired Eunice Sybia, a corporate social-responsibility professional and the only African woman in the division management ranks. Eunice honored me with a *braai*, or cookout, at her home in Soweto. I learned more about corporate social responsibility in South Africa than I had learned in all of the division offices' conference room presentations. Eunice kept track of compliance with the Sullivan code, delivered grants to community groups, and coordinated the company's corporate social-responsibility efforts with our bottlers and the corporate social-responsibility programs of other US companies.

We retained the services of internationally renowned New York public relations firm Burson-Marsteller to work with our team to ensure our messaging was as consistent in South Africa as it was in the US. Chairman and CEO Harold Burson, who was also Roberto's personal PR advisor, became my hands-on consultant in matters of communication and media relations, and he assigned his top professionals to work with Brant and Eric on the ground in South Africa.

We had laid a lot of groundwork in Atlanta and in Johannesburg for a fundamental shift in our South Africa business strategy. A meeting I had requested several months earlier with Bishop Desmond Tutu, the outspoken leader of the anti-apartheid movement and recipient of the Nobel Peace Prize, had finally materialized. Without his input and without his buy-in, our new strategy would have no credibility.

Meeting Tutu in Soweto

Our car snaked slowly through the silent streets of Soweto, which was surrounded by concrete barriers and barbed wire. We took a circuitous route to evade police roadblocks, which were set up at the main thoroughfares to enforce the 9 P.M. curfew. The place was eerily vacant of people, the only sign of life being perhaps the occasional flicker of light behind a drawn curtain.

Being stopped would have been very bad for us. That week brought the anniversary of the Soweto uprising. On June 16, 1976, 15,000 schoolchildren gathered in Soweto to protest the government's ruling that classes in secondary schools must be taught in Afrikaans.

Parents and teachers protested this ruling that required their children be taught in the language of the oppressor. To no avail.

During the student protests, police opened fire on children who had only sticks and stones to defend themselves, killing and wounding hundreds of them. The massacre sparked international outrage and was a turning point in the battle against apartheid.

As always around the anniversary of the uprising, black South Africans turned out in remembrance of the children who died in the massacre. And, as always, the government feared that there would be violence. So the curfew was imposed, and even if blacks had the papers that the government required them to carry, they would be in trouble if they were out after 9 P.M.

But more than keeping people out of Soweto that night, the police wanted to keep anyone inside Soweto from going out. The paranoia that drove the minority-white government to control the movements of the majority-black South African population was heightened by the pent-up anger, resentment, and frustration of the oppressed. These feelings simmered among the people of Soweto, and the government feared it might boil over and spread violence into the privileged white areas of Johannesburg. The police would ask no questions before doing whatever they thought necessary to stop anyone who looked suspicious.

Three of us were in the car—an Asian, Yusef Surtee; a white colleague of mine, Brant Davis; and myself, who for all practical purposes was a black South African. A police officer peering into the car would not be happy with the mix. The races were required by law to be separated in all aspects of life, especially after dark in Soweto.

Yusuf was at the wheel and drove side streets and back alleys that I imagined only he knew, steering us clear of police blockades.

Yusuf's relationship with Bishop Tutu made our meeting a reality. That night, Yusuf's mission was to get me to the bishop's home in Soweto on time and in one piece, if possible.

Many black and white South Africans assumed, before they met me, that with a name like Carl Ware, I must be white. In fact, when the Tutu meeting was being set up, the bishop directly inquired about my racial identity. When he was told I was an African American who shared his deep concern about the welfare of the black majority, he is reported to have laughed and said, "Well, tell Mr. Ware that he is most welcome in our humble church!"

We were headed to the Tutu home on Vilakazi Street, a modest brick house painted white and enclosed by a high concrete wall. His wife, Leah, in a colorful African print wrap dress, greeted the three of us warmly at the door. She wore the kind of wide smile that put me at ease. She ushered us into the living room, where we awaited an audience with the bishop. I was in awe of the moment. I had never met a Nobel laureate, and I felt extremely blessed.

When Bishop Tutu entered the room, wearing his colorful dashiki and dark slacks, he welcomed us to his home with his signature singsong voice. I knew I had thirty minutes to state the company's preliminary thoughts about disinvestment and hoped our approach would be consistent with the ANC strategy to end apartheid.

It was a lot to accomplish in one meeting. At the rate events were moving, and considering the number of constituencies and players competing for Bishop Tutu's ear, I knew this might be my only chance. Without his support, our goal to be on the right side of change in South Africa would be meaningless.

Bishop Tutu was a very keen listener. Over the years I would come to know him and work with him, I would learn that he was the consummate ecumenical leader who always sought common threads of belief in both religious and secular matters. He was willing to listen to other people's positions and respect them even if they didn't line up with his own thinking. That quality also made it impossible to know what he was thinking until he spoke his mind.

As plainly and succinctly as I could, I told the story of why I was given the South Africa assignment by Roberto and Don and what my team had accomplished over the past several months. I explained to Bishop Tutu we had arrived at the position that mere adherence to the Sullivan Principles was not enough. And I further stated that the guiding principles of our thought about disinvestment were our abhorrence of apartheid and our commitment to help prepare black South Africans for a new South Africa.

As I spoke, I felt I was getting a fair hearing. But still, when I was done, I did not know whether my words had swayed him. I had the sense that while the bishop was certainly cordial, he was also skeptical. Instead of giving me a definitive answer, he invited Brant and me to join him the next morning for the Eucharist at his church, St. Mary's Cathedral in downtown Johannesburg.

After the service, Bishop Tutu invited us to join him for his staff meeting, which he oddly began without introducing me. There Brant and I sat, the only people in the room wearing business suits, with the bishop's people eying us and wondering why we were there. Then the bishop got everyone's attention. He said, "I'm going to make an announcement. I'm issuing this press release."

He held up a piece of paper and read aloud: "Coca-Cola and all American companies must leave South Africa now, unconditionally."

My heart sank. Not only had Tutu rejected my proposals, but he had also put Coke atop the list of companies he wanted out of South Africa. His announcement would be news around the world, and it would carry enormous weight both inside and outside South Africa. He was the conscience and the voice of the anti-apartheid movement.

Once he issued his press release, anything short of Coca-Cola cutting all ties in South Africa would be viewed as falling short of doing the right thing. I don't know what came over me at that moment. I can only describe it as something I had been taught all my life never to accept: a feeling of complete and utter failure.

I didn't argue with Tutu when he made his devastating announcement to his staff in the church sanctuary. I didn't try to convince him not to have his press conference calling on Coca-Cola and all other American companies to leave South Africa unconditionally. Instead, I said, "Bishop Tutu, would you mind having a prayer with me so I can get the strength to have a press conference of my own?"

I wasn't sure what I was going to say at a press conference. But I knew that Coke would have to respond to Tutu's announcement, and I knew I couldn't say what I had hoped to say, which was that we had reached an agreement on a disinvestment plan that had the endorsement of Bishop Tutu.

So, we had our prayer together, Bishop Tutu and I. In his prayer, he called apartheid "immoral, inhuman, and unjustified, a sin against God." It was the first time I had heard apartheid described in religious terms, and it resonated with me deeply.

When we were done praying, something amazing happened.

152

Bishop Desmond Tutu changed his mind. He said, "I'm not going to do the press conference just now. I'll let you know my decision later."

To this day, I can't say why it happened. I can only attribute it to the trust he felt for me when I asked him to pray. That was the end of the meeting, so I returned to the company's headquarters in downtown Johannesburg to regroup. I had to confer with my local colleagues as well as our bosses in Atlanta. We looked at our strategy, and I asked how we could get Bishop Tutu to agree not to issue that press release. And what's more, to get him to chair the independent foundation that we had decided to fund as a part of our plans to disinvest.

21

THE COKE WAY

The Coca-Cola Company operates in 200 countries around the world and has seen everything through that little bottle of Coke, from world wars and civil wars to coups and revolutions, from the fall of the Berlin Wall to the disintegration of the Soviet Union.

The brand has survived and prospered in tumultuous environments because of the Woodruff principle: "We want to be a welcome part of every community where we do business." The countries where we operate are our hosts, and, as business guests, we adapt to the local culture and political structure. We don't back governments, nor do we champion or denounce any political ideology or form of government. That's the Coke Way.

South Africa would become the exception to this operating principle.

The independent foundation that the Coca-Cola Company envisioned, and, we hoped, would be chaired by Bishop Tutu, would become the largest privately funded, black-controlled foundation in South Africa. After much debate in Atlanta and Johannesburg, Claus Halle made the recommendation, and the company board of directors approved a $10 million contribution to create the Equal Opportunity Foundation.

Doing so was a monumental statement. We strongly felt that anything less would not be substantial enough to make an impact.

The Coca-Cola Company would have no control over the foundation other than to offer technical assistance. A completely independent board of trustees would administer the foundation. Board of trustee members would be drawn from across a spectrum of political, business, civic, and religious leaders. For example, the Zulu-dominated Inkatha Freedom Party members would be sitting at the same table with their ANC rivals and making decisions on critical education and development programs for South Africa's neediest.

I went back to Bishop Tutu to reconfirm our plan for the foundation and other aspects of the disinvestment. He informed me that he would consider serving as chairman of the foundation. But then he recommended that I meet with the exiled ANC leaders in London, and he graciously offered to arrange a meeting for me with the two highest-ranking leaders, ANC president Oliver Tambo and minister of communication Thabo Mbeki.

The meeting took place a couple of months later in London's Islington borough, at 28 Penton Street, the exiled government's headquarters that had been bombed by operatives of the apartheid regime a couple of years earlier.

Thabo Mbeki was an economist who would serve as the second post-apartheid president of South Africa, from 1999 to 2008. His father, Govan Mbeki, was a South African politician known worldwide as one of the distinguished ANC leaders imprisoned on Robben Island with Nelson Mandela, Ahmed Kathrada, Walter Sisulu, and others charged with treason and terrorism.

Oliver Tambo had then already served as president of the ANC for more than twenty years. Together, the men were disarming. Mbeki smoked a pipe, and Tambo wore spectacles and carried himself more like a professor than the president of a government in exile. Mbeki and Tambo were no ordinary men of power, which became apparent the moment we sat down.

I knew that Tambo, Mandela's former law partner, was trained in guerilla warfare and that he had planned and led several attacks against the apartheid regime in his early years with the Umkhonto weSizwe ("Spear of the Nation"), the armed wing of the ANC.

The ANC had close ties with the South African Communist Party and was ideologically socialist. It was unclear then in the minds of the ANC, or of anyone else in the world, whether the ANC was going to nationalize industries in South Africa once it came to power.

When we sat down, I could see right away that in Tambo's and Mbeki's eyes I was first and foremost an executive of the Coca-Cola Company, not necessarily an ally because I was an African American. However, I knew it was beneficial that Tutu had made the introduction, and I felt comfortable sharing my background with the ANC leaders.

I told them about growing up in rural Coweta County in the Jim Crow South, working my way through college in Atlanta at the height of the civil rights movement, being elected Atlanta's first black city council president, and helping to build the black economic and political power base in the city. As I spoke, I sensed the two men were captivated by my story, and I felt we bonded around a shared empathy for each other's causes.

My purpose for sharing my personal story was to get Tambo and Mbeki to see the Coca-Cola Company through me and to understand that the company's highest-ranking leaders, Goizeuta and Keough, knew that black South Africans would eventually prevail. And the duo wanted the company to be on the right side of change in South Africa.

I then talked about two other very important elements of our evolving thinking around disinvestment: the creation of an independent, black-controlled education/development fund to help black South Africans prepare for the new South Africa, and black ownership of a significant part of the Coca-Cola business in South Africa.

At that time, the African National Congress demanded that all foreign companies completely disinvest from South Africa. I pointed out that when the Coca-Cola Company disinvested, a South African company would probably assume its role in the South African economy. Whether you are a South African company or an American one, you're still going to pay taxes to the apartheid government.

I argued that Coca-Cola was committed to figuring out a smart way to deny the South African government tax revenues while preparing black South Africans to gain ownership within the Coca-Cola system so they would be better prepared for the future in an ANC-ruled South Africa.

They were socialists, and I was pushing ideas about economic empowerment, free enterprise, and capitalism. Although I left that meeting not knowing whether the ANC would support the Coca-Cola disinvestment proposal, I felt good about the meeting because if they had not liked what I said, they would have told me so. And the one thing I thought I could count on was Oliver Tambo being a visionary.

Soon after I returned from London to Johannesburg, Bishop Tutu officially agreed to chair the fund. That was a pivotal first step, although I knew that recruiting the remaining board members would require extreme sensitivity and diplomacy.

And so, with support from Tambo, Mbeki, and Tutu, I set out to get Chief Gatsha Buthelezi's support and to ask him to designate a representative from KwaZulu-Natal. He was the undisputed leader of six million Zulus, the largest ethnic group in South Africa. He was also the president of the Inkatha Freedom Party, the largest black political movement in the country. Buthelezi supported a policy of negotiation and appeasement with the government of President P. W. Botha. Even so, the Zulu leader was critical of South Africa's new constitution, which established the Tricameral Parliament that granted limited political rights to coloured people and Indians but denied the country's twenty-four million blacks any political role whatsoever.

In fact, according to a now-declassified 1985 CIA report, the American government expected Buthelezi to support US policy in an upcoming meeting with Ronald Reagan. Buthelezi had split with the African National Congress in the 1970s and was openly critical of its tactics, accusing its leaders of a plot to assassinate him. He was also critical of Tutu, the CIA reported: "In a recent letter to Tutu, Buthelezi castigated him for 'playing to the galleries,' noting that 'as a Bishop of my church you should be playing a conciliatory role. You shame the cloth you wear and you turn the accolades you received in being given the Nobel Peace Prize into a farce.'" Buthelezi also was at odds with the United Democratic Front, headed by Rev. Allan Boesak.

Amid this supercharged political environment, Don McHenry and I stood outside Buthelezi's headquarters in Zululand one blistering day in February, awaiting an audience. I remember remarking to Don that the concrete was so hot you could fry an egg on it.

An aide escorted us into Buthelezi's antechamber, where we awaited his arrival.

Buthelezi wore a business suit and quickly got down to business. Don and I explained our vision of one fund representing all of South Africa for the benefit of all. At the end of our conversation, the Zulu leader expressed his support for the Equal Opportunity Foundation as well as for our black economic empowerment initiatives, and he agreed to designate a representative from the Inkatha Freedom Party.

Over the next several weeks, I worked with Bishop Tutu to identify, vet, and recruit the remaining trustees for the board. We enlisted Arthur Chaskalson, director of Legal Resources Centre, South Africa's leading legal aid organization. Already distinguished, he would go on to serve in the Mandela government as president of the Constitutional Court of South Africa from 1994 to 2001 and as chief justice of South Africa from 2001 to 2005.

We enlisted the support of Rev. Allan Boesak. He was important as head of the United Democratic Front, a forceful anti-apartheid coalition of more than 400 worker, church, civic, and student organizations. Rev. Boesak launched the UDF in 1983 to denounce the Tricameral Parliament. He was also the elected president of the World Alliance of Reformed Churches, which had seventy-five million members globally and was an extremely vocal and public critic of apartheid.

Boesak nominated professor Jakes Gerwel, rector of the University of the Western Cape, for the board. The rector was a leading intellectual and a member of the ANC, and he would eventually become director-general under the presidency of Nelson Mandela. We added such leaders as Pali Francis Mohanoe, professor in the Department of Didactics at the University of the North.

Sheila Sisulu was education coordinator for the South African Council of Churches and married to Mlungisi Sisulu, grandson of Walter Sisulu. She would become the first female South African ambassador to the US, the last appointment Mandela would make in office. I later hosted a party in her honor at the exclusive Cosmos Club in Washington, DC, following her official presentation at the White House, where she met with President Bill Clinton for the first time.

Professor Gertrude Mncube, who was a nurse with a master's degree from Columbia University and an examiner for the South African Nursing Council, would bring needed expertise, as some of the grants would very likely be made to health clinics.

Yusuf Surtee became a trustee as a representative of the black South African business community, where he not only owned the Gray's men's clothing chain but also served on the board of directors of several South African and multinational corporations. He was also an active member of the United Democratic Front.

The first board of the Equal Opportunity Foundation would also include Coca-Cola's Ernest Mchunu, then president of the Black Management Forum, where he worked tirelessly at night and on weekends to train the next generation of black business leaders. Entrepreneur and investor Ebrahim Bhorat was valuable because of his work as a director at numerous trading companies and real estate firms.

When we announced the fund publicly in March 1986, *New York Times* reporter Kathleen Teltsch interviewed me in our New York offices. Others quoted included C. Payne Lucas, head of Africare in Washington, DC. Lucas was quoted as saying, "Personally, I think it's wonderful that respected indigenous people will be given the power over disposition of the funds."

Dr. James Joseph, president of the Council on Foundations, also praised our plan. "These new foundations, controlled by non-white South Africans and funded generously by a major United States corporation, break new ground for corporate responsibility," he said. Dr. Joseph would become US ambassador to South Africa, and we would enjoy a lifelong friendship.

Rev. Jesse Jackson, head of the Rainbow Coalition, who was also quoted in the *New York Times* story, was critical. Coca-Cola's $10 million gift, he stated, "represents a victory for those who want to get profits from the South African oppressors and give contributions to the apartheid opposers." Nothing could have been further from the truth.

On April 2, 1986, Brant Davis and I attended the foundation's first board meeting. Later, in remarks to the Coca-Cola Company board's public issues committee on July 17, 1986, I said, despite the imposition of the state of emergency, and despite enormous pressure from US disinvestment activists, the trustees stood their ground and the fund became a functioning reality. It had an office in Cape Town. Alex Boraine, a white Progressive Party parliament member, served as its interim executive director. He would later become one of the main architects of the Truth and Reconciliation Commission and its deputy chairman under Desmond Tutu.

The trustees established an investment policy to dedicate at least half of the trust corpus to the creation of an endowment and then pay out the remainder in grants. Almost immediately, the foundation received nearly 100 grant applications, but the trustees decided not to make any grants until they first settled on a set of guiding principles. The purpose would be to dedicate the fund to the cause of change and to helping build the economic, social, and political infrastructure of post-apartheid South Africa.

Despite the goodwill it could create, the fund was not an insurance policy to protect the Coca-Cola Company in the US. It was an investment in South Africa, I told the committee. It did, however, allow us to develop a relationship of mutual respect and trust with many of South Africa's most prominent black leaders.

Many other American companies had previously attempted to establish foundations in South Africa. They failed because not one of them had been able to convince prominent black South Africans to serve on their boards. What made Coca-Cola's South African foundation attractive was that we promised them independence, and we kept that promise. Coca-Cola succeeded because we supported the cause of black liberation, and in post-apartheid South Africa, that would be extremely important.

The fund was only a piece of our overall approach to South Africa. Equally important were our public statements of opposition to apartheid, our programs to increase and strengthen black management within the company, and our efforts to sell some of our South African holdings to black investors.

The common thread linking these efforts was the realization that, sooner or later, black South Africans would succeed in their struggle for freedom. If we continued our initiatives on all fronts, when that day came, the company would be a welcome, prospering participant in a new South Africa.

Until that day came, however, we would do what we did best: adapt.

For example, I recall going for a jog one Saturday morning with my white Coke colleague Peter Rosen in downtown Johannesburg. A parade in progress meant the usual jogging routes were blocked, so Peter and I jogged a few blocks over to the Johannesburg College of

Education athletic field track to avoid the downtown traffic. After all, I had been there just the day before to present the college with a check—money to finance several student work-study projects that would help train rural Zulu mothers in KwaZulu in the areas of home economics, healthcare, and basic education.

Having been there already, I felt safe returning to the campus. However, as Peter and I lapped the track for the third time, we heard loud voices from the football field stadium shouting, "Kafir, leave!"

We looked up into the stands to see several white South African teenagers. They were clearly telling me to get off their field and using the African equivalent of the N-word.

Peter said, "What should we do, Carl?"

"Why don't you just go up there and tell them that I'm an honorary white?" I said. "Just kidding, Peter."

The thought of my father telling me to never run away from a white man resonated in my mind. Peter and I kept jogging as the threats from the white boys got louder. We finished our run and then walked up the stadium steps toward the hecklers.

I spoke. "Gentlemen, how's your morning? I hope you have a nice rugby game."

They stared at me, realizing by the sound of my accent that I was an "honorary white," protected by their country's own insane racial laws. But I also realized afterward that I had been a bit naive. In hindsight, I know that if I had been a black South African, they would have had the right to detain me or even do me bodily harm. The absurdity of apartheid!

22

KILIMANJARO

A few months after my first presentation to the committee, another major piece of the disinvestment plan fell into place. Swaziland agreed to allow Coca-Cola to build a new concentrate plant there so that we could shut down the plant in Durban, thereby depriving the South African government of hundreds of millions of dollars in tax revenue.

As part of these negotiations, and more a formality than anything else, I shared a meal with the newly crowned, eighteen-year-old king Mswati III, as the details had already been decided with his ministers. King Mswati is Africa's last absolute monarch. At the time he was also the youngest absolute monarch in the world.

As we broke bread, the young king proudly told me about the Dlamini dynasty, which could trace its roots back to the beginning of the nation, long before the 1200s and the beginning of recorded time. His father, King Sobhuza II, had ruled for sixty-one years and left behind seventy wives, who bore him 210 sons and daughters. At Sobhuza's death, he had an estimated 1,000 grandchildren.

The Durban plant was important to Coca-Cola strategically because it supplied the majority of the Southern African Development Community nations of Southern Africa, including Botswana, Lesotho, Namibia, South Africa, and, of course, Swaziland. The new Swaziland plant would eventually become the supply point for other countries, such as Angola, Mozambique, and Mauritius.

Later, when Mswati visited Atlanta, we held a reception in his honor at Coca-Cola headquarters to celebrate the deal, which by then was formalized. I struggled to come up with an appropriate gift until someone told me the young king fancied boom boxes.

The tip was music to my ears. I sent a staff member out to find the best boom box that money could buy. I like to think the boom box was inspired—the king was visibly pleased with the gift, and whenever we saw each other again, whether at a UN meeting or one of my business trips to Swaziland, we would share a chuckle about it.

But the negotiations had gone smoothly because the move was a win-win for both sides. The taxes Coca-Cola paid would make up 50 percent of Swaziland's entire tax base, bringing much-needed roads, schools, and hospitals to an independent black nation. Coca-Cola's supply point for the concentrate plant in sub-Saharan Africa would not change significantly, thanks to Swaziland's location some 300 miles north of the previous supply point in Durban. We would still be able to manufacture and distribute the concentrate in almost the same manner as before.

Before the disinvestment plan was signed, on September 5, 1986, Don McHenry and I were honored with invitations to attend Desmond Tutu's enthronement as Lord Archbishop of Cape Town at St. George's Cathedral. Some 2,000 guests packed into the Cape Town church, including dignitaries from afar, such as Coretta Scott King. Tutu's elevation as the first black head of the Church of the Province of Southern Africa and the spiritual leader of three million Anglicans in South Africa, Lesotho, Swaziland, Namibia, Mozambique, and the island of St. Helena was led by Archbishop of Canterbury Robert A. K. Runcie, spiritual leader of 65 million Anglicans worldwide.

That day brought many moments of spontaneous eruptions of joy and applause regarding the plight of black South Africans and the steps that would be needed to free them from apartheid. The service was an emotional one for me. I felt the circumstances of the blacks in that country so deeply. How I wished my mother and father could have been there to share this solemn religious and spiritual occasion.

Among the most poignant Tutu quotes from that day was this one: "If we could but recognize our common humanity, that we do belong together, that our destinies are bound up with another's, that we can be free only together, that we can survive only together, that we can be human only together, then a glorious South Africa would come into being where all of us lived harmoniously together as members of one family, God's family."

Once the entire disinvestment plan was complete, the newly enthroned Archbishop Tutu called it a "model" that other companies should follow. The Coca-Cola disinvestment was designed to strike a blow against the apartheid government by depriving it of tax revenue. At the same time, the disinvestment did not entail the loss of any jobs in the Coca-Cola system in South Africa. We knew that once the Coca-Cola Company pulled out of South Africa, we would no longer employ anyone there. But we wanted to preserve job opportunities for our South African employees, roughly 80 percent of whom were black.

Because Coca-Cola goes to market through a local franchise bottler system, we were able to come up with a creative solution. We issued a license to a new company in South Africa, National Beverage Services. The employees would work for that licensee, and Coke would have no role in its ownership or its operations. This arrangement would also ensure that our brands remained in the marketplace and that we had a working business system in place inside South Africa once apartheid fell.

The Equal Opportunity Foundation would also remain to help black South Africans continue to fight against apartheid. Ingrid Saunders Jones would lead the technical support team for the Equal Opportunity Foundation from Atlanta after we left South Africa.

Even though the Coca-Cola Company was no longer in the country, we were able to create economic empowerment opportunities for black South Africans. We would enable black ownership by creating the first black-owned bottling franchise ever in the history of South Africa. We would then offer shares of our largest, publicly traded bottler, Amalgamated Beverage Industries, to black South Africans who were our employees, wholesalers, distributors, and spaza/shop owners through a special placement on the Johannesburg Stock Exchange. Doing so would create broad ownership in the soft drink industry and give black South Africans a financial stake in the Coca-Cola bottling system for the first time.

After the disinvestment plan was approved and set in motion, the next step was to communicate it to the world. These days, when you want to get the word out quickly, you can announce it on Twitter in 280 characters. When a company had something serious to say back in the 1980s, it did so in a press release that was mailed or faxed to news organizations.

I knew the press release announcing Coke's disinvestment had to be strong enough that Archbishop Tutu and anti-apartheid leaders could use it to pressure other companies to disinvest. I stood with the cleric near a fax machine in Coca-Cola's Johannesburg offices, anxiously awaiting a draft of the press release from Atlanta. We were both disappointed with it when it finally arrived. It was just the facts. It lacked the moral urgency needed to be effective.

On September 17, 1986, however, the final press release quoted Don Keough: "Our decision to complete the process of disinvestment is a statement of our opposition to apartheid and of our support for the economic aspirations of [black] South Africans." What it said to the world was that we were disinvesting not for economic reasons, but because of our abhorrence of apartheid. We not only opposed apartheid, we were essentially joining hands with the African National Congress. We weren't just rejecting the South African government, we were supporting black South Africans to continue their struggle internally. And we were putting our money where our mouth was.

The headlines the next day bore out these intentions. *The Atlanta Constitution*: "Coke to sell its assets in South Africa. Bottler operations being sold as apartheid protest." *The Washington Post*: "Coke to Sell All Holdings in South Africa." And, finally, *The New York Times*: "Coke Plans Pretoria Pullout. Opposition to Apartheid Cited."

"Coca-Cola also is believed to be the first American company to at least publicly express plans to sell its South African operations to black investors," the *Los Angeles Times* wrote the next day. The *Times* continued:

> And it is also one of the first to acknowledge political as well as economic reasons for its withdrawal. Most US companies have said they were withdrawing solely because of deteriorating business conditions.
>
> The Atlanta-based firm said it plans to sell its 30% share of a major bottler and a 55% share of a canning operation within six to nine months. Those operations employ about 4,300 workers, mostly black South Africans, making Coke one of the largest US employers in South Africa.

A month later, on October 21, 1986, the *Los Angeles Times* reported that General Motors, the largest employer in South Africa, announced its plans to pull out by year's end and to sell its auto assembly plant in South Africa to local managers. The company is quoted as being "disappointed in the pace of change in ending apartheid." The deterioration of the South African economy and the fact that GM had been losing money on its operations there for at least three years "are believed to have made the decision easier," the story concluded.

The headlines were great, but the overall reaction was mixed. People who understood our business model and those with whom we had consulted were very supportive. Critics complained that our disinvestment plan was a sham because our brands would still be on the ground in South Africa.

The strongest criticisms of our disinvestment strategy, however, came from the American side, not the South African side. Don McHenry counseled that it was not the American critics whose approval we needed, but that of black South Africans. Throughout my time there, Don helped me understand and navigate the intricate political, governmental, racial, and ethnic mazes of that challenging international assignment.

However good the initial headlines, I knew an effective communication strategy entailed more than press releases. We needed to mount an all-out effort to explain our disinvestment plan across a broad spectrum of American audiences. These audiences were allies of the struggle to end apartheid and could be found on college and university campuses, at civil rights organizations' annual meetings, and within business and political groups.

One of my most humbling personal memories of the disinvestment was a celebratory reception hosted by Chuck Morrison at the company's headquarters on North Avenue. He succeeded me as head of special markets. To the sound of applause and cheers, I entered the central reception area, which was filled with employees. Chuck and some of our associates held a big banner that read, "Congratulations, Carl, on achieving mission impossible!"

If my life had taught me anything until that moment, it was that nothing was impossible.

Identifying South Africa's First Black Bottler

Communicating our message in the US was an urgent task, to be certain, but we did not lose our focus on the absolute imperative of effectively executing the disinvestment plan on the ground in South Africa. We began intensifying our efforts to identify potential bottling-franchise candidates. This search would turn out to be one of our more difficult tasks.

First, we had to figure out where the franchise would come from, meaning which of the current franchise bottlers would be willing to give up part of its territory in order to refranchise that marketing area to a black owner/operator.

My role was to identify those investors and get them ready to make the acquisition. That proved challenging because, in 1986, there weren't that many black South Africans with the financial wherewithal and operating experience needed to successfully own and operate an independent bottling franchise.

Richard Maponya was an obvious choice because he was already a distributor in Bophuthatswana and had expressed a strong interest. We asked Richard for other names, and he pointed us to Gibson Thula. Both were strong businessmen but neither had the capital to swing the entire deal.

Much like the process of selling the Philadelphia bottling franchise to an African American franchisee, we discussed a strategy that would entail finding more individual black South African investors who would have the financial ability and willingness to participate.

The other side of the equation was identifying and carving out a franchise that we could sell to black investors. We started with Coke's largest bottling franchiser, Amalgamated Beverage Industries, a subsidiary of South African Breweries (SAB) headed by CEO Meyer Kahn. ABI was publicly traded on the Johannesburg Stock Exchange, and it became clear to us all that carving out a territory from ABI's franchise would be more cumbersome than working it out with one of the privately held, family-owned bottlers.

In the end, we sat down with all of the franchise owners, including the Phil Gutsche family, which owned Port Elizabeth-based Sabco, and the Cook family, which owned the Nigel and Heidelberg territories. The Nelspruit franchise, which would eventually be sold to the Kunene brothers, was partly owned by the Forbes family, which also owned the Cape Town franchise, Peninsula Beverages. The Suncrush group, owned by Robin Hamilton, controlled the KwaZulu-Natal and North West franchises. The white franchise system owners were very reluctant to release any of their territory to create a black-owner franchise.

Just when I thought we had reached the end of our rope, Robin Hamilton offered his franchise in the Eastern Cape city of East London to create the first black-owned Coca-Cola bottler in South Africa.

I remember being somewhat surprised that it was Robin who had ultimately come through. Later, I asked him what motivated the decision. He replied, "I did what I did because I thought it was the right thing to do, and I wanted to save the Coke system."

With the franchise territory and investors in place, a new company called Kilimanjaro Holdings was created to purchase the East London bottling franchise. When I asked Richard Maponya why the investors had settled on the name "Kilimanjaro," he told me it was the highest peak in Africa, and this deal was the highest peak in terms of business for black South Africans in the nation's history.

23

At the Leeds Castle Meeting
and the Dakar Conference

From my perspective, the period between the September 1986 announcement of the Coca-Cola Company's disinvestment in South Africa and the February 1990 release of Nelson Mandela from prison encompassed a series of significant events that foretold the inevitable demise of apartheid.

The first event was actually a mission, embarked upon by the Commonwealth Eminent Persons Group, itself established to conduct an on-the-ground inquiry into the then-current state of affairs of apartheid South Africa. The Commonwealth of Nations, often referred to as the Commonwealth, is an intergovernmental organization made up primarily of former colonies of the British Empire. The members of this elite group of seven hailed from five different continents and were black, white, and brown.

Over the course of its six-month mission, this Eminent Persons Group consulted with the African National Congress in exile, held political talks with Nelson Mandela in Pollsmoor Prison, and met with in-country black South African political and business leaders—as well as with the heads of the Frontline States, a loose coalition of African countries, including Angola, Botswana, Lesotho, Mozambique, Swaziland, Tanzania, Zambia, and Zimbabwe. The Frontline States were committed to ending white minority rule in South Africa and Rhodesia.

The peace mission, however, was brought to an abrupt halt on May 19, 1986. As the Eminent Persons Group was in the process of negotiating with Prime Minister P. W. Botha and his government, the South African Defence Force (SADF) launched assaults against three neighboring Commonwealth countries, attacking the capital cities of Botswana, Zambia, and Zimbabwe.

In its final report on June 12, 1986, the EPG recommended economic sanctions and concluded that the South African government was "not yet prepared to negotiate fundamental change, nor to countenance the creation of genuine democratic structures, nor to face the prospect of the end of white domination and white power in the foreseeable future."

June 12, 1986, a Thursday, fell four days before the tenth anniversary of the Soweto uprising. It was the very day South Africa's government declared a nationwide state of emergency that restricted political funerals, imposed curfews, and banned news crews with TV cameras from filming in areas of political unrest.

It appeared to me that the Botha regime, instead of negotiating a peaceful resolution to the country's apartheid problem, recoiled and entrenched its resolve to maintain and defend at all costs that atrocious system of oppression.

So, from May through June 1986, dozens of black Africans were killed, many more injured, and an estimated 70,000 left homeless in what became known as the Crossroads-KTC Holocaust. Crossroads and KTC were sections of Khayelitsha. These squatters' camps near Cape Town grew from a need for blacks to get to their jobs in white areas and circumvent daily commutes as long as nine hours from the townships where they were forced to live.

The government blamed armed vigilantes for the violence in which women and children were burned alive in shacks, but dozens of affidavits were filed by squatter leaders alleging South African security force participation, according to an article published in the August 2, 1986, issue of *The Black Sash*.

A United Press International story by John Iams dated June 14, 1986, a Saturday, stated: "By Wednesday of this week, with the death toll over 65, Bishop Desmond Tutu, the archbishop-elect of Cape Town, stepped in to mediate a cease-fire.

"Following a visit to the ravaged KTC camp, Tutu was visibly shaken," the reporter observed.

In the story, Tutu is quoted as saying, "The situation is so terrible. You think you will wake up and discover it isn't true."

At the same time, the United States Congress was working to

170

pass economic sanctions against the apartheid regime. Doing so wasn't a fait accompli. US president Ronald Reagan vetoed the Anti-Apartheid Act three months later in September 1986, branding economic sanctions "economic warfare."

In October, Congress overrode Reagan's veto, thanks in no small part to the efforts of US Senator Dick Lugar from Indiana, my former National League of Cities colleague. Dick led the Republican Party's opposition to its own president and stated on the Senate floor, "We are against tyranny, and tyranny is in South Africa!"

The second event unfolded behind the scenes and focused on the planning of a private meeting at Leeds Castle in Kent, England, among chief executives of multinational companies doing business in South Africa. The meeting was being organized by Rev. Leon Sullivan. I kept in direct contact with Rev. Sullivan, and Ernest Mchunu and Eric Mafuna kept me briefed as plans unfolded in South Africa.

The Sullivan Principles were necessary reforms, but they put business in lockstep with the South African government's strategy of so-called constructive engagement, which had run its course as a justification for the United States to continue to do business in South Africa. Profit motives no longer mattered. It had become a question of business ethics and each company's moral obligation to its shareowners.

The Leeds Castle meeting was being designed to explore how multinational companies could collectively leverage their enormous economic power to prevent a bloodbath in South Africa.

The initial correspondence from Rev. Sullivan to Roberto to request his attendance at the March 9, 1987, meeting came in a letter dated July 1, 1986. Roberto's first instinct was to delay a firm answer to the invitation. In addition to listening to me urging him to accept, he discussed the matter with other company executives, including Don Keough and Claus Halle. No doubt Roberto consulted members of his board of directors before he made a final decision about attending the Leeds Castle meeting.

More than six months later, on January 20, 1987, I received a note from Bill Newton, Roberto's executive assistant: "I am passing along the attached transmission from Reverend Sullivan. As you will see, he lists RCG as expected to attend," Bill wrote in longhand. "P.S.

RCG did not see this." "RCG" was, of course, Roberto Crispulo Goizueta.

Bill's note could have been interpreted as a polite way of questioning whether I had committed Roberto to attend the Leeds Castle meeting without his consent. My reply was equally circumspect. Just as I had been kept informed of Sullivan's plans, I had also kept Rev. Sullivan up to date about the prospect of the company's disinvestment, I told Bill.

I further said to Bill that Rev. Sullivan was most likely presuming upon Roberto, and before him, J. Paul Austin (as well as upon his personal friendship with me), in adding Roberto to the "expected to attend" list before Roberto had accepted. But it really didn't matter how Leon got from point A to point B. I knew that it was critical for Roberto to attend. The Coca-Cola Company was the iconic American brand that everyone watched closely in South Africa. The meeting in Kent would be no different.

On January 20, 1987, six months after the initial talks of the Leeds Castle meeting began, Rev. Sullivan sent a more formal invitation that included a list of invited individuals. The list featured top executives of virtually every major American company doing business in South Africa, including such companies as IBM, Johnson & Johnson, Mobil, Colgate-Palmolive, and, of course, General Motors, where Leon was a board member and enjoyed 100 percent support from his chairman and chief executive, Roger B. Smith. UK companies included Consolidated Gold Fields, Unilever Limited, International Cadbury Schweppes, and British Petroleum. Nestlé of Switzerland, Henkel of Germany, and Alfa Laval of Sweden were also on the final list of invitees. The agenda for the meeting was also enclosed.

I briefed Roberto and recommended that he accept immediately. He didn't hesitate. He picked up the phone and called Rev. Sullivan to say that he would be there.

&

Immediately preceding the Leeds Castle meeting, I was in Naples, Florida, for a Coca-Cola management retreat. Knowing that Mary and I would be flying with Roberto and his wife, Olguita, to London,

I was a bit nervous because I had never been on a long flight with Roberto. I was aware that Roberto didn't sleep much on airplanes, and I knew he would be full of questions.

Coca-Cola executive vice president Garth Hamby, my direct boss at that time, who often acted as Roberto's right-hand man, gave me some excellent advice on how to manage seven hours of conversation with the chairman.

"Roberto doesn't like chitter chatter," Garth said. The chairman of the Coca-Cola Company did not like talking about sports or care who was winning the World Series. Garth advised me to talk business with Roberto. That meant knowing a little bit about everything that the Coca-Cola Company did.

"And be prepared to say what your favorite Coke drink is," Garth added.

We had just introduced Diet Coke, and I was a consummate consumer of the sugar-free product.

Sure enough, during the flight Roberto asked what my favorite soft drink was.

"Of course, it's Coca-Cola," I said, "but I drink more Diet Coke than I do Coca-Cola."

Roberto nodded in approval and then turned to Mary to ask what her favorite Coca-Cola product was.

Mary didn't miss a beat: "I drink Coca-Cola!"

That got us off to a pretty good start. Roberto was just an avid Coca-Cola man.

During the lengthy flight, I shared with Roberto what it was like growing up black in the Jim Crow South and how we still faced our own racial problems in the US, ones that we confronted daily. The difficulties we dealt with as African Americans, I stated, paled in comparison to what black South Africans faced.

We landed at Gatwick on Sunday morning, March 8, and checked into the Berkeley Hotel in Knightsbridge.

That evening, Mary and I had dinner with Olguita and Roberto. Garth Hamby joined us, along with Ralph Cooper, president of Coke's Northwest European division, for a total of six. We dined at the Berkeley, Roberto's favorite hotel in London, an establishment that would eventually become my favorite hotel and the venue where I would one day meet Nelson Mandela and South African ambassador to the US Barbara Masekela.

After dinner, the four men took a stroll through the streets of Knightsbridge, an affluent area of grand Victorian homes and gardens that borders London's Hyde Park. Roberto was dressed immaculately, as usual, in his ascot and a nice blue suit. We were all in business attire.

As Roberto and I walked, a little ahead of the rest of the group, he told me about how important it was for the Coca-Cola Company to get the South Africa problem right—and how important it was for him personally to see that we got it right. What's more, he said, the company was depending on me to lead the right solution.

◈

The next morning, I awoke early and shared a car with Roberto for the nearly two-hour drive from Knightsbridge to Kent. Built as a Norman stronghold in 1066, Leeds Castle was later used as a residence whose most famous occupants were Henry VIII and his first wife, Catherine of Aragon. The "loveliest castle in the world," as it is known, has a fairytale moat, breathtaking gardens, a hedge maze, a nine-hole golf course, and conference facilities.

Leeds Castle was an ideal setting for such a critical meeting. Despite the high-profile attendees and sensitive nature of the topic to be discussed, the meeting was kept out of the press. Attendance was by invitation only, and the event was somehow planned and executed out of the public eye. To have done otherwise would have made it unlikely the CEOs would attend.

We arrived well ahead of 9:30 A.M., the start of the meeting, along with thirty or so other participants. The mood was decidedly somber, as every single attendee seemed laser-focused on the seriousness and urgency of the business at hand.

We met in the castle's boardroom while the featured speakers assembled at a head table and each made remarks from a podium. The CEO participants were seated around an oval table with their support staff in a circumference behind them. I sat directly behind Roberto.

I looked at all of the distinguished persons around me and felt that the collective power gathered in that room could weigh heavily in changing the course of history in South Africa.

Rev. Sullivan cochaired the meeting with former British prime minister Sir Edward Heath. Leon was confident and charismatic, a religious leader who pastored the largest black congregation in Philadelphia. Importantly, he spoke the language of business with passion.

Being surrounded by corporate leaders at Leeds was a familiar one to the civil rights leader, who had personally visited every major American, British, and South African corporation doing business in South Africa to secure signatures and promises of adherence to the Sullivan Principles. In his introductory remarks, he told the room of multinational chiefs that unless corporations did something urgently, South Africa would go up in smoke.

His remarks were followed by ones from A. M. Rosholt, chairman of Barlow Rand; Dr. Sam Motsuenyane, chairman of the National African Federated Chamber of Commerce and Industry and chairman of Africa Bank; and J. J. Steyn, executive chairman of the Urban Foundation. Together they painted a bleak picture of the current conditions in South Africa that included the government's most recent declaration of a state of emergency, the military raids on neighboring countries, the fear of unrest in the townships spilling into white areas, and the imminent threat of civil war.

Dr. Motsuenyane, in particular, made the point that freeing black businesses to operate in white areas was something that black business leaders were becoming increasingly impatient about. I knew Sam from my time working in South Africa. He was one of the people I consulted about things like identifying the first black bottler.

Once Sam and his fellow panelists finished, Malcolm Fraser, former prime minister of Australia, gave a review of the Commonwealth Eminent Persons Group Initiatives. Fraser cochaired the group of seven with General Olusegun Obasanjo, former head of the Federal Military Government of Nigeria and that country's future president.

The EPG's intensive six-month probe into apartheid South Africa resulted in the June 1986 report titled *Mission to South Africa: The Commonwealth Report*, which Penguin Books published and made an overnight bestseller.

"Put in the most simple way, the blacks have had enough of apartheid. They are no longer prepared to submit to its oppression, discrimination and exploitation. They can no longer stomach being treated as aliens in their own country," the Commonwealth Report warned. "Unlike the earlier periods of unrest and Government attempts to stamp out protest, there has been during the last 18 months no outflow of black refugees from South Africa. The strength of black convictions is now matched by a readiness to die for those convictions. They will, therefore, sustain their struggle, whatever the cost."

A foreword to the report by Commonwealth Secretary-General Shridath Ramphal states,

> The message is clear: apartheid must end. It will end—if necessary, through a bloody struggle whose cost in lives may be counted in millions and whose agonies will reverberate in every corner of our multiracial world. But it could end by peaceful means—by a genuine process of negotiation—once white South Africa accepts that the evil system by which it has sustained its dominance must end and is ready by deeds to bring it about. The Group's account shows with unique authenticity how far the Government of South Africa is from that acceptance and that readiness. It shows too that not all white South Africans stand rooted on the banks of the Rubicon; some are ready and willing to cross. And the Group's Report confirms that on the other bank those so long oppressed in South Africa, the victims of apartheid, are ready even now to join in a peaceful process of building a new South Africa in which all its people, black and white, coloured and Indian, will share in fairness and with dignity.

The Commonwealth Report focused on the violence and atrocities that occurred during the EPG's visit, including the practice of the South African police shooting their guns randomly into peaceful black crowds and torturing black schoolchildren. "Indeed, we heard, with depressing repetition, accounts of violence directed by the security forces against children, of children brutally whipped, of schoolrooms teargassed and of difficulties experienced by parents in locating children taken by the police," the Eminent Persons Group found.

Among its conclusions, the Commonwealth Report included this key observation: "We are convinced that the South African Government is concerned about the adoption of effective economic measures

176

against it. If it comes to the conclusion that it would always remain protected from such measures, the process of change in South Africa is unlikely to increase in momentum and the descent into violence would be accelerated. In these circumstances, the cost in lives may have to be counted in millions."

The Commonwealth EPG advocated for the immediate suspension of business and for the implementation of international sanctions against the apartheid government.

At 12:30, the speakers and participants continued discussions over lunch. During the single thirty-minute break, Roberto and I left the meeting room to explore the castle's interior and discuss the morning session.

Nothing the speakers said was new to me, but for Roberto it was a revelation to hear all this in one setting. And that was the important thing. "Our guys inside of South Africa have not been telling us the whole truth, Carl," he told me, clearly moved after hearing the grim facts about the situation from such prominent experts on the subject.

I had been hearing the whole truth and seeing it and reporting it back to Atlanta. That day was the first time Roberto had actually heard about the horrors of apartheid from peers and from such people as Sam Motsuenyane. He had never been in this kind of session before. It was as if a light bulb had turned on for him.

In the afternoon session, Sir Edward Heath, former British prime minister, led a discussion on how companies could accelerate the Sullivan Principles efforts in terms of equal-rights employment, education, black business development, housing, the elimination of statutory apartheid, and the establishment of political rights.

These multinational chief executives had been hearing about "reform" and "constructive engagement" from their staffs on the ground in South Africa all along. At the Leeds Castle meeting, they came to understand that reform was no longer considered a viable option. Apartheid had to be dismantled.

In his closing remarks that day, Sullivan stressed that Botha's "reforms" did not scratch the surface when it came to mitigating the impact of apartheid on the lives of blacks in South Africa, and that business and industry had to unite to demand the end of every single vestige of the evil system.

As we were packing up to go back to our hotels, Leon took me aside to ask how I thought the meeting went.

"This is a turning point," I assured him. "What you've done here is monumental, assembling all of these powerful executives in the same room." I advised him to continue the conversation individually with all of the participants, especially the South African business leaders.

☙

Back in Knightsbridge that evening, Roberto hosted a dinner at Mosimann's Club that was attended by all of the Coca-Cola UK business partners, approximately twenty-five executives, and no spouses. Halfway through the dinner, Garth Hamby leaned over to me and said, "Roberto wants you to speak to the group about South Africa. He just told me to tell you."

I put down my knife and fork and took a sip of water. "Okay, give me a minute," I said. I excused myself to go to a quiet corner in the men's lounge to ask the Lord to give me the strength, the courage, and the wisdom to deliver this extemporaneous speech.

Five minutes later, I returned to my seat.

"Are you ready?" Garth asked.

I told him I was, and I stood and gave a ten-minute talk about the meeting at Leeds Castle, the dangerous situation in South Africa, the stubborn apartheid government, the resolve of the ANC and the impatience of black South Africans, the role of business, and the necessity for Coca-Cola to be on the right side of change in South Africa. I also pointed out that the Coca-Cola Company had never before used its power to say to the South African government, *we are disinvesting—not because of economic reasons, but because of our abhorrence of the system of apartheid.* But I further stated that the time might soon be approaching when the Coca-Cola Company had to stand on principle.

Divine intervention must have been responsible for putting the right words in my mouth and for giving me the strength to deliver that important speech, which put me in front of Coca-Cola's key business partners in the UK. Not far into it, I could already sense the audience was impressed by how conversant I was with the problem and the way forward.

In the Q&A session that followed my remarks, our business partners asked questions about the African National Congress and its ability to lead the country once apartheid was abolished. I talked about my meetings with exiled leaders of the ANC, including Oliver Tambo, Thabo Mbeki, and Johnny Makhathini. I talked about Desmond Tutu, Allan Boesak, and the black business leaders in the country. I said that while the Sullivan Principles had greatly enhanced the movement toward workplace justice, they fell short of providing a viable solution for companies doing business in South Africa.

The impromptu talk went off without a hitch, and I could tell that Roberto was very proud. He had a lot of confidence in me, and I was proud of that fact, and that he believed in me. I was humbled to be in a position at that moment to deliver.

❧

The Leeds Castle meeting marked the first all-out effort by South African business leaders to dismantle apartheid. Some of them were Afrikaners and supporters of the government that employed their family members and friends. In reality, companies such as Barlow Rand, Anglo American Corporation, and the Premiere Group defended and propped up the apartheid regime—until their business interests were threatened.

Perhaps the most important outcome of the Leeds Castle meeting was not that US companies would have to leave South Africa because of economic sanctions but, indeed, that the South African companies were motivated to initiate direct contact and dialogue with the exiled ANC leaders.

By the time the Leeds Castle meeting ended, the Institute for Democratic Alternatives in South Africa (IDASA) had gained tremendous credibility as a conduit between the exiled ANC government and the allies of the anti-apartheid movement. I was not surprised to learn that, indeed, white South African business leaders were already in dialogue with IDASA.

Three months later, the now historic Dakar Conference in Senegal took place July 9 through July 12, 1987. The founders of IDASA, Alex Boraine and Frederik van Zyl Slabbert, two white members of the South African parliament, were outspokenly opposed to apartheid and committed to a peaceful solution to the South Africa problem.

Of course, the South African government outlawed such meetings. So, the first one, which few people other than the participants knew about, was set to take place outside the country. The problem was that most of the ANC delegates didn't have the money to cover travel and other expenses needed to attend the meeting in Dakar.

The white South Africans involved with IDASA were already taking risks by opening a dialogue with a "terrorist" organization whose existence was banned in their country. Providing financial assistance to ANC members would have placed them in more serious jeopardy.

A month after the Leeds meeting, Alex Boraine asked to see me for dinner one evening at my usual Cape Town address, the Mount Nelson Hotel. He said the matter was urgent, confidential, and politically sensitive. He asked if the Coca-Cola Company could help with the Dakar meeting by picking up the ANC delegates' travel tab. It was a big ask, but I knew what was at stake and agreed to fund the travel expenses for the ANC delegates to Dakar.

Although few people even knew the meeting was taking place, fewer still would know of Coke's involvement. It was clear to me that this was the right thing and another step toward putting the Coca-Cola Company on the right side of history. Indeed, the Dakar Conference would go down in history as a major turning point.

I didn't realize it then, but my role in South Africa, and the rest of Africa for that matter, was only beginning. After my negotiating the disinvestment plan, anti-apartheid leaders across the continent trusted me. Some called me for advice. Others saw me as a possible conduit to American power centers needed to support the anti-apartheid movement.

24

Meeting Two South African Presidents

After the disinvestment, two events that drew responses from me based on my gut instincts also drove business decisions and had large impacts on the way Coca-Cola was perceived by the ANC's leaders. Those responses were small acts of kindness outside my usual corporate domain.

In July 1988, the Soweto home of Winnie Mandela, wife of imprisoned ANC leader Nelson Mandela, was burned to the ground, along with all of its contents, including wedding pictures. It had been the Mandelas' family home since the 1940s. The government described it as a garden-variety fire caused by schoolchildren. However, many people believed that security police had firebombed the house. That kind of thing was happening to anti-apartheid activists across the country in an overt campaign of intimidation.

But I wasn't concerned about the cause of the fire. Its result left Winnie Mandela—determined wife of Nelson Mandela, and the person who "freed" her husband's voice as he sat in prison year after year—homeless, as were the Mandelas' children. I asked my South African colleagues at Coke, specifically Fred Meyer, Hennie Viljoen, and Ernest Mchunu, "What can we do to help this lady? What can we do to help Mrs. Mandela?"

We sent Ernest to do an assessment of the Mandela family's needs. When he returned, he said, "Well, they can rebuild the house but they have no stove, no refrigerator, no beds, no furniture, no nothing."

"We can easily buy these things for Mrs. Mandela and her children," I said. "We should do this." That was it. We really didn't discuss it much because it seemed like such a small gesture for a family who had given and lost so much while fighting injustice.

The Last Apartheid President

There was one powerful enemy of the anti-apartheid movement, however, whom I wanted to meet because he was the one man who had it in his power to immediately alter the course of events in South Africa. I made known my desire to meet South African president F. W. de Klerk, and soon word came back that he also wanted to meet me. A long time passed. And then, on June 10, 1989, I received the summons to meet him.

The practice of the South African government was to convene for six months of the year in Cape Town and convene in Pretoria for the other six months. My meeting was scheduled for the presidential offices in Cape Town. I was to meet with De Klerk for fifteen minutes, starting at 11:15 that morning, and I was told that he would be on a tight schedule. At noon, De Klerk was set to depart for Nigeria, where he would meet with Nigeria's head of state, Ibrahim Badamasi Babangida, the first such meeting by a South African president with his most powerful adversary on the continent.

I arrived at the presidential offices without much hope of getting my full fifteen minutes. My experience with African heads of state was that scheduled meeting times didn't mean much. If you were supposed to start a meeting at 11:15 A.M., you might get in at 12:15 P.M. or you might get in at 2:15 P.M. It was open ended. With a plane waiting to whisk De Klerk away at noon sharp, I knew that I would be lucky to see him even for a brief handshake and photo.

But De Klerk surprised me. I was ushered into his office on time. My fifteen minutes came and went. The meeting continued. We spoke past the thirty-minute mark. Eventually, the meeting stretched beyond forty-five minutes.

De Klerk did most of the talking. I did most of the listening. He had already begun preparing white South Africans for the possibility of a transition to a one-man, one-vote democracy. He told me how difficult it was for him to do that as an Afrikaner and as the head of the Nationalist Party, which had instituted apartheid.

The president recounted what happened to him on a then-recent trip to his hometown. He was used to being greeted as a hero there. He would go into restaurants where everyone would give him standing ovations and people would come up and shake his hand. His last trip home, however, came after he said publicly that he would consider ending the ANC ban and that he was thinking of releasing Nelson Mandela from prison. He did not say that he was going to release Mandela after more than two decades, just that he was thinking about it.

The mere idea was enough to set off feelings of betrayal and waves of rage among white South Africans, especially De Klerk's fellow Afrikaners. So instead of being welcomed home with open arms that time, he was pelted with rotten eggs.

The president said he wanted to talk to me about what was happening in his country. He said he especially wanted to speak with an American businessman who understood the necessity and inevitability of what he was going to do for South Africa. He said he had heard that I was well connected in the anti-apartheid movement in South Africa, as well as in business and political circles in America.

There were two things he wanted to convey to corporate America. "The first is that change is coming, and it's coming pretty fast," De Klerk told me. "Second, I'm catching hell."

These were new and extraordinary sentiments to hear in the corridors of power in South Africa. For years, the usual response to outsiders regarding criticism of the white power structure was either to ask for patience or, more often, to tell others not to meddle in South Africa's internal affairs. De Klerk was signaling that the wait for change would soon be over and that he could use some outside help to weather the storm that might erupt over what he planned to do.

I understood and admired the courage it took for De Klerk to take the path he had chosen. There was legitimate concern about what the true believers within his own political party and ethnic group would do in order to preserve white supremacy in South Africa. There were Afrikaners who thought white dominance over blacks was the result of a covenant with God.

The most extreme elements within De Klerk's party publicly spoke of resorting to violence to prevent his move toward democracy. There were questions about which side the South African security forces would take. They had been enforcers in the government's campaign to preserve apartheid, following orders to harass, persecute, kidnap, torture, and even murder persons the government deemed dangerous. What would these loyal thugs do if they decided the danger now came from inside the government?

No doubt, there were individuals who delighted in the prospect of South Africa's whites at each other's throats, fighting among themselves until they were so weakened that the country's long-oppressed people of color could pick up the pieces and claim control. But I agreed with Tutu and others who saw a peaceful transition into democracy as the best hope for all South Africans, especially the majority. I was happy to carry President de Klerk's message back to America and to urge support for what he was doing.

Over the next few months, De Klerk made good on his promise that change was coming to South Africa. He took steps ranging from ending the ban on the ANC to allowing blacks to use beaches that previously had been designated "whites only." On February 11, 1990, eight months after our meeting, De Klerk released Nelson Mandela from prison with no restrictions on what he could do once he was free, a defining moment in the country's history.

De Klerk continued to make statements to allay the fears of South African whites, warning, for example, that majority rule was "unacceptable in the South African context" because it would lead to persecution of the white minority. Yet, for many, De Klerk's release of Mandela marked the point of no return in South Africa's march toward democracy.

Madiba

Once Nelson Mandela was released from prison, he became the man everyone wanted to see. He was the most popular and recognizable person in South Africa, perhaps the world, despite not having been seen in public for more than twenty years. Confined to a cell, he was denied direct contact with the outside world, yet he symbolized freedom for millions of South Africans. Everyone wanted to meet him. I was fortunate to be the first American businessman to do so.

I met Mandela for the first time on March 21, 1990, thirty-eight days after he was set free and literally hours after Africa's last colony, Namibia, gained independence. That day dawned in Windhoek, Namibia, where Don McHenry and I attended ceremonies marking the nation's independence from South Africa.

Until then, Namibia was called South West Africa, essentially created and controlled by South Africa as a country of convenience. I watched as President F. W. de Klerk handed over the reins of power to Sam Nujoma, the country's first black president. So many world leaders were in attendance the event was hailed as a "mini United Nations."

It was another sign of De Klerk's commitment to change. Once the ceremony was over, I boarded Coca-Cola's Gulf Stream jet with Don McHenry and Rev. Allan Boesak for the flight to Johannesburg to meet De Klerk's longtime nemesis and, at that time, his future partner in forging the new South Africa.

Don would accompany me to meet with Mandela, as he had done numerous times to confer with other South African leaders. Once we deplaned in Johannesburg, we headed straight to Shell House, the Shell Oil Company's high-rise office building in downtown Johannesburg. At the ANC's national headquarters I would meet the most revered man in South Africa.

Inside, ANC security met us and immediately escorted us into Mandela's office, where he greeted us graciously. My first impression of him was that he had both a regal bearing as well as a down-to-earth quality. He was reserved, certainly, but not in a guarded way. I thought he was the most majestic person I had ever met and felt humbled in his presence. Before me stood a man who had spent a total of twenty-seven years in prison, eighteen of them at labor in a rock quarry, yet he remained unbeaten by all he had endured. He actually seemed happy.

Mandela looked me directly in the eye and said, "I'm finally happy to meet a comrade who has meant so much to me and my family and to the struggle." He told me about the first time he had heard of me, about how his wife, Winnie, visited him in prison and spoke of an African American businessman who had helped her and their children after their home was burned to the ground.

He talked a bit about his life and about his experiences in prison. We, in turn, spoke to him about our philosophy of corporate responsibility. I outlined our intentions to help in creating the new South Africa. Coke wanted to empower black South Africans, I said, by preparing them to move into managerial positions. We would sponsor developmental training, including for Coca-Cola suppliers. We would make certain that blacks were owners and operators within the new Coca-Cola system in South Africa.

We talked about what Coke could do to help prepare his nation for its first free, democratic elections. And we outlined our vision and plans for moving forward in a democratic South Africa. I assured Mandela that we would reinvest in South Africa once a new government came into power.

At the time, the Coca-Cola Company neither owned nor operated anything in South Africa. Just as we had to come up with a plan for getting out of country, we had to come up with a plan to reenter when the time was right.

Don McHenry and I discussed future relationships between the ANC, South Africa's government in waiting, and the US government, and we offered to help in facilitating a positive working relationship between the two governments.

One of the things Mandela especially needed help with was countering the perception that the ANC was a Communist organization that would nationalize all of South Africa's industries and install central control over the economy as soon as it came to power. Mandela and the ANC suffered from the same misperceptions that plagued Dr. King and the civil rights movement. Because avowed Communists joined the ANC in fighting apartheid, people painted it as a Communist organization. But Mandela was no Communist. He wanted all South Africans to have the opportunity to share in the country's wealth. Instituting government policies that would cripple the nation's economic engines wasn't his intention.

I promised to reassure American political and financial leaders about Mandela's true intentions. By speaking to the Business Roundtable and the US Chamber of Commerce, using Coca-Cola connections on Wall Street, testifying before Congress, appearing on college campuses, and carrying Mandela's message to other audiences, including non-US businesses, I would become among the most vocal spokesmen in America for reinvestment in South Africa.

In all of these talks, I emphasized the depth and breadth of business-friendly leadership within the ANC. I rattled off names including Trevor Manuel, who became Mandela's minister of finance; Tito Mboeni, who became governor of the Reserve Bank of South Africa; Jakes Gerwel, who became chief of staff for Mandela; Alec Erwin, who become Mandela's minister of trade and industry; and Thabo Mbeki, deputy president.

The first meeting with Mandela went extremely well. After that, it was rare for me to miss an opportunity to visit with him at his family residence whenever I was in South Africa. Our working relationship developed into a true friendship. Whenever we met, we always talked about personal and family matters before getting down to whatever was on the official agenda.

I became a mentor to some of the Mandela children and grandchildren, and I helped a few get into American colleges. I was honored when Mandela invited Mary and me to be his personal guests at his inauguration as South Africa's first truly democratically elected president. One of my prized possessions is a signed painting Mandela brought to me when he visited the United States in July 1993. Above his signature is a note: "To a comrade who lent his life and influence to the struggle."

People often ask me how I could tell that the South Africa I encountered the first time I visited the country was gone and that a new South Africa had emerged. I think they expect me to talk about the most visible signs of the black majority's political power, the election of Mandela as president, and the blacks serving in parliament or as judges or running government ministries.

Instead, the first sign was something much more subtle: the appearance of black professionals in places where, when I first arrived in South Africa, I never saw them. They were in restaurants, in hotel lobbies and country clubs, just walking on the streets. It seems strange in retrospect, but before the transformation began in earnest, I usually saw only a handful of black professionals in the offices where they worked. It was as if even the best and brightest among South Africa's blacks "knew their place" in society and that they were forbidden to stray outside it. But with the coming of freedom, they began to show themselves in everyday places, where they seldom ventured previously.

25

THE MAKING OF CLARK ATLANTA UNIVERSITY

In late 1986, as I was preparing to return home after three weeks in Johannesburg, I got a call from my secretary, Linda Wight, in Atlanta. Atlanta University Board of Trustees chairman Tom Cordy and vice chairman Prentiss Yancey had just called and told her they "urgently" needed to meet with me as soon as I got back.

I had been serving as chairman of the Clark College Board of Trustees since 1984 and worked with board members from the other schools in the Atlanta University Center on a regular basis. Seldom was our business "urgent."

On the flight, I thought about Linda's message again, finally concluding that the two trustees wanted to discuss a million-dollar contribution that the Coca-Cola Foundation was considering for Atlanta University. The money was under discussion, but I thought they were going to ask us to forward-pay the contribution to shore up Atlanta University's desperate financial situation.

That night, back in Atlanta, I rang up Tom Cordy at his home. I was half right about what motivated the ominous request—Tom and Prentiss indeed wanted to speed the Coca-Cola contribution along. But more importantly, they wanted to have a confidential meeting with me to discuss a possible combination of Clark College and Atlanta University.

My initial reaction was that I could not put Clark's future in jeopardy, considering the Atlanta University bankruptcy crisis, which I knew only too well. The grand old institution had overspent its endowment and borrowed to the point that no bank in Atlanta would lend it a dime. Enrollment was declining, the faculty was jumping ship left and right, and its academic standing had plummeted.

When Dr. Eldridge McMillan, head of the Southern Education Foundation, nominated me to chair the Clark College Board of Trustees, he said nothing about leading a bailout of a failing Atlanta University. As far as I could tell, the biggest issue Clark faced at that time was fundraising, which I tackled immediately. I raised $11 million in a silent capital campaign within the city limits.

Saving Atlanta University by combining it with Clark College would be a daunting task, if it could be done at all. I didn't dismiss the request out of hand, tempting as that might have been.

I knew that entertaining the question meant bringing in academic consultants, lawyers, and accountants just to get an accurate picture of Atlanta University's condition. Assessing AU's assets and liabilities had to be done before any creative thinking could occur.

Dr. James P. Brawley, a mentor of mine and president emeritus of Clark College, recommended that I talk with Dr. Thomas W. Cole, chancellor of the West Virginia Board of Regents and one of four African Americans to head a state system of higher education.

Tom Cole had a long history with Atlanta University as head of the Department of Chemistry and as its vice president and provost. After Dr. Brawley's recommendation, I consulted Tom Cordy, and we agreed that I would pay a visit to Dr. Cole's office in West Virginia.

Once there, I told Dr. Cole what we were trying to accomplish. I explained the proposition of a possible merger of Clark College and Atlanta University. I knew that it would be a stretch for him to consider leaving the prestigious post of chancellor of the West Virginia university system to lead the consolidation effort.

I invited him to Atlanta to advise Cordy and me on the matter of consolidation. When he sat down with us at a private meeting in my office, he was surprised by our offer to him to lead the consolidation. Having obtained the approval of the board of trustees, I offered him the presidency of Clark College.

I explained to Dr. Cole that, in this position, he would become the principal operating officer overseeing the consolidation. He was impressed with our vision of a new university that would combine the academic and institutional strengths of Clark College and Atlanta University. Because Atlanta University did not have a president at that time, Dr. Cole would, in effect, be running both institutions simultaneously. He took our offer seriously, and, on his next visit to

Atlanta, informed us that he would be honored to lead such a historic venture in black higher education.

As I set those wheels in motion, I decided to do a little research of my own so that I would be informed by the historical intentions of both institutions. I started with Dr. Brawley's 1977 book, *The Clark College Legacy*, a scholarly work of the type that is often ignored by book reviewers. Until the question of consolidation came up, I had only thumbed through it myself. Dr. Brawley, of course, was the strong Clark president most remembered for shepherding the school through the turbulent days of civil rights.

Clark College was founded in 1868 by the Freedmen's Aid Society and the Methodist Episcopal Church and, over time, had four different campus locations. The first was a sprawling 122-acre farm in the Summer Hill area of Southwest Atlanta. It soon became the first four-year liberal arts college in the nation to offer degrees to African American students, with a curriculum that focused on training those students to become teachers and ministers for the church.

In 1872, the campus relocated to Whitehall and McDaniel streets, where the Clark Theological Seminary opened. Within eight years, the institution had to relocate yet again, this time to the South Atlanta site, which encompassed 150 acres to allow for present and future expansion.

The curriculum also expanded to bachelor of arts degrees in carpentry, blacksmithing, agriculture, and eventually "domestic economy." That last curriculum can be credited to Rev. E. O. Thayer, Clark's young president, who had definite ideas on the education of women and proposed a model home in which young ladies would receive practical training in housekeeping. The students would live in the model home, called Fisk Cottage, for two years and learn sewing, among other domestic arts.

In the early decades of the twentieth century, Dr. Brawley notes, industrial training as a complement to an academic education was recognized as a critical component of higher learning, and Clark University was known to have "one of the best-located as well as one of the best-equipped industrial schools south of the Ohio [River]," according to *The Christian Educator*.

As I read Dr. Brawley's book, I learned that from its inception, the school had welcomed students of all races and, of course, that its first presidents and faculty were white. Clark's higher calling to serve primarily African American students became clear in an 1888 report from the school's president, Dr. Atticus G. Haygood:

> It is settled that the Negro must be educated, not at all because he is a Negro, but because he is a man.... It is settled that mere book-learning is not enough for the Negro race, because it is not enough for any race.... People who are to succeed, who are to be what they can and therefore ought to be, must know how to do things also.
>
> If these people are to be a self-sustaining race, they must earn more than enough for the cheapest sort of living.... They must have money in the savings bank; they must have capital.... To have capital they must save money...to save money they must be able to earn more than just enough to live on.

The agriculture department also flourished. In 1909, Dr. Brawley quotes a report of its progress from an instructor named P. H. Parks:

> The following crops have been grown on the university farm in the past year: 350 bushels of corn, 11 bales of cotton, 80 tons of hay, and 300 bushels of oats, 40,000 heads of cabbages, 2,000 pounds of salad, 40 bushels of okra, 300 dozen bunches of onions, 125 bushels of sweet potatoes, and 40 bushels of white potatoes. In addition to the above-named crops, we have made 2,500 pounds of pork, 300 pounds of butter, and 7,300 gallons of sweet milk.

As I read, I learned that Dr. Brawley himself became dean of the university in 1926 and then became dean-registrar in 1929. He would continue to make structural reforms that would modernize the curriculum and record-keeping systems. What's more, I learned that talk of merging Clark College and Atlanta University had been under consideration as early as 1922, though nothing came of it then.

Not long after Dr. Brawley came on board, the Great Depression hit, and colleges and universities across the country were crippled by the lack of funding. Many struggled to keep their doors open. At one point, Clark didn't even have the funds in its coffers to pay the faculty, yet every single professor agreed to continue teaching without a paycheck.

One of the survival strategies was for all of the historically black colleges and universities to band together. Until then, they had all been competitors. The shift in thinking was for the institutions to work together to find the natural synergies that would help each, in turn, to survive independently. A shared statement of purpose outlining how Atlanta's HBCUs would cooperate was signed, and discussions began about another relocation of the Clark campus so that it would be in proximity to the other schools.

After the move in 1941 to Atlanta's west side, the Atlanta University Center included Clark College, Spelman College, Morehouse College, Morris Brown College, Atlanta University, and the Gammon Theological Seminary, and the relationships between all of them were further defined and solidified. Principles included mutual respect and confidence, unity, careful planning, reciprocity and economy, and a sense and spirit of togetherness.

In terms of facilities, the combining meant that although Clark maintained its own library, Clark students nonetheless had access to the Atlanta University library. In the new setting, Clark had no athletic facilities but used the gymnasium of Morris Brown, and so on. Students who attended Atlanta University Center schools could choose from a wider variety of course offerings as the institutions coordinated and consolidated their efforts. Teachers employed by one institution could also teach courses at the others.

Preserving a Black Brain Trust

Like Clark, Atlanta University could also trace its roots back to the period immediately following the Civil War, when thousands of freed blacks flocked to Atlanta for safety, writes Dr. Clarence A. Bacote in his 1969 book, *The Story of Atlanta University*.

At the end of the war, just 5,000 of the 462,000 blacks in Georgia could read and write. Instead of shelter and a way forward, the newly emancipated found chaos, with widespread hunger and epidemic illness in a city that had quite literally been burned to the ground. Against this backdrop two formerly enslaved men, James Tate and Grandison B. Daniels, opened a school for "freedmen in an old church building [located] on Jenkins Street, the original home of the present Big Bethel African Methodist Episcopal Church," according to Dr. Bacote.

Soon after that founding, the American Missionary Association, the most important Northern benevolent society dedicated to the advancement of freedmen, came to Atlanta and offered to take over and expand the school. Tate and Daniels were happy to hand over the reins to experienced educators. As for the "first founders," my research revealed that they went on to become members of the city's emerging black middle class—Daniels as a railroad worker and Tate as a grocery store owner.

Famously, some of the first classes were held in a boxcar purchased by Big Bethel AME for $310. A few years later, in 1867, Atlanta University was granted a state charter. By 1900, it had the third-largest black library in the country, with 11,000 volumes. Only Howard and Lincoln had more. Of the white universities in Georgia, only Emory, UGA, and Mercer had larger collections.

Over time, the Atlanta University Center library, which would become known as the Robert W. Woodruff Library, grew into a national repository of rare historical artifacts, including slavery narratives, Frederick Douglass items, and autographed Phillis Wheatley poems.

The care in building the library was a direct reflection of the faculty that molded the minds of great intellectuals such as Richard Wright, John Hope Franklin, and W. E. B. Dubois. They left Atlanta University not only as scholars and future leaders in their fields but also as highly disciplined and socially conscious activists.

Renowned Harlem Renaissance poet James Weldon Johnson, another famed graduate, also led the NAACP. Through it, he became a major force behind the anti-lynching bill. He served his country as a diplomat: President Theodore Roosevelt appointed him US consul to Venezuela and, later, to Nicaragua. He was the first black professor at New York University and a professor of creative literature at Fisk.

Atlanta University could boast graduates including Clayton R. Yates, co-owner of the Yates & Milton drugstore chain, where the Atlanta Student Movement began. Yates also served as chairman on the boards of several local black banks, including Citizens Trust Bank and the Mutual Federal Savings and Loan Association.

North Carolina Mutual Life Insurance Company founder and self-made millionaire John Merrick was an Atlanta University grad, as was Jo Ann Robinson, who led a one-day boycott in Montgomery, Alabama, following the arrest of Rosa Parks for refusing to give up her bus seat. The faculty included such distinguished figures as professor George Towns, father of Grace Towns Hamilton, the first black female legislator in the Georgia General Assembly.

Atlanta University's history of high educational standards was documented as early as 1870. The Georgia legislature was about to make an $8,000 appropriation to the school, which meant it came under the same oversight and regulations as the University of Georgia. That resulted in three days of rigorous testing of students in all subjects by the school's harshest critics: white former slaveholders. Alongside the stellar results recorded lay this statement from one of the examiners: "the blackest student could demonstrate clearly problems in Algebra and Geometry, and read smoothly in Latin and Greek."

In its first twenty years of existence, Atlanta University educated white students as well as black. Dr. Bacote quotes an 1887 report written by the Georgia Board of Visitors: "We find in attendance…a number of white students of various ages and both sexes, most of them having more or less connection with the members of the faculty and other officers, and one at least, entirely unconnected with the officials." When this fact could no longer be ignored, the state legislature threatened to pull funding if the practice continued. It was necessarily ended.

Until the Supreme Court's *Brown v. Board of Education of Topeka* decision in 1954, Atlanta University was the only school in the South where blacks could earn graduate degrees. The decision "was a moral victory worthy of celebration" that struck a blow to most black colleges and universities in the late 1960s, "but Atlanta University felt it almost immediately," writes Dr. Thomas Cole.

By the early 1980s, borrowing from the endowment to cover funding shortfalls was standard practice, and the school had been operating at a deficit over four consecutive administrations.

Saving Atlanta University was a big moment in the history of Atlanta, but history was also on our side. Atlanta city leaders—black and white—had a track record of coming together in times of crisis. Given all of our Fortune 500 companies and prosperity as a city, if we failed, what would it say to other struggling HBCUs that operated in places with fewer resources? Atlanta's African American leaders faced a call to action. What would it say about us if we allowed Atlanta University to fail?

As chairman of the Coca-Cola Foundation, I used my clout to get the ball rolling. This challenge was in our backyard. Mr. Woodruff's name was on the Atlanta University Center library. Coca-Cola had been the lead contributor to the Atlanta University Center schools, and Coke executives served on their boards.

I made a grant to Clark College that would fund the consolidation study and bring in consultants including Dr. Vernon Crawford, former chancellor of the Georgia Board of Regents. He would provide guidance to the consolidation committee's work. The grant funded advisors on academic restructuring, lawyers, accountants, and other specialists that neither Atlanta University nor Clark could afford.

The consolidation committee was formed out of the two school boards, and we looked for synergies between Clark College and Atlanta University as the study was being completed. Obviously, there were many to be found.

Much of the work that made the endeavor successful took place behind the scenes in a tight-knit group that included Tom Cordy and Prentiss Yancey from AU; Eldridge McMillan; Lamond Godwin, founder of Peachtree Asset Management; and myself. Throughout the consolidation, the five of us would meet at one another's homes once a week. We trusted one another's integrity and agreed to put emotional issues aside to focus on business issues as if we were merging two corporations. In that environment, we were able to debate and decide most major issues. By the time the board met, the votes were already in hand.

As cochairs of the consolidation committee, Tom Cordy and I made a pact: we would always be together publicly. We could disagree and agree to disagree privately, but when we came out on an issue, Tom Cordy and I would be as one. That, I believe, was the key to leadership and the eventual smoothness that characterized the merger.

We decided that instead of a merger, in which Clark College would use its healthy balance sheet to absorb Atlanta University, we would consolidate the two schools, thereby creating a larger, stronger institution. In 1988, Clark Atlanta University was born with a combined enrollment of 2,000 undergraduate students and 1,000 graduate students, making it the largest of the Atlanta University Center schools.

After the consolidation, Tom Cordy nominated me for chairman of the new Clark Atlanta University Board of Trustees. The board consisted of some of the most prominent leaders in Atlanta, including Marvin Arrington, president of the Atlanta City Council; Lamond Godwin, first vice president of American Express Bank, who chaired the finance committee; Dr. Cornelius Henderson, my pastor at Ben Hill United Methodist Church in Atlanta, who provided spiritual counseling and advice; and James R. Kuse, president of Georgia Gulf Corporation, who privately made and kept pledges for the new institution.

Other board members were Dr. Delores Aldridge, chair of the Department of African American Studies at Emory University, and Dr. Eldridge McMillan, whom I credit with selling the efficacy of the consolidation throughout the network of Southern Education Foundation schools. My consolidation committee cochair, Tom Cordy, was peerless in keeping us on track in our weekly one-on-ones throughout the process and in being very candid about identifying and defusing land mines before they became obstacles. There was savvy Myrtle Davis, a member of the Atlanta City Council, who became secretary of the new board.

We were fortunate to have such entrepreneurs as Michael Hollis, founder of the first black-owned passenger airline, Air Atlanta; George Puskar, chairman and CEO of Equitable Real Estate Investment; Prentiss Yancey, a partner in law firm Smith, Gambrell & Russell; and Senator Sam Nunn, who, as a former trustee of Atlanta University and stalwart supporter of black higher education, kept the doors open to the right corridors in Washington, DC. Another influential trustee was Allen Franklin, CEO of Georgia Power and a strong advocate for the consolidation in the Atlanta business community.

As chairman of the Clark Atlanta University Board of Trustees, my job continued to focus on university governance, recruiting strong trustees, and ensuring board oversight of the new university in every aspect, including student enrollment and recruiting, as well as retaining a strong faculty. I continued to spend time fundraising and reaching out to alums of both legacy institutions.

The Carl & Mary Ware Academic Center

By the end of the 1990s, Clark Atlanta had not had a new academic building in thirty years and was in need of a classroom building that would, among other things, galvanize the strength of the combined institution.

I was keenly aware of the need and also keenly aware of the fact that my own net worth had grown significantly, to the point of my being in a position to create a lasting legacy that would demonstrate my commitment to Clark Atlanta University and to black higher education.

Mary and I shared this vision and together agreed to donate $2 million as a lead gift to get a new classroom building started. It was enough. The fact that I had dug into my own pockets for the money made it more palatable for philanthropic interests such as the Woodruff foundation, the Campbell foundation, and corporate donors to step forward with the remaining $15 million needed for construction.

What made the fundraising even more personally meaningful to me was that I asked Tom Cole, the immediate past president of CAU, along with Walter Broadnax, the new president, to accompany me on the fundraising campaign. They both accepted in a rare show of unity for such high-level administrators. The building was quickly funded.

In 2005, *Ebony* magazine quoted Dr. Broadnax describing the result of our efforts: "When the last brick was laid, the last window installed, and when the construction workers left the site, they were paid in full; the university owned the building lock, stock and barrel."

We had built a state-of-the-art academic building with twenty-eight classrooms, wireless Internet and other electronic learning technologies, a videoconferencing facility, conference and lecture rooms, a large study lounge, and a copy and printing center, as well as a coffee shop.

At some point before the building was completed, the CAU Board of Trustees informed me that they wanted the new classroom building to feature a portrait of Mary and me in the main lobby. Our name was already on the building, and it smacked of self-aggrandizement, so I immediately pushed back.

Ingrid Saunders Jones and Walter Broadnax changed my mind. "These kids need to see your portrait so they can see that you and Mary were like them. And that if you two did it, they can do it. That's why it should go in there."

That was enough to convince me. To make the most of the inspiration, I told Ingrid that her assignment was to find the most prominent African American portraitist in the country to paint our picture.

Ingrid didn't hesitate: "I've got just the person," she said. "Simmie Knox."

I had heard of Simmie Knox—he had painted the official portraits of Bill and Hillary Clinton, not to mention Frederick Douglass and Thurgood Marshall, as well as contemporaries of mine such as Alexis Herman and Oprah Winfrey. I was sold.

Mary and I invited the artist to our home in Atlanta. As we got acquainted, I learned that, like me, Simmie was also a type 2 diabetic, but he had licked the disease through diet and exercise. From that moment on, I made it my personal mission to do as Simmie had done, so right away our connection to each other went beyond the business at hand. Before he left, he took photographs of us. We awaited the proofs and eventual unveiling of the new classroom building's portrait.

Whatever my misgivings, the dedication ceremony for the opening of the Carl & Mary Ware Academic Center turned out to be the proudest moment of my life. Mary and I met at Clark College, we both graduated from the institution, and there we were, in a position to do something meaningful for it.

But the event was more than emotional; it was spiritual, like the fulfillment of a calling. Once the ceremony was over, Mary and I agreed we had done the right thing, that this gift was the ultimate way to give back to the institution that had meant so much to us and to thousands of other black kids like us. In fact, two of those kids happened to be our grandchildren: our granddaughter Renita Ware graduated with the class of 1988, and our grandson Aaron Ware graduated with the class of 1989.

In making that gift, I had become the largest single individual contributor in the university's history. Mary and I would eventually contribute more than $4 million of our personal wealth to the institution. I thought to myself, *Emory had a multi-billion-dollar endowment largely through the philanthropy of Robert W. Woodruff and other wealthy donors. Although my donations are small in comparison, I have become Clark's Robert W. Woodruff.* The thought was fitting because, as Mr. Woodruff said, and as I also truly believe, "There is no limit to what a man can do or how far he can go if he doesn't mind who gets the credit."

Stemming from our modest gift to Clark was a recognition that I thought was worthy of a slight deviation from the Woodruff philosophy. On March 9, 2007, the United Negro College Fund presented Mary and me with the President's Award at a gala in New York City for our philanthropy in black higher education. We were honored to be corecipients of the award that evening, along with President Bill Clinton and President George H. W. Bush.

The Carl & Mary Ware Academic Center was a high point for me but not the end of the Clark story, of course. I am now chairman emeritus, but I continue to work on behalf of the school behind the scenes. In fact, there are two extremely exciting projects on the drawing board right now that will catapult CAU to the top ranks of institutions of higher learning: the Prostate Cancer Research Center, which has yet to be built, and a new School of Communications and Fine Arts.

Atlanta's HBCUs have always trained their grads to be broad thinkers and strong professionals and to be grounded in spiritual and ethical behavior; to be leaders in society and to be socially conscious activists, aware of inequities whether they exist in the United States or abroad.

The ethical and moral training that HBCUs provide is focused on the black race but by no means limited to the black race. No other framework in America, including churches or civil rights organizations, has done more to further the cause of equality. As such, these stalwart American institutions have a right and a responsibility not just to survive, but to thrive.

Honoring Tutu and Mandela

Atlanta's historically black colleges and universities have repeatedly been on the cutting edge of social change. To have been able to act as such a central player I can attribute only to a miraculous convergence of fate and power in my life. As a senior vice president of the Coca-Cola Company, I used my position to make real social change for African Americans in corporate America and black Africans in South Africa.

One of the results of this convergence occurred in February 1992, when, as chairman of the board of trustees, I presided over a convocation in which Clark Atlanta conferred an honorary degree upon Archbishop Desmond Tutu. Mary and I felt privileged to host Desmond and his wife, Leah, overnight at our Ryland home during the festivities and to host a special dinner in his honor, with guests including Andrew Young, Ingrid Saunders Jones, and Tom and Brenda Cole, among others.

The most memorable outcome stemming from my leadership roles was a sequence of events that took place from July 9 through July 12, 1993.

On July 7, 1993, I sent a memo to my boss, John Hunter, president of Coca-Cola International, stating that I would take a company jet on July 9 to Los Angeles to pick up Nelson Mandela and bring him back for a special convocation. Mandela was then traveling the United States on a two-week fundraising tour for his presidential campaign in the run-up to South Africa's first democratic elections the following April.

In Los Angeles, I joined Mandela for a fundraising dinner—hosted by Peter Guber, chairman and CEO of Sony Entertainment—that was attended by attorney Johnnie Cochran, Los Angeles mayor Richard Riordan, Sugar Ray Leonard, Los Angeles Lakers coach Pat Riley, US congresswoman Maxine Waters, San Francisco mayor Willie Brown, and Hollywood celebrities including Danny Glover, Robert Guillaume, Sidney Poitier, and Arsenio Hall.

The next day, on the flight from Los Angeles to Atlanta, Mandela clearly wanted to spend quiet personal time with his two daughters and his grandchild, who were accompanying him on tour, so we

200

didn't discuss business. It was a pleasure for all of us to watch this great man interact with his beloved family from whom he had been separated for so long.

The company plane, *The Wind Ship*, touched down at Fulton County Airport and taxied to our hangar. A studious person might notice that all of our planes were called *The Wind Ship*, a clever play on *Winship*, the *W* in the middle of Robert W. Woodruff's name.

I escorted Mandela and his entourage to the downtown Ritz-Carlton, where they were lodging. That evening, Mayor Maynard Jackson held a dinner in Mandela's honor that featured speeches by Atlanta civil rights leaders Coretta Scott King and Rev. Joseph Lowery. Evander Holyfield, Mandela's favorite boxer, sat at our table. The two got along famously and even posed for a mock Mandela-Holyfield match, which drew much laughter and mirth from everyone.

The next day, Sunday, July 11, 1993, Clark Atlanta University held a convocation with full academic regalia to honor Mandela at Symphony Hall in the Woodruff Arts Center. The city's entire diplomatic, business, and civic corps turned out to honor him. Dignitaries included Georgia governor Zell Miller, Senator Sam Nunn, Congressman John Lewis, Atlanta mayor Maynard Jackson, Ambassador Andrew Young, South African ambassador Barbara Masekela, Coretta Scott King, Rev. Joseph Lowery, American poet Maya Angelou, and all seventeen presidents of the other historically black colleges and universities that joined Clark Atlanta in bestowing the honorary doctoral degrees.

Clark Atlanta president Dr. Thomas Cole had the honor of officially robing Mandela. As chairman of the board of trustees, I had the honor of giving the introductory remarks welcoming all to the historic event and introducing Mandela to the audience. I knew how important this visit to my city would be in fundraising for his presidential campaign, for the future of blacks in South Africa, and for the hope of every African descendant around the globe who believed in freedom and equality.

"We must remind ourselves that, yes, great strides have been made, and yet Nelson Mandela cannot vote in his own country," I said, coming to the end of my remarks. "And, as he [Mandela] points out, much work remains—for all of us—to ensure that free and open democratic elections take place. The struggle still demands spiritual enlightenment, moral courage, and financial support from every quarter, including all of us herein assembled, including the international business community and Western democracies, especially the United States."

The event was heavily covered by local and national media. I still treasure a news photo that was published on the front page of *The Atlanta Journal-Constitution*. In the picture, I am standing next to Mandela with my right fist proudly raised and clenched in solidarity with our South African brothers and sisters as we sang the ANC national anthem.

The next morning, when I arrived in my office, I was greeted by a summons from my boss, John Hunter. My remarks introducing Mandela had amply highlighted the positive work of the Coca-Cola Company in South Africa, so I was surprised by the cold reception.

John didn't hesitate to tell me that it was not an appropriate gesture for a senior executive of the Coca-Cola Company to be seen with a clenched fist on the front page of the newspaper.

I responded with equal certainty: "John, that photo of my gesture of solidarity with Mandela was also published in South Africa newspapers and elsewhere around the world. It very likely assured our smooth reentry into South Africa and will solidify Coca-Cola as the favorite brand in South Africa."

I was amazed but not thrown off my stride by my Australian colleague's arrogance and narrow-mindedness. I pondered how a modern president of the Coca-Cola Company could be so shortsighted and lacking in vision.

Shortly after the galling conversation with John, I headed to Roberto's office to brief him on the luncheon he would be hosting later that same day to honor Mandela in the company's atrium dining room. I never mentioned the episode to Roberto because I didn't want to spoil the day.

I greeted Mandela personally in the central reception area and took him to my office. We then went to see John in his office for pleasantries.

The luncheon was a proud moment for Roberto and the entire

Coca-Cola family, and Atlanta's Who's Who attended the event. True to form, Roberto did not sit for the meal but made an appearance to personally greet Mandela and pose for photos.

Mandela's table seated nine. John Hunter and I sat to his left and right, respectively. The other guests at the table were Yusuf Surtee, tailor and a close confidant to Mandela; Neville Isdell, president of Coca-Cola's Northeast Europe/Middle East Group; Jack Stahl, president of Coca-Cola USA; South Africa ambassador Barbara Masekela; Doug Daft, president of Coca-Cola's Asia-Pacific Group; and Ralph Cooper, president of Coca-Cola Europe.

Two weeks after Mandela's return to South Africa, I received a letter dated July 29, 1993, which I treasure and share here in its entirety:

> Dear Carl,
>
> It is always a difficult task to find words adequate enough to express the depth of our indebtedness to somebody as special in our life as you have become, Carl.
>
> When the history of our struggle is properly reviewed in the near future, only then will the world be privy to fully understand your catalytic role in that struggle. We in the ANC know of countless contributions made to innumerable individuals and organizations in our country through your direct intervention. This you did, not only in your capacity as one of the decision-makers within Coca Cola, but also in your own right as a conscientious human being of African descent.
>
> Nothing could underscore this assessment more than the diverse roles you played to make my recent visit to the United States the unqualified success that it truly became. The ease in travelling; comfortable accommodation; the most moving convocation at Clark Atlanta; the camaraderie of that homecoming dinner you jointly hosted with Mayor Maynard Jackson; and then the grand finale hosted by President Goizueta at your Headquarters. To be sure, every word and every expression of previous and continuing support remain our greatest source of inspiration that spur us on to greater victories.
>
> So today Carl, I wanted to personally thank you for all that you are and becoming to us. We value most profoundly, your friendship!
>
> Sincerely
>
> NELSON R. MANDELA
> President

26

BECOMING COCA-COLA'S AFRICA GROUP PRESIDENT

From my earliest days in marketing, I dreamed of one day running a Coca-Cola business unit. That idea was always on the back burner, simmering in my thoughts.

During the countless trips I made to work on Coca-Cola's disinvestment in apartheid South Africa, I often traveled with my assistant, Brant Davis, who joined me to attend meetings with South African leaders. He was an easy traveling companion, and so, over time, we became not just business professionals working together but also friends.

On one of those long flights back to Atlanta from Johannesburg, I confided in Brant about my dream of one day heading up the Africa business.

"That would be a great thing for Coca-Cola!" Brant replied. "Once you have the South Africa disinvestment nailed down, you could come back to head up the business in Africa."

Back in the office, Ingrid was equally encouraging: "What better person would there be to run the Africa business?"

But in 1990, when I attended a joint meeting of senior worldwide Coca-Cola and McDonald's executives in Palm Springs, California, I guess you could say the Africa dream pursued me.

Every two years, the largest beverage company in the world and our largest customer, the fastest-growing restaurant chain in the world, met at such places as Walt Disney theme parks; Scottsdale, Arizona; Hawaii; and Pebble Beach to talk business and strengthen relationships. We heard speakers including Ronald Reagan, Indira Gandhi, Henry Kissinger, Margaret Thatcher, and Colin Powell, who collectively kept us informed on geopolitics and public policy issues affecting our business.

Don Keough, then-president of the Coca-Cola Company, was at

the Palm Springs meeting. During one of the breaks he found me and said, "Carl, I want you to come to my suite. I want to talk to you."

I had no idea what he wanted to discuss. I was quite curious but not overly concerned about being fired—or about being given a bonus, for that matter.

Once we were both seated in his suite and sipping on cold Coca-Cola, he said, "Now that you've solved our problem in South Africa, what are you going to do?" He added, "You're a hero in South Africa. You're a hero in America. You're a hero in the Coca-Cola Company—so, what's next for you, Carl?"

"Don, I think I'd like to run a business unit," I said.

"How would you like to run the Coca-Cola Africa business?" he asked, as if reading my mind. "We will start you off as deputy group president of the Northeast Europe/Africa Group reporting to Neville Isdell. This position will be the first step in the process of grooming you to become a general manager and senior operating officer."

I was ecstatic over the offer. "These past few years have provided me with exposure to virtually every aspect of the Africa system," I said. "I am very excited, I'm honored, and I'm confident that I can build Africa into one of our top-performing business units." And then I hesitated a moment before bringing up my only concern. Africa was a huge, complex business, and I knew I would need to know much more about operations, particularly in the areas of finance and the technical side of the business.

"Whatever you need to know, we'll teach you. We will design a crash course on how to run the Coca-Cola Africa business." He added, with his trademark chuckle, "You've done very well giving away the company's money. Now you can make money for the company."

Don had already asked Doug Sorrell, head of human resources, to find the best program to prepare senior executives who were transitioning to the next level in the organization. They selected Harvard University's International Senior Management Program, an eleven-week course in Cambridge, which I began in April 1991. It was a fully integrated and highly immersive program for senior executives who were being positioned to oversee large international businesses.

My class had ninety-four participants—among them, five Americans and executives from thirty-two countries around the world. The curriculum focused on examining how major companies operated across borders, and we analyzed more than fifty of them, representing various industries including transportation, emerging technology, retail, consumer goods, and manufacturing. At the end of the course, I felt better prepared to take charge of the Africa business.

Not long after I returned from Cambridge in July, Don called me into his office again. "We want you to go to live in London," he said. "And we want you to focus your attention on Africa."

Mary and I had just finished the construction of our new home on Ryland Trail in Niskey Lake, an affluent neighborhood in Southwest Atlanta. Our new neighbors were professionals just like us. They were doctors, lawyers, college presidents, and corporate executives. We built on a three-acre lot in a lovely neighborhood, not a subdivision—an ideal setting for helping to raise our grandchildren, Renita and Aaron, and entertaining guests.

We had already planned our first big reception in honor of John Jacob, president of the National Urban League, who was in Atlanta for the organization's big annual convention that July. The guest list featured my city's top community, civil rights, business, and religious leaders, as well as media and sports figures. Nate Goldston, a Road Dog and owner of Gourmet Services, the leading African American-owned catering and food service company in the country, catered this event and many others at our home.

From then on, our doors were open for hospitality—hosting dinners for Desmond Tutu, Andrew Young, Deval Patrick, the CAU Board of Trustees, United Way, class reunions, political campaigns, and many other worthy causes that repeatedly gave Mary and me the honor of raising money and connecting with local, national, and international leaders.

Two weeks after Don called me into his office, Mary and I were in London to look for a place to live. We would both be commuting back and forth across the Atlantic, but that didn't faze us one bit. The new international assignment was what mattered. Mary and our grandson, Aaron, then just a toddler, would come for visits. And, of course, I returned to Atlanta frequently for business and holidays. I was turning forty-seven, and for the first time in my life, I was going to live in another country.

After being shown several outrageously expensive apartments in Central London, we finally settled on a flat in Chelsea Harbour, a completely enclosed modern complex with garden apartments and a high-rise condo building that, by London standards, was more American than British. We chose a unit that overlooked the River Thames from the seventh floor.

The place was ideal for my business and personal needs, and it featured a five-star Conrad hotel with conference and meeting facilities. It also had three great restaurants, upscale boutiques and antiques stores, and laundry and dry-cleaning services. And it had a fully staffed gym where I spent a great deal of my time when not working in the Windsor office or flying out to the job somewhere in Africa.

I met some interesting luminaries there, including Princess Diana, who frequently exercised in the gym (mostly swimming laps in the pool). I also met British actor Michael Caine, who lived in the penthouse. We sometimes made small talk on the elevator, but one incident caused us to meet and exchange closer greetings than either of us anticipated.

You see, we both used the same dry cleaner at Chelsea Harbour. One Saturday, I picked up my navy blue suit and packed my suitcase for a trip to Abidjan, Ivory Coast. I was flying out Sunday morning and scheduled to give the keynote address that evening to a group of government officials, the Coca-Cola Company business partners, and customers.

Only after I checked in at the hotel in Abidjan and began to dress in my navy blue suit did I realize the dry cleaner's mistake. It was immediately evident because Michael Caine is 6' 2" and I am 5' 7". When I put on the pants, I knew the suit was a nonstarter. A sports coat and trousers would have to do for the evening.

Although I felt a bit underdressed, the speech I gave went well. Normally, I would use a French translator in a French-speaking country, but I had fun astonishing my staff by insisting on delivering the speech myself in French, which I hadn't spoken since my college French class. When I was introduced, I pretended to fire the translator and commenced reading the speech myself. The crowd, 99 percent of whom were French-speaking, loosened up, laughing as I stumbled and mispronounced words.

From this, my staff learned that it's okay to lay bare your own humanity and add a bit of levity in a business setting. My staff and I were pleased that the stunt had the effect of freeing the moment for more open and relaxed business conversation. As Don Keough used to say, "I don't take myself seriously, but I take my business very seriously."

Once I returned to Chelsea Harbour, I pointed out the error to the dry cleaner, who informed me that Michael had my suit. Michael and I met in the lobby of our apartment building to exchange garment bags, and we shared a hearty laugh about the mix-up. It turned out that he, too, had experienced suit-sizing issues while getting dressed for a London event where he had also been a featured speaker that same Sunday night.

Chelsea Harbour was an amazing place to live. Whether I was running a staff meeting or negotiating with Africa bottling partners— including Leventis of London, Heineken from Amsterdam, or Castel from Paris—it proved an ideal venue for conducting business. Whether we were enjoying brunch or dinner with family or entertaining guests from the US, the location had all of the amenities we needed, including a convenient ride on the river taxi down the Thames to the best restaurants and sightseeing tours of historic London.

At the same time that we were looking for a place to live in London, I was getting daily briefings on the Africa business and being introduced by Neville Isdell to my new Africa management team and bottlers. Neville was a rock star group president who was leading the company's business in two of the world's most volatile political environments, Eastern Europe and Africa. Three significant geopolitical events were occurring simultaneously in those markets—the fall of the Berlin Wall, the breakup of the Soviet Union, and the imminent collapse of apartheid.

The wonder was that Neville even had time to personally introduce me to the Africa division, but he did so with poise and professionalism, ownership and pride. He introduced me as his new deputy in charge of Africa and explained that I would be succeeding Mike Hall as head of Coca-Cola Africa.

The first round of introductions took place at a members-only restaurant in London called Mosimann's. Over cocktails and dinner, I met the European bottlers and the members of Neville's senior management team, including Muhtar Kent, the Turkish American executive who succeeded Neville as chairman and CEO of the Coca-Cola Company in 2008.

The next day, Neville and Mike introduced me to the entire Africa division staff, including directors of finance, marketing, technical services, human resources, bottler operations, legal, and the very special person who became my "Linda in London," my executive assistant, Priscilla Ellis.

I often felt that this task must have been an awkward, if not difficult, one for Mike, who was handing over the reins of the organization he had built. But, like Neville, Mike was a consummate professional. He always seemed to take business seriously but did so with a sense of levity and plainness that made everyone around him feel at ease.

Over the next several weeks, Mike and I, along with support staff from our Africa headquarters in Windsor, flew the company Gulf Stream II to our regional offices in Lagos, Nairobi, Abidjan, and Harare. These trips were not simply to introduce me to field operations staff and bottling partners. They were designed to acquaint me with real business opportunities and challenges throughout the continent.

I felt completely at home with the people of Africa. The thing that bothered me about using the multi-million-dollar Gulf Stream jet was deplaning in sometimes desolate places and being greeted by bottlers who were struggling to pay for concentrate and keep their businesses afloat. To me, it was almost offensive to arrive in a "chariot," as some of the local bottlers referred to the Gulf Stream. Indeed, it cost in excess of $3 million to operate annually. Once I became group president of Africa, selling the Gulf Stream was one of my first cost-cutting measures.

Many of the introductions were to people I had already met on my first visit to Africa in 1983. What caught my attention most, though, was the fact that our Africa businesses were still being run by Europeans and Americans. Throughout the divisions and regional offices, all of the managers were white males. The noteworthy exceptions were the community and governmental affairs managers, including Percy Wilson, an African American from Washington, DC, whom I helped recruit into the Windsor organization.

Upon my return to the Windsor office, I invited Paul Graves, an African American senior human resources executive from Atlanta, to help me develop a strategy to "Africanize" our Africa business. That meant devising a plan to recruit, train, and develop African managers throughout the continent. It was unacceptable that we had no Africans in our ranks with either profit-and-loss responsibility or decision-making authority when the overwhelming majority of our division's retail customers were African and most consumers of our product were African.

I also knew we needed to dispel long-held colonial myths, such as the idea that you can't find African employees who are capable of running a business. Another such notion suggested that if you find a Kenyan who does well running things in Kenya, don't even think of moving him to another country in Africa. The colonialists believed that Nigerians couldn't work in Kenya, that Tanzanians couldn't work in Zimbabwe, that Ghanaians couldn't work in Zambia.

"If We Believe in Africa"

After these initial introductory visits throughout Africa, Mike would no longer be running the business—I would. I returned to Windsor and convened my first staff meeting. I started with a direct question to my team of division and region managers: "What would it take for you to identify, recruit, and train your successor who happens to be an African? I want each of you to go away and think about that question. I want you to bring me back a plan on how we can Africanize the Africa business."

If we believe in Africa, I said, our European employees in Africa will find Africans who can do their jobs. If we believe in Africa, we'll reset goals that are much higher than our roughly 500 million cases a year to a billion cases a year. If we believe in Africa, we will invest heavily in plants and equipment and bring in new international investors to grow the Africa business.

I said, if we believe in Africa, we can stand in front of the president of Kenya or Nigeria or Zimbabwe and say, "Mr. President, when you reduce the burdensome taxes on soft drinks, we will sell twice as much, and that will mean twice as much revenue to the government."

210

If we believe in Africa, we will do a better job of training our staff in the plants. If we believe in Africa, we will make sure that every Coca-Cola to come out of every plant in Africa tastes the same as it does in Atlanta, Georgia.

That recurring phrase became the theme of every meeting and business plan presentation throughout the Africa business system. That was the beginning of the "We Believe in Africa" initiative.

It was obvious to me that my mission in Africa would be a much bigger calling than overseeing a broken, obsolete business system. The system was not aligned with the reality of the changing sociopolitical environment that was gaining momentum across the continent. Aside from what I had observed of our internal deficiencies, external forces were also at play. As more democratic elections were held, as more free market policies were introduced, and as the deregulation of the African economies began to take form, African governments started to recognize the necessity of a strong private sector. This realization meant that several governments in Africa that had nationalized the Coca-Cola bottling business were primed to discuss privatization.

I knew that a critical success factor would be understanding the impact of the World Bank, the International Monetary Fund, and donor countries on these changes occurring throughout Africa. As these policy initiatives took hold, gross domestic product growth in many African nations would rise, bolstering consumer purchasing power, which meant greater opportunity for Coca-Cola.

In the meantime, the most dramatic and historic event in the history of the continent was beginning to unfold in South Africa, which would change significantly the way we did business on the continent of Africa. The first democratic elections in South Africa were held on April 27, 1994. I had been on the ground in South Africa a few days before the election, but then I returned to Atlanta.

I kept in constant communication with my friends and my business and political contacts in South Africa. That Wednesday, mid-morning, I sat in my office on the 24th floor, my eyes glued to the TV, marveling at the massive turnout of black voters. It was a monumental achievement, getting 22 million South Africans to the polls, the majority of whom were black voters casting ballots for the first time. The elections were among the greatest political triumphs of the twentieth century, if not for all of history; the world watched as voters patiently formed lines that snaked around for miles. There they waited, determined to claim their freedom.

᠈᠊

I had been in London for about two and a half years, serving as Neville Isdell's deputy for Africa, when some significant changes were made in the company's structure: sub-Saharan Africa was established as a stand-alone operating unit in 1994. I was named president of the new Africa Group, with operational responsibilities for forty-eight sub-Saharan African countries. Neville became president of a new fifty-two-country Northeast Europe/Middle East Group.

As group president leading the continent's largest private-sector employer, I was a member of the company's senior operating committee, alongside the group presidents of Asia, Europe/Middle East, Latin America, and North America. The chief financial officer and the chief marketing officer also served on the operating committee. Don Keough, chief operating officer, presided over the meetings, whereas Roberto attended only when major issues and decisions were being debated.

My new position placed me at the center of the company's plan to reenter South Africa, some ten years after I began spearheading the effort that got us out of there.

From the very beginning of my new role, all of my business trips to Africa began or ended in Johannesburg. It became apparent to me in the frequent meetings with Nelson Mandela and other ANC leaders that a fundamental shift in economic policy was beginning to unfold. The ANC was coming to grips with the fact that nationalizing industry was not the right public policy strategy for managing the diverse South African economy. The new government would face the task of trying to level the economic playing field while dealing with the issues of redistribution of wealth and ensuring that black South Africans could participate fully in the formal economy that they had been denied access to under apartheid.

Mandela also made it clear to industry leaders that the new government wanted local and multinational corporations to develop economic empowerment programs that would ensure meaningful levels of black ownership, management control, and economic advancement.

Indeed, when the African National Congress government came to power in 1994, one of the first principles of empowerment enacted was the Reconstruction and Development Programme, requiring equity participation in all industry sectors and black participation in the governance of companies across all industry sectors.

Soon after the election results came in, the phone rang. The caller was professor Jakes Gerwel, one of the original members of the Equal Opportunity Foundation, who would become Mandela's chief of staff and most loyal advisor in the first five years of his presidency. I could hear the sheer pleasure in his voice as he extended a personal invitation to Mary and me to join him in Pretoria for the inauguration.

27

INAUGURATION OF PRESIDENT
NELSON ROLIHLAHLA MANDELA

May 10, 1994, the inauguration of South Africa's first democratically elected president, was a beautiful day in Pretoria, administrative capital of South Africa. It was a fitting honor for Nelson
Rolihlahla Mandela, who had put sunshine into the hearts of millions
of South Africans and people around the world.

Mary and I held hands in silent prayer as we were driven up the
stately driveway leading to the grand entrance of the Union Buildings,
the official seat of the South African government and the offices of
the president of South Africa. We were in a line of black limousines,
each with diplomatic flags identifying the country of VIP guests inside, including many heads of state and members of the diplomatic
corps.

We shared the same thought, Mary and I: *How on Earth is it that
we are so privileged and blessed to have the honor of attending the inauguration of Nelson Mandela?* The day before the inauguration in Pretoria,
he had been officially elected by South Africa's parliament in Cape
Town.

The Union Buildings were decked out with all of the regalia,
pomp, and circumstance befitting such an occasion. The stage was set
with seating for heads of state and other national and international
dignitaries to witness the most important event in the history of the
continent of Africa. I had visited the Union Buildings a few times
before for business meetings, but this time a protocol officer escorted
us to our seats on the right side of the stage, in full view of the podium where President-elect Nelson Mandela would take the oath of
office.

The deputy president-elect, Thabo Mbeki, was seated next to

Mandela. To this day, I have a clear picture in my mind of Mandela standing there in all dignity and majesty, being sworn in by Chief Justice Michael Corbett. Nothing else in my life came close to the awe, tearful pride, and honor I felt in the midst of world leaders paying tribute to the most iconic man of our times.

I saw in Mandela's inauguration a beacon of real hope for the future of South Africa. Because I had spent time talking with him over the previous three years, I knew of his commitment to nation-building founded on the principles of forgiveness and reconciliation. He was truly a remarkable man, a great man, and a compassionate man. I saw on this occasion the true meaning of his struggle and the extreme personal sacrifices that he made to bring freedom to black South Africans and to bring freedom to their oppressors. Who else would have invited his former white jailer, Christo Brand, as a VIP guest to his inauguration as president?

I was moved to tears when I heard Mandela say in his inaugural speech: "Today, all of us do, by our presence here, confer glory and hope to newborn liberty. Out of experience of an extraordinary human disaster that lasted too long, must be born a society of which all humanity will be proud.... Never, never and never again shall it be that this beautiful land will again experience the oppression of one by another.... The sun shall never set on so glorious a human achievement!"

As the inaugural ceremony concluded, Mary and I were promptly escorted to our car and driven back to Johannesburg, not wondering or worrying about exchanging a personal greeting with our friend, the new head of state of the Republic of South Africa. So we were overwhelmed to be invited back to Pretoria two days later for a private meeting with President Mandela at his presidential office inside the Union Buildings.

We were greeted again at the Union Buildings, this time by ANC stalwart Pallo Jordan, a newly appointed cabinet minister, along with my old friend professor Jakes Gerwel, who left his post as chancellor of the University of the Western Cape and the Equal Opportunity Foundation board to join Mandela as chief of staff. We were scheduled for twenty minutes, precious time for a world leader.

Mary and I were ushered into the presidential chambers, which were imbued with power through their design in an Italian Renaissance style for gatherings of national and ceremonial significance. The space was a sacred one where decisions of historic importance were made. Although Mandela had been in the office only a few days, his majestic presence filled the rooms as if he had been there all along.

The new president greeted me warmly, calling me by my first name before quickly turning to Mary with a welcome embrace and his trademark smile. "Mary, how does such a lovely, charming lady end up with such a fellow as Carl?"

We settled in a formal sitting area. Hot tea was served in the presidential chambers, and I quickly got down to the purpose of our visit: the Coca-Cola Company's plans to reinvest in South Africa. Mandela listened thoughtfully as I revealed the company's heretofore-unannounced plans to establish a new Southern Africa division headquartered in Johannesburg. I stated that our plans were to dramatically increase investments in microbusinesses such as spazas, kiosks, taxi ranks, and wholesalers, thereby creating thousands of jobs and hundreds of new business owners in townships throughout the country.

As a part of our return, we would begin to invest heavily in the new South Africa as a means of galvanizing South Africans across racial groups and income levels. "Mr. President," I said, "our research has revealed that the area of competitive sports is the most potent vehicle capable of bringing together South Africa's racially divided communities."

He nodded in approval.

I assured President Mandela that the Coca-Cola system in the new South Africa was committed to black economic empowerment and black managerial development, and that we had already begun the process of investing in human resources: hiring, training, and developing talented black South African people capable of running our business in the future.

I stated that the crown jewel of our reentry plan would be the creation of a major black-owned bottling franchise and that we were already making good progress in the negotiations with the Kunene family to that end. I pledged to the new president that I would personally keep him informed and notify him in advance of the transaction being made public.

With apartheid over and sanctions being lifted, I said, we would unleash the power and know-how of South Africa's bottler system to help develop Coca-Cola across the continent. I finished my presentation by telling President Mandela that I had been appointed president of Coca-Cola Africa and, going forward, I would have the authority to fully implement our reinvestment plans.

President Mandela congratulated me and asked me to convey his sincere appreciation to Roberto Goizueta, whom he had met in Atlanta at Coca-Cola headquarters a year earlier.

The meeting ended within the allotted twenty minutes with a quick photo session to immortalize the day. A photo of me with the president appeared in newspapers in South Africa and back home, signifying his welcoming the Coca-Cola Company back to South Africa.

After we left, Mary couldn't stop talking about how sincere and down-to-earth this great man was. I had experienced the same feeling when I first met him four years earlier at Shell House in Johannesburg. Later that day, I saw Mary off at Jan Smuts International Airport and returned to the division office, which was still operating as NatBev, soon to become our Coca-Cola Southern Africa division headquarters.

I gathered my staff in a conference room to get a real-time snapshot of where the business stood in terms of restructuring to implement our core black empowerment initiatives, including management development, supplier development, and equity participation. I informed them of my pledge to Mandela that the creation of black owners and operators in the Coca-Cola system would be the cornerstone of our reentry.

The impact of Mandela's election would reverberate through every aspect of South African society. The fall of apartheid was not really complete for black South Africans or even coloured South Africans until Mandela's election. Shortly after the election, my personal driver in South Africa, Brendon Van Stavel, who lived in Cape Town, made a comment to me that I'll never forget. "Mr. Ware," he said, "frankly, coloureds don't want to be called 'coloureds' no longer. We are Africans. We are Mandela." Brendon, who was always an extremely reliable and conscientious driver, would go on to build his own company in Cape Town, BVS Transport Consultants.

The Kunene Bottling Franchise

Eric Mafuna, my friend and our South Africa consultant, first introduced me to Keith Kunene in 1992. Keith was an attorney and one of five well-educated brothers. His other siblings included Dudu, a medical doctor; Zanosi, a business manager and economist; Menzi, an accountant; and Zoli, a specialist in industrial law. I saw huge potential in the family becoming bigger players in the Coca-Cola system in the new South Africa.

Like most consumer product companies, Coca-Cola was dependent on black distributors in the townships to reach millions of black consumers in urban South Africa. The Kunenes alone distributed 670,000 cases of Coca-Cola products in the townships of Vosloorus, KwaThema, and Katlehong. I was intrigued by their success and went to see their operation in Vosloorus in person.

As background, Fortune Kunene, the patriarch, launched the family business in 1978 as a fresh-milk outlet in the sprawling Vosloorus township, located about eighteen miles outside Johannesburg. By 1992, the Kunenes were distributing everything from milk and Coca-Cola products to beer and liquor. I was impressed by the scale and variety of their distribution business, and I took particular notice of the fact that they knew our business very well.

In those years, the Coca-Cola Company was not doing direct business in South Africa but kept a foothold in the country through the license agreement with NatBev, which ran marketing, operations, and franchising in accordance with the contractual agreement of 1986. That meant the Coca-Cola Company could not legally force NatBev to restructure the South Africa bottling franchise system to allow for black ownership.

It also meant that the Kunenes had to deal with NatBev directly, a relationship that got off on the wrong foot. Through conversations, I could sense that the brothers were frustrated by the lack of sensitivity of NatBev's white managers, who were not supportive of their aspirations to own and operate a Coca-Cola bottling franchise.

Even though we were still out of the country, Coca-Cola wanted to be ahead of the curve, to be seen as the multinational corporation leading the way toward black empowerment in post-apartheid South Africa. For that reason alone, I knew it would be critical to make black ownership in the system the centerpiece of our return.

Creating the second black-owned bottling franchise became a personal passion I followed relentlessly. The first black-owned bottler—Kilimanjaro Holdings, created in 1986 in East London—was fairly straightforward in comparison with the process that led to the establishment of the second black-owned bottling company. What became known as the Coca-Cola Fortune bottling deal took a great amount of know-how, guts, effort, and patience from both the Kunene brothers and from the Coca-Cola Company.

The Kunenes started distributing Coca-Cola in the mid-1970s. The then-fledgling business suffered losses because of political strife that ignited lawlessness, violence, protests, and all manner of boycott campaigns in the black townships. Just when the Kunenes were running out of ideas about how to keep the family enterprise afloat, Zanosi Kunene took the lead in pursuing a distribution arrangement with the Cook brothers, who were, of course, white, as well as owners of the Highveld Coca-Cola Bottling Company.

Their business arrangement proved mutually profitable, but Zanosi was keen on pursuing a formal partnership between the Kunenes and the Cooks. Zanosi was impressed with how the Cooks—who were different from other white businessmen the Kunenes had dealt with—did business. They were upfront and honest, firm but fair. He believed the partnership would allow his family enterprise to learn all aspects of the soft drink business so they might one day run their own bottling company. Owning a Coca-Cola franchise would be what Zanosi called "the cherry on top of what our father, Fortune Kunene, struggled to build into a service to our black community."

The Cook brothers, while actually supportive of the Kunenes' aspirations, just weren't prepared to sell any portion of their family-owned operations to the five brothers. As the deliberations between NatBev and the South African bottler system continued into 1994, Zanosi became increasingly impatient with what he perceived to be red tape and corporate bureaucracy blocking progress toward the establishment of a Kunene bottling franchise. His determination, however, signified the extent of his family's commitment to move out of liquor retailing and into soft drink bottling.

Eric Mafuna gave me regular feedback about the Kunenes' discussions with NatBev, which were often confrontational, stemming in part from their distrust of white business operators "out to cash in on unsuspecting black partners." For this reason, during my visits, Eric and I invested a considerable amount of time coaching, encouraging, and guiding Zanosi and his brother Zoli to adopt a more businesslike approach in their dealings with NatBev executives.

Close up, the Kunene brothers reminded me of a pride of male lions at play. On one hand, they didn't seem to realize that their boisterousness generated fear and unease in the hearts and minds of their guests. On the other hand, they were aware of the fact that their brotherhood was intimidating, and they knew how to use their outsized physicality and numerical dominance to their advantage. They were out to win a Coca-Cola franchise and learned how to convey their aspiration with disarming humility, honesty, and candor.

At one point in the process, the Kunenes invited Don McHenry and me to join them for Sunday dinner at Keith Kunene's family home in Vosloorus. Don flew in from Atlanta for the occasion. As we approached the middle-class, ranch-style home, the brothers burst out of the front door onto the manicured lawn to greet us with smiles and bear hugs, as if our joining them was no run-of-the-mill business call. Following the brothers were many Kunene sisters, wives, and children, who also gathered around us in warm greeting, exuding the same sense of pride and strong physical presence as their men.

Over a mouthwatering South African *braai*, the local barbecue, the brothers talked to Don and me about the unfinished legacy their father had left for them to accomplish. They explained that they were eager to understand what they needed to know and what they needed to do to acquire a Coca-Cola bottling franchise. And they promised to restructure their many business functions to focus on building a Kunene Coca-Cola bottling franchise, if and when they got the opportunity to acquire one.

Don and I saw a wonderful family—great people with great values. They had business acumen, entrepreneurial zeal, family cohesiveness, vision, and determination—everything we prized in a Coca-Cola bottling family. By the time we left later that evening, the success of the Kunenes had become our mission. They would be the next black South African family to enjoy a bottling franchise for generations to come.

It seemed almost prescient that I had played a primary role in the establishment of the first African American-owned and operated Coca-Cola bottling franchise. The Philadelphia Coca-Cola Bottling Company deal taught me a lot about franchise deal-making and offered a sort of playbook on how to make the Kunene deal work. Coca-Cola's global business succeeds in large part because of locally focused ownership, social uplift, and economic empowerment in communities. Like the Bruce Llewellyn deal, the Kunene acquisition would be done for sociopolitical reasons as well as out of business necessity.

After visiting the Kunenes that Sunday, I invited the brothers to meet me in Windsor. The invitation was intended to test their resolve, and their willingness to travel to make a formal presentation was a strong indicator to me of their commitment to the deal.

As it happened, all five of the brothers boarded the same aircraft from Johannesburg to London. And then they shared a London taxicab from Gatwick Airport to my office at 56 High Street. It startled me momentarily. It was probably all right for all of them to ride in the same taxi, I advised, but key people in major businesses should always travel on separate flights.

Despite their natural business acumen, the Kunenes' business practices did not meet the standards that the Coca-Cola Company demanded of its bottlers. To overcome this obstacle, I advised them to structure the Kunene enterprise as a basic operating company with documented business procedures. Only one brother could be designated as "Coca-Cola bottler," or general manager and chief operations officer, I explained. That person would be required to attend the twelve-week Coca-Cola University program in the US, where he would learn best practices firsthand alongside other Coca-Cola executives from all over the world. Their cohesiveness as a group was such that they immediately and unanimously elected Zanosi to fill the lead spot.

For counsel on financial and organizational structure, I pointed the Kunenes to the Johannesburg branch of Ernst & Young. It helped that the Coca-Cola Company was one of the accounting firm's largest international clients. The managing partner was a white South African gentleman named Graham Royston, who headed E&Y's financial advisory practice.

With those items out of the way, I informed the Kunenes that we had identified an opportunity for them to acquire a bottling franchise. There were no guarantees, I said, and instructed them to return to South Africa to prepare themselves to make a proper pitch. After they left, I learned that they had rebooked their travel plans for the return journey from London to Johannesburg. They took their first corporate business lessons from me very seriously, including the risk of all five brothers flying on the same aircraft together.

Fortunately, the Kunenes' first meeting with Graham was a big success for both parties. At that time, in 1992, Graham and his partners at E&Y had never before had a black client. He told me later that he came away knowing instinctively from that first meeting that a Coke deal could be put together with the Kunenes. Graham knew the time was right because a deal of this magnitude could signal, for the first time, that the playing field was beginning to level in South Africa and that such a shift would create limitless opportunities.

The entrepreneurial spirit of the Kunenes thrust them into the rare category of being the "first through the door" with respect to black ownership of a major franchise brand in the new South Africa. This watershed transaction was also a masterstroke for Graham and his company. It mattered that all three of us—Zanosi, Graham, and I—were avid golfers. We spent long hours together after rounds of golf with me mostly listening, absorbing, and advising them about the deal.

As the Kunene financing and organizational structure were being designed under E&Y's guidance, I worked closely with the new Coca-Cola South Africa management team headed by Neville Kirshman, whom Neville Isdell and I recruited from the Canadian Coca-Cola system to help prepare the company for reentry to South Africa. Kirshman would become the first division manager of the new Coca-Cola Company in South Africa. He had the right skills and temperament for the job.

Kirshman reported to me, and I found in him a strong ally, a

Coke executive who had vision and who shared our sense of urgency about black empowerment. He, too, became an ardent supporter of the Kunenes'.

Together, Kirshman and I visited the family-run Nelspruit South Africa bottling plant known as Coca-Cola Bottling Mpumalanga, in which NatBev had purchased a 62-percent interest. It was the right-sized business, one that would not be overwhelming as a first venture for the Kunenes. Mpumalanga would be fairly uncomplicated. As with the Philadelphia deal, the Coca-Cola Company would sell off its interest to the Kunenes. Like Llewellyn, the Kunenes would also have to arrange their own financing to acquire the Nelspruit operation.

Kirshman and I secured approval of the deal financing structure from headquarters in Atlanta. I then directed Kirshman and Royston to provide guidance to the Kunenes in navigating this process, which led them to David Lawrence, a managing director of First Corporate Merchant Bank who was eager to be a part of this important black-empowerment deal. Coca-Cola's backing made it work.

The Coca-Cola Company officially reentered South Africa in October 1994. Shortly afterward, I flew with my boss, John Hunter, head of Coca-Cola International, from Atlanta to Johannesburg to make the historic announcement of "a first joint venture of its kind for Coca-Cola in the new South Africa."

Coca-Cola and the Kunene family formed Fortune Investment Holdings Ltd. to acquire the Nelspruit Mpumalanga franchise. The business would be owned and managed by the Kunenes. It took almost three years to accomplish. The historic transformation of the Coca-Cola Company from the apartheid era through disinvestment and now reentry was nothing short of a well-planned and well-executed business strategy.

Even now, I am humbled when Zanosi Kunene introduces me to his staff and business partners as the "single most important reason" they are where they are today. I attribute their stunning achievements to their strong family values and ingenuity.

The Kunene story is an inspiring one. From a humble milk outlet in a black township under apartheid conditions, an enterprising black family built one the largest unlisted investment holding companies in South Africa. Kunene Brothers Holdings' portfolio of investments features companies such as Action Ford, Alcatel-Lucent, Kunene Ovations, and Ovations Technologies. As Zanosi stated, the most prized asset in the portfolio is Coca-Cola.

Sports and Management Development

Despite the fact that the Coca-Cola Company made contributions to a variety of community programs in South Africa, the corporate social responsibility investments had fallen behind the urgent needs of the emerging democratic society. What the country needed most amid such change were investments that served to unite its citizens.

Sports, of course, has historically been central to brand Coca-Cola marketing locally. But because of apartheid, South Africa was banned from participation in such international sports competitions as the Olympics and the FIFA World Cup. Isolated in this way, South Africans became internally focused on their sports teams, which promoted a fierce sense of national pride but fell short of their aspirations to compete on the international stage.

Over and above investment in traditional corporate social responsibility programs, the new Coca-Cola system in South Africa would channel millions of dollars into sports sponsorship. Doing so would be a natural outgrowth of the Coca-Cola marketing programs. The key factor at that time, however, was the scale and thrust of marketing investments in soccer, rugby, and women's sports.

The most famous example of the effectiveness of this strategy was the 1995 Rugby World Cup, staged in Johannesburg. Most white South Africans are crazy about rugby, so they were in ecstasy when the Springboks, South Africa's national rugby team, was in the championship against the powerful New Zealand All Blacks. The South Africans were solid underdogs relative to the New Zealanders.

For the white population, the match at Ellis Park was their World Series and Super Bowl in one. Their emotional well-being rode on the outcome of the game, it seemed. Black South Africans weren't nearly as invested. Soccer was their passion. There were very few black South African rugby players—an athlete named Chester Williams, in fact, was the only black on the entire national Springbok team. Black South Africans so closely identified the Springboks with their white oppressors that they often rooted against the team.

Nelson Mandela changed all of that with one magnificent gesture that summer night. Before the game, he donned a Springbok jersey and walked onto the field. He put his arm around South African team captain Francois Pienaar and said, "You go out and beat these guys. You go and win this one for our country." And that was exactly what happened: the Springboks defeated the New Zealanders, 15 to 12. In that moment, Mandela put all South Africans—black and white—on the same side.

As I sat in the corporate suite next to President Mandela's heavily guarded presidential suite that night at Ellis Park, I said to myself, "This is the beginning of a true reconciliation in the new South Africa." The best reminder I have of that night is also one of my most prized possessions today: a rugby ball from the historic match, signed by both Mandela and Pienaar.

The 1996 Olympic Games held in Atlanta was another example of how Coca-Cola investments in South African sports yielded great results. Josia Thugwane, the black South African distance runner who won the gold medal in the marathon race, was sponsored by Coca-Cola South Africa and returned to South Africa as a national hero for all South Africans to revere. The return of South Africa to Olympic competition ushered in a new era in the psyche of the nation.

Developing People Power

The Coca-Cola reentry plan that I discussed with Mandela would require us to establish an aggressive management program to recruit, train, and develop black South African managers who could run the Coca-Cola business. This program would complement the government's policy of filling the void of competent black managers in the country as a whole.

I took a personal interest in this business imperative, spending countless hours interviewing prospective candidates to fill critical positions in management, finance, marketing, media, and government relations. This process was what "We Believe in Africa" was all about.

Because there were so few qualified black professionals in the country (many were in exile), the competition for talented black professionals was fierce among all companies, local and multinational alike. And these highly sought-after people knew their worth in the marketplace. We recruited aggressively on a local level and, when necessary, brought in expats from other African countries and the US.

One recruit whom we ultimately lost to Mandela's new government was Sakumzi "Saki" Macozoma, one of the country's most prominent businessmen and civic leaders. Saki was imprisoned on Robben Island for five years after leading a student protest, and he worked as a business development manager at South African Breweries for just one year before his election to parliament in 1994.

Saki would spend three years as Mandela's media representative and would help Mandela craft his first speech after his release from prison. It famously begins, "My friends, comrades and fellow South Africans, I greet you all in the name of peace, democracy and freedom for all. I stand here before you not as a prophet but as a humble servant of you, the people."

Our recruitment strategy was to demonstrate that Coca-Cola was the employer of choice for aspiring black professionals. That meant we would offer the best working environment, competitive salaries, and a solid career path in order to retain people once we hired them into the Coca-Cola system.

There were several great hires that came out of this effort to transform the Africa division. The most notable were Charles Rukwava, a marketing manager from Zimbabwe; Subu Mgadi, a South African communications and government relations specialist; Kevin Williams, an African American, whom we brought in as deputy division manager; Mike Steel, an African American marketing specialist; William Asiko, general counsel; and Rute Moye, operations and business development manager.

The people development process in South Africa was top priority then, and it continues to this day to be the strongest competitive advantage in doing business in South Africa and throughout the continent.

28

"WE BELIEVE IN AFRICA"

During the December 1994 meeting of the Coca-Cola Company Board of Directors, I made the most important business plan presentation of my entire career. That meeting was my first as group president of Africa, and my presentation outlined the plan for reinvestment in South Africa as well as the overarching business strategy for the forty-eight sub-Saharan African countries that fell under my purview.

Our main objective was to grow the Africa Group's case sales volume by 10 percent over the three-year plan period, from 1995 through 1997. Our long-term plan was to double the Africa business from 500 million annual case sales to a billion. Our success throughout the continent would hinge upon our success in South Africa. But the plan was not without risks.

One of the things you go into the board meeting knowing is that the board members are not just listening to your business plan—they are also evaluating you. They evaluate your leadership potential and where you fit into the management succession plan. I took every session with the board seriously, whether it was over dinner, cocktails, or a formal presentation. It wasn't just business results they were assessing. They were sizing up your ability to deliver the business-plan results.

Before presentations, much preparation occurred that entailed working with a business communications consultant, Sandy Linver, of Speakeasy, based in Atlanta. We conducted several meetings on the presentation, including style, clarity of content, elocution, and body language. After the sessions with Sandy, I used my staff to critique me and ask questions as if they were coming from the board members themselves.

On many occasions, whether preparing for a board presentation or for an important public address, I would head to Newnan, to the farm, my sanctuary, where I rehearsed while standing on the dock at the lake and visualizing my audience. Nothing matches the spiritual preparation gained from such a sacred environment.

Some group presidents read their presentations while standing behind the lectern and using notes. I always felt sufficiently well-prepared and confident enough to stand in front of the board without notes to discuss my business plan.

On financial plans, I studied the numbers until I felt as knowledgeable as the CFO. On the people issues, I knew everything about my key managers and presented the board a description of how we were developing our staff. I spoke at length about Africa bottler restructuring and conveyed to them why the Coca-Cola Company needed to invest hundreds of millions of dollars to restructure the business and so double our volume and profits over a five-year period.

Let me hasten to add that business plans are never rubber-stamped by a conscientious board. A board's job is to make sure that the business plans are in lockstep with the company's overall business strategy. Board members' collective and individual approval of the annual business plans convey to the shareowners their commitment to the financial projections and overall business objectives. Only rarely did the board reject any of our business plans. Sometimes, though, a group president's financial projections or business restructuring plans needed further review. Such was not the case with my plans.

The 1994 Africa business plan was aggressive, considering the facts that South Africa, the plan's engine of growth, was in the fourth year of a recession and its economy was in recovery with 50 percent unemployment. Inflation had grown from 7 percent to 10 percent, which cut deeply into discretionary income, meaning consumers had less money to spend on soft drinks.

Labor strikes were endemic to the new South Africa. Coca-Cola bottlers and some of our largest customers and suppliers were familiar targets for labor union work stoppages.

We also faced competition from another well-known international brand, Pepsi, which had already announced its own South Africa reentry plans.

One question raised in that first board meeting came from board member and former US ambassador Don McHenry. "Some African governments are notoriously corrupt," he began. "Can you explain how we manage around the reality of this corruption in some of these countries?"

I explained that we simply had a zero-tolerance policy regarding fraud and corruption, backed up by a stringent code of ethics and business conduct. It was true. Our legal department conducted ongoing mandatory training programs for all of our managers and employees. Part of our business routine entailed constantly reviewing our code of business conduct and the consequences of violating it.

The presentation went well and, based on the response of board members, including Warren Buffett, Herb Allen, and Don McHenry, I felt confident I could move on to the job of executing the business plan without any reservations or constraints from the board.

I must admit that after the board presentation, the competitive threat from Pepsi was troubling to me. Pepsi was fanning the flames of the all-too-familiar "Cola Wars." Even though Coca-Cola already had 80 percent of the carbonated soft drink market in South Africa, we simply could not ignore the Pepsi threat.

So, when I returned to South Africa, all hands were on deck to mount a system-wide offensive to deny Pepsi even a modicum of success in its South Africa relaunch.

Pepsi's strategy was to undercut our stronghold by painting a picture of Coca-Cola as the apartheid-era soft drink company. The Pepsi plan was to form strong business alliances with aspiring black South African entrepreneurs and well-known African American celebrities, including athletes, entertainers, and prominent business figures.

Through an arrangement with such big-name black celebrities as Whitney Houston, Magic Johnson, and Earl Graves, PepsiCo of Purchase, New York, found investors who would form a joint venture with black South African business partners to act as the franchisee for the new Pepsi venture in South Africa. Through this scheme, they hoped to use the powerful images of African Americans in partnership with black South Africans to popularize brand Pepsi in the black consumer market. Furthermore, it was communicated throughout political channels in South Africa—in particular, to Mandela and the ANC—as the kind of competition needed to break up the Coke "monopoly."

The Pepsi launch was about public relations and political posturing. We had yet to see any real evidence of serious investments in such infrastructure as plants, trucks, or distributors in townships. Likewise, they hadn't done much to penetrate supermarkets, convenience stores, or cold-drink vending machines.

The most noise, at that stage, had come from a Whitney Houston concert whose promoters insisted that all Coca-Cola signage in the stadium be covered and only Pepsi products be sold. The problem with this demand—for PepsiCo, anyway—was getting the Pepsi product to the stadium, since they had no nearby production facility. The closest Pepsi distributor was in another country, Namibia.

We knew instinctively that the only way for the Pepsi franchise to gain traction was through massive product distribution in the townships. At that time, they had neither the production capability nor the distributor network to get their products to market.

Nothing gets the Coca-Cola system in South Africa geared for war like a Pepsi competitive threat. Throughout the townships, all customers—from spaza shop owners to street vendors and warehouse distributors—were incentivized through sales promotions, merchandizing, and training on how to sell more Coca-Cola at higher profit for their businesses.

Over the decade I had been traveling to Johannesburg, first as deputy to Neville Isdell and later as group president, I always stayed at the InterContinental Sandton Towers Hotel. My room was on the eighteenth floor—number 1856, to be exact. Because the hotel was like a second home, I was on a first-name basis with the hotel staff, including the general manager, the bellmen, front desk clerks, waiters, the concierge, and the maître d'. But I was especially friendly with the staff members who ran the business center, where I spent a good deal of my time.

One evening, after a long flight from London, a staff meeting, and dinner, I returned to my room and was reviewing materials for a trip the next morning to Cape Town when the doorbell rang. I opened the door, and a bellman handed me a sealed package marked, in block letters, "CARL WARE."

At first I set the package aside as airplane reading for the next day. But my curiosity got the best of me, and I opened the envelope. Inside was an unsealed, unmarked, plain manila envelope. It contained the entire Pepsi South Africa launch and reentry plan. It went into detail, with names and profiles of key investment partners, organizational charts, budgets, financials, and investment timetables, not to mention the locations for two new Pepsi bottling plants. It also contained information on the number of bottling lines, trucks, forklifts, and other equipment. It outlined brand and product launches and included a list of prospective wholesalers and distributors.

As I scanned the pages, the feeling that came over me was literally indescribable. I felt something between shock and elation. I put the document back the way I found it in the unsealed envelope, placed that back in the hotel envelope, and called the business center to let them know a package had been delivered to me by mistake. I asked them to send the bellman to fetch it and to bring me a clean envelope without my name on it.

When the bellman arrived, he said innocently, "Mr. Ware, I was told that Pepsi was owned by Coca-Cola and this package belonged to you." True story.

≈

Our overarching Africa strategy included restructuring the bottler system in Africa. As background, during the late eighties and early nineties, the Coca-Cola Company established an elite global network of top bottler operations called "anchor bottlers." They were international companies that consistently outperformed their peers in distinct geographical areas. For example, Coca-Cola Femsa became anchor bottler in Latin America. In the US and parts of Europe, Coca-Cola Enterprises held that title, whereas in other parts of Europe and Australia, Coca-Cola Hellenic held sway.

We selected Coca-Cola Sabco as our as anchor bottler to lead the all-important restructuring throughout East Africa. Initial countries in that region were Mozambique, Tanzania, Uganda, Kenya, and Ethiopia. Sabco, with its record of outperforming other South African bottlers, entered the anchor bottler network in November 1995 to become the seventh anchor bottler of the Coca-Cola Company worldwide.

I invited Sabco owner and CEO Phil Gutsche to a December 8, 1994, meeting in London, where Coca-Cola International president John Hunter and I informed Phil that we had decided to offer Sabco the opportunity to become the anchor bottler for East Africa. Phil accepted our offer enthusiastically and said, "Coca-Cola Sabco is a can-do, able-to-do, and willing-to-do company."

I felt confident that Sabco was the right choice to develop our business throughout East Africa, having experienced in February 1993 Phil's pioneering spirit and Sabco's capability and willingness to take on the franchise in Mozambique. Sabco had invested in Mozambique when other South Africa bottlers thought it was laden with too many political risks, especially because of Mozambique's staunch support of the ANC military wing against the apartheid-backed South Africa security forces. These factors, along with the fact that Mozambique had the lowest per capita income in the Southern Africa region, gave other South Africa bottlers great pause.

Sabco was initially unable to raise the money in South Africa or overseas for the expansion into Mozambique. Only after Phil's perseverance with the governor of the South Africa Reserve Bank were funds released to Sabco for investment. I remember distinctly Phil explaining the enormous benefits that would be forthcoming to South African industries and also the wisdom of having an economically prosperous neighbor such as Mozambique.

The governor of the South Africa Reserve Bank gave Sabco permission to transfer $5 million, half in assets and half in cash, and a new plant opened in Maputo on May 25, 1994, coincidentally just two weeks after Mandela was inaugurated.

After the Maputo plant opening came the 1997 opening of the Chimoio plant in Mozambique. I was proud to attend both plants' openings, at which Mozambique prime minister Pascoal Mocumbi praised Coca-Cola for the foresight we showed by investing in his country. He cited the role that Coca-Cola was playing in Mozambique with regard to employment and development of the economy.

Among the people attending the Chimoio ceremony was Graça Machel, representing her Mozambique Children's Fund. She was then the widow of Samora Machel, the first African president of

Mozambique, and would later become the first lady of South Africa as Mandela's wife. I presented her with a substantial check from the Coca-Cola Foundation for her fund.

The Mozambique experience with Sabco was followed by an impressive string of investments by the anchor bottler, starting with the opening of the new Dar es Salaam, Tanzania plant, which was officially opened by his excellency Benjamin Mkapa, president of Tanzania, and Doug Ivester, then-president and COO of the Coca-Cola Company. I was on the stage alongside Phil Gutsche and Reginald Mengi, one of the original owners of the Tanzania operations who became a joint-venture partner in the new Coca-Cola Kwanza-Tanzania bottler operations. We all proudly celebrated the sparkling-new $35 million bottling plant.

To me, the most impressive photo of that day was not one of the official dignitaries attending the opening but a of huge crowd of more than 300 Tanzanian employees celebrating the opening of their new workplace. The $35 million investment was a huge economic boost for Tanzania's economy, whose average per capita income was $1,800 a year, or less than $5 a day. Using the multiplier of 12, that meant at least 3,600 new jobs would be created for Tanzanians.

While Sabco was expanding rapidly outside South Africa into East Africa, what became abundantly clear was that it needed new management capability to handle the rapidly expanding business outside South Africa. This requirement came as no surprise, and we were prepared to augment Sabco's efforts.

The Coca-Cola Company had embarked on an ambitious worldwide management recruitment and development program, which we called the global management training initiative. The goal was to recruit at least fifty high-potential general managers from within the Coca-Cola system, and elsewhere, to fuel the rapid growth of the Coca-Cola business worldwide.

My goal was to find Africans and African Americans who would become the next generation of business leaders for Coca-Cola Africa. Martin Jansen, a German, was an exception I made in order to find managerial talent ready to hit the ground running with the Sabco business. I first met Martin in the Frankfurt airport business lounge. Having studied his CV against a global management training initiative competency model, I felt good about his manufacturing and operating skills. I structured the two-hour interview with him to explore his people skills and how he would adapt to Africa. After the interview, I felt confident that he would be a top candidate for Sabco and arranged an interview with Phil Gutsche at Sabco headquarters in Port Elizabeth.

A week later, Martin was in South Africa to interview with Phil. At some stage during the interview, they reached a mutual agreement that Martin would be the right person to embark upon a transformation process to meet the demands of a rapidly changing Sabco operation. If that sounds unglamorous, it was. It was business.

Indeed, Sabco was on a mission in East Africa. They opened the Flamingo Bottlers in Nakuru, Kenya, in 1998 and the Mbarara plant in Uganda in 1999. Following the Nakuru venture came a $25 million bottling plant in Embakasi, an area east of Nairobi's central business district.

In 2001, an impressive new Coca-Cola Sabco plant opened just outside Kampala, the capital city of Uganda. The Uganda investments were preceded by negotiation sessions with top Ugandan government officials, including the minister of finance and the minister of industry and trade.

From the beginnings of our negotiations with the Uganda government, I had numerous face-to-face discussions with Uganda president Yoweri Museveni in his chambers in Kampala about removing the obstacles that hindered direct foreign investment by Sabco. Our first meeting was arranged by Dr. Martin Aliker, a member of the Coca-Cola Africa Advisory Board. Aliker was a dental surgeon, entrepreneur, and businessman who came to Nairobi originally as a Ugandan expatriate during the brutal dictatorship of Idi Amin.

I also met with Museveni at Uganda's Washington, DC, embassy, headed by Ambassador Edith Sempala. There, we discussed preconditions for Coca-Cola investment in Uganda, which included lowering excise taxes on soft drinks and reducing the burdensome import levies on concentrate and raw materials, as well as ones on equipment such as trucks, bottling lines, and everything else that could not be sourced in Uganda. Revisions to the Ugandan investment code were necessary to allow for repatriation of profits by investors as well as to allow for private ownership of property, which heretofore had been owned by the government.

Our discussions paved the way for the introduction of Sabco as the investor and franchisee in partnership with the government. Sabco would also become the operator. The two plant sites selected were Kampala and Mbarara. Although return on investment in the Mbarara plant was not as strong as in the Kampala plant, Mbarara was the next-largest population center in Uganda. In addition to that, it was President Museveni's home territory, from which he led the national resistance movement in the rebellions that toppled Idi Amin in 1979.

I had gone to assess the bottling situation and what Coca-Cola would do with its plants once the civil war was over and Museveni was in power. A perhaps eerie aside about my first visit to Kampala took place when I checked in at the Sheraton, the only decent hotel in town, if not the whole country. Outside, on the hotel grounds, I saw these big, grayish-brown birds walking around. I remarked to my host, Davis Sebukema, the manager for Coca-Cola Uganda, how peaceful these birds seemed. They looked like big beautiful birds to me, but they were vultures.

"You didn't know this is where the captured troops and Amin loyalists were executed?" Davis said. Their bodies lay in that area for days and days, he explained. That's when the vultures came. Long after the bodies were gone, the birds stayed.

I had the honor of escorting President Bill Clinton and his entourage during his Africa tour of the newly opened Namanve plant near Kampala. Building a plant in the forest, a national reserve, required special dispensation from the government and extraordinary investments to protect the pristine environment. Clinton praised the Coca-Cola investment and said he was impressed by the efforts we had made to preserve the integrity of the Namanve Forest.

An interesting sidebar to the bottling investments centered on Uganda's growing unlimited amounts of oranges, pineapples, and other citrus fruits, which grew unabated across Uganda in its rich, fertile soil. President Museveni wanted me to explore the idea of exporting oranges from Uganda for Minute Maid, a subsidiary of the Coca-Cola Company.

To that end, I flew to Houston—Minute Maid headquarters—where I had an exploratory discussion with the company's technical and procurement folks. I asked whether they would be willing to send a team from Houston to Uganda to explore the possibility of us exporting Ugandan oranges for Minute Maid. Soon thereafter, a team from Minute Maid spent three weeks on the ground, doing soil tests and testing the fruit. As it turned out, the fruit was so rich that you could not feasibly ship it from Uganda to a processing plant before the produce would rot. Unfortunately, building a Minute Maid plant there wasn't economically feasible.

Remaking Coke's Bottler System

In 1999, on a hot, sunny Sunday morning, I boarded a private six-seater aircraft to Addis Ababa, Ethiopia, normally a three-hour flight from Nairobi. With me were Stuart Eastwood, head of our East Africa division, and Phil Gutsche. It would be my most frightening airplane ride during a decade of flying in Africa.

In midflight, we lost cabin pressure, which produced excruciating heat, and there was no escaping it. We were flying at a low altitude across the mountain range between Kenya and Addis Ababa, meaning the two safe landing spots were the airport we had just departed and our final destination in Addis. We landed safely, by the grace of God, and all of us were completely drenched with perspiration.

Needless to say, after my meetings with our Ethiopian business partners, I returned to Nairobi via commercial airliner.

Sabco continued its aggressive East Africa expansion in Ethiopia with a $6.4 million upgrade of the Addis Ababa plant. Sabco formed a joint venture with Ethiopian investors in 2003. One of the Ethiopian partners was an astute businessman named Bereket Haregot, at the time head of ExxonMobil's Southern Africa and East Africa lubricants business. Bereket later sold his interest back to Sabco and relocated to the US, where I was proud to introduce him to Patricia Woertz, head of Chevron's downstream business. He was hired and became a rising star executive at Chevron, and he is still based at its San Ramon corporate headquarters.

I realize I'm spending a good deal of time on the Sabco Africa expansion, but the Sabco success story didn't end with Africa. In 2004, Coca-Cola Sabco acquired bottling rights from the Coca-Cola Company for Vietnam, Sri Lanka, Nepal, and Cambodia, thus making its first move out of Africa. Together these East Asia markets encompassed 150 million consumers with more than 2,000 employees. Coca-Cola Sabco had become the leading emerging markets specialist for the Coca-Cola system.

Coca-Cola Sabco was by far the most pioneering operator in the anchor bottler network. It led an aggressive investment and restructuring throughout Southern Africa and East Africa. It's no surprise that the Coca-Cola Sabco story was the most exciting and impactful part of our overall Africa bottler strategy, which was to consolidate into fewer bottlers that were larger and that had the financial wherewithal and technical and managerial talent to become better aligned on the continent. Our objective was to be the low-cost soft drink producer throughout every region. We believed in the long-term future of Africa, and this belief drove our strategies and investments.

Bom Jesus

At different times in various countries, as I oversaw operations in Africa, the environment discouraged investments in the infrastructure needed to grow our business. Over some periods, there might be political stability, transparency, and relative economic prosperity. At other times, the atmosphere was far from ideal for Coca-Cola or any other company. We were forced to find a way to build entirely new businesses in countries where impediments existed, including government ownership of our bottling operations, low regard for the rule of law or property rights, weak legal systems, corruption, and civil war. Learning how to run a legitimate business while mitigating inherent risks became an essential skill.

I recall a fascinating story with origins in Angola that I encountered during the bottler restructuring in Africa. I was riding in a motorcade with the country's minister of finance. We were heading to a little village called Bom Jesus on the Kwanza River, about eighteen miles outside Luanda, the capital city. The government had proposed to lease a parcel of land to Coca-Cola for a new bottling plant. South

African Breweries was our franchise-bottling partner in Angola. The Luanda municipal water source and infrastructure were so unreliable as to render impossible the making of our products in the dilapidated old Luanda plant.

As our motorcade moved toward the village of Bom Jesus, two military helicopters gave us an escort from above while a military crew swept the road and the field where the new plant was to be built to make sure there were no hidden land mines. These precautions were essential. A state of civil war existed inside the country. The Soviet Union and Cuba supported the side led by President Eduardo Santos's ruling MPLA Party while South Africa lined up behind the other side, led by the UNITA Party's Jonas Savimbi.

For people to have to live in such conditions was terrible. We pushed governments to institute economic policies that were more business friendly to companies wanting to invest in their countries the way Coke had. Our presence made those countries better places for people to live, and stable, predictable governments that promoted peace and prosperity were good for Coke's bottom line.

Fast-forward to one of my proudest Coca-Cola moments: returning to Bom Jesus a few years later to see a state-of-the-art, modern production facility amid a new industrial park and infrastructure (compliments of the Chinese government), this time without the escort of helicopters or military policemen brandishing AK-47s.

President Jerry Rawlings

There were times when we had to be flexible and willing to compromise on important issues to do business in some countries. But on some things, we simply could not compromise. The best example of that I can offer is how we handled a delicate negotiation with the national government of Ghana, headed by President Jerry Rawlings.

One of the promises I made when I launched the "We Believe in Africa" strategy was that we would ensure that the quality of our products in Africa matched the quality of products we sold in Anytown, USA. To that end, I started looking for trouble spots where product quality was unacceptable. One place I visited was the Coca-Cola bottling plant in Accra, Ghana. It was under the control of the government and run through a parastatal organization called the

Ghana National Beverage Corporation.

The plant was a dump with greasy floors, its antiquated equipment producing an inferior product that tasted like flat, watered-down soda but certainly not like Coca-Cola. I went in with my staff of engineers and plant technicians and did an assessment. It was the most deplorable production facility I had seen since my first visit to Luanda. From our perspective, nothing at the plant was salvageable, and the only solution was to shut down operations in Ghana and build a new, state-of-the-art bottling facility that would meet our standards.

From London, we began negotiating with the Rawlings government officials toward terms that would let us identify a greenfield site in Accra on which to build a new bottling plant. Our differences were wide from the start, with Rawlings saying he would be happy to have Coke build a new plant, but the government would still own and operate it just as it had the old plant. Such terms didn't fit any model for how the Coca-Cola Company wanted to operate. They were completely unacceptable, in fact.

We were so far apart that it became clear we needed serious, face-to-face negotiations to attempt to hammer out a deal. I flew back to Ghana with my team to sit down with Rawlings and his team, including his ministers of finance, commerce, and industry, as well as the manager of the parastatal.

Being in the same room didn't improve the prospect for success. The Ghanaians just didn't want to budge. In fact, they clearly wanted 100-percent control—business as usual. We came to a moment in the meeting when I realized we were not going to reach an agreement by the end of the day. Then, to my surprise, Rawlings excused everyone else from the room. He wanted to talk to me alone.

Now, Jerry Rawlings is a big man. He was 6' 2", and he seemed about that wide. He was one of the most massive human beings I had ever met in my life. But he wasn't fat. He was wide and muscular. His body was very sculptured. His reputation for having an intimidating presence as a physical force and ferocious fighter would be believed by anyone as soon as they laid eyes on him.

Once our aides were out of the room, Rawlings began pounding his fist on the coffee table and yelling, "You're just an envoy for a big company! We know you're just here talking for the white guys, saying what they've told you to say. The way it's going to be is the way I say it's going to be."

I looked at him and replied evenly, "Mr. President, respectfully, we can't do business the way you want us to."

That was it. The meeting was over, and I asked to be excused. I would be lying if I said I wasn't nervous about the outcome of that meeting and what was to come next.

Eventually, cooler heads prevailed. Rawlings must have realized that bluffing and blustering were not going to be effective negotiating tactics. Clearly, losing an investment in Ghana of the magnitude of a new Coca-Cola bottling facility was not the right signal to send to the Ghanaian people—or to donor countries or to any of the multilateral agencies such as the World Bank or IMF.

We reached an agreement wherein Coke would identify private investors who would form a joint-venture company with the government. That new company would construct, own, and operate the new bottling franchise. The government would continue to own a significant interest in the franchise, but for all intents and purposes, it would be operated as a private enterprise. The government wouldn't be allowed to mismanage and run another Coca-Cola plant into the ground.

I will never forget sitting on the stage in 90-degree heat at the 1994 ribbon-cutting ceremony for the gleaming new Coca-Cola bottling plant in Ghana. President Rawlings sat next to me. At one point, he leaned over to me and said, "By the way, Mr. Ware, you were right. I'm sorry that I didn't see the vision the way you did. You were right."

"Mr. President," I said, "you don't need to and never should apologize to a mere businessman like me."

We laughed, and we were on friendly terms from that moment on.

Old-School Capitalism

With regard to the human capability aspect of our strategy, our system in Africa had some of the most talented local employees on the continent. Our challenge was twofold: to develop systems for training, upgrading, and retaining these talented employees; and to attract talented general managers who could lead at the highest level of our business system throughout all regions of Africa.

Alex Cummings, whom I recruited from Pillsbury International, was one of those people. He first ran the business in Nigeria and eventually succeeded me as group president. Bill Egbe, a French African, who was recruited from France, was put in charge of the West Africa Francophone business. Kevin Williams, whom I recruited from a US-based pizza operation, was deployed as deputy division manager in South Africa, reporting to Charlie Frenette, who had joined my team as head of the Coca-Cola South Africa division from his post as chief marketing officer of the Coca-Cola Company. Charlie was a good teacher.

Once we had bottler and company alignment on investment strategy, building new production capacity, bottling plants, trucks, and distribution infrastructure, the goal of a billion cases sold in Africa became more realistic. We went to market. We developed dealer and customer incentives. We developed road shows, promotions on truck backs, sales rallies using outdoor cinema, media blitzes, and newspaper and radio advertising.

We developed collectors' clubs like the ones for the famous Ndebele bead bottles featured at the Atlanta Olympics. We sponsored promotions like the Nigeria Coca-Cola Table Tennis Festival. We sponsored the Nigeria Under-23 football team.

We continued to invest in communities throughout Africa, an example of which was Coca-Cola and the Nigerian Bottling Company's donation of two blocks of classrooms to a grammar school in Ota. Africans are natural engineers, taking the worst of scrap and making usable tools from it. For instance, in Tanzania, we deployed a unique mode of transport, a bicycle made completely of wood, including the wheels, to transport Coca-Cola.

In Ghana, we opened 500 new outlets and built new ice plants. We instituted a program called "Operation Red" to recruit blitz teams from all bottler territories and literally paint the market Coca-Cola red. This concept was similar to one we deployed throughout urban markets in the United States.

One of our biggest dilemmas in serving customers in Africa was how to keep Coke cold 24/7 in a climate where 90-degree weather was the norm. Just as the Coke formula was designed to be sweetened with cane sugar rather than beet juice or high-fructose corn syrup, it was also formulated to taste its very best at 30 degrees, the temperature that would produce the *Ahhh* after a consumer took a nice long swig. Of course, that *Ahhh* became synonymous with the product and was captured over and over again in our commercials and advertising.

To solve the problem, we developed a paraffin-fueled cooler that would keep the product at 40 degrees so that Africans could experience Coke closer to the way it was meant to be enjoyed. We deployed hundreds of these coolers in urban areas of South Africa, where vendors could fill them at the ice plants in the morning and have cold product to sell all day. As a result of our microbusiness development, vendors started selling more Coke and employing more people.

Sure, we made money. But the benefit of Coke being in Africa was the uplifting of the people in Africa. It was old-school capitalism. Then, it's all there was. There was no telecom, or Internet, or Bill Gates on the scene.

In 1996, Diet Coke had its Nigerian launch. Within a week, 19 percent of all soft drink sales in Lagos were of Diet Coke. In Abidjan, Cote d'Ivoire, we introduced a product availability program by developing the informal market with iceboxes and pushcarts in high-density areas to penetrate previously untapped outlets and channels with our products. In Nairobi, we used Olympic consumer promotions in supermarkets to drive sales throughout the territory.

Kenya was viewed as a giant among nations in terms of its locally sponsored Olympic trials and participation in the Olympic Games. We instituted programs such as basic production management training. The one that I visited was held in Douala, Cameroon, with attendees from the Yaounde, Bafoussam, Garoua, Libreville, N'Djamena, Abidjan, and Douala bottling plants. Also participants came from Dakar, Ouagadougou, Bobo-Dioulasso, Bamako, and Niamey plants. All of them were French-speaking employees, but we all shared a common language called Coca-Cola.

With regard to our suppliers, the objective was to lower cost, to improve quality, and to ensure continuity of supply by using economies of scale with sugar purchases, glass bottles, crates, and trucks.

Our strategy with the government was to demonstrate that government policy in Africa by and large presented a barrier to growth. Therefore, we focused governments' attention upon the impact of the Coca-Cola system on local economies and our system's contributions to local communities vis-à-vis jobs and support of human services such as schools and health clinics. We commissioned economic impact studies to demonstrate to African government officials the multiplier effect of the Coca-Cola business at local and national levels.

We believed in the long-term future of Africa, and this belief drove our strategies and investments. The bedrock of our business strategy in Africa was to activate the vast entrepreneurial potential of Africa's macroeconomy and become the premiere economic empowerment vehicle in Africa. Our goal was to bring thousands of small retailers into the Coca-Cola system by teaching economic empowerment through retailing. Furthermore, we aimed to earn sole supplier status of soft drinks in Africa. The truth of the matter is that the economics of Africa mandated that we become the sole supplier of carbonated soft drinks in Africa. That was our mindset.

29

THE WARE REPORT

On October 18, 1997, Roberto Goizueta, my friend and longtime mentor, died of cancer at age sixty-five. That day was one of the saddest of my life. We were colleagues for twenty-three years, the last seven of which I intimately felt the power of his influence. I was at our Ryland Trail home in Atlanta when I got the news.

"Go get a loan, never sell your Coca-Cola stock," I could almost hear him say. I knew this, of course, but I hung on every word he said, often as I inhaled the fog emanating from his True Menthol cigarettes, which he would smoke one after another at our regular Monday lunch.

He was too much of a gentleman to call anyone a "liar." But at the historic Leeds Castle meeting in London, he had said, "Our South African managers have not been telling us the whole story." Those words reminded me how he had been a champion of integrity and the truth.

And then there was the time he came to my office (which simply never happened; people went to Roberto). On that occasion, he asked whom I would recommend to replace me as head of corporate external affairs once I was promoted to head the Africa Group.

"Ingrid Saunders Jones," I said without hesitation.

"I couldn't agree with you more," he responded and promptly left my office without another word.

And finally, I smiled as I recalled these words: "You can tell a man's character by the way he cares for his shoes," Roberto had said. "Your shoes are always shiny and coordinated with your suit." Of the other unfortunate executive, he remarked, "His shoes are always scuffed." Roberto was an immaculate dresser and took pride in every detail of his appearance.

Trouble

Roberto's funeral was held at Holy Spirit Catholic Church in Atlanta, and it set into motion what I can describe only as a very weird series of events within the Coca-Cola Company. Roberto's death left a huge void of leadership at the company. He goes down in history as the greatest CEO of Coca-Cola since Robert W. Woodruff. By then, Don Keough had become the heart of the company's operating success and was sometimes called "the real boss."

Roberto was the brains, the visionary, the champion of shareholder value, an aristocrat who created a company ethos, a swagger that was the envy of Wall Street. He was the darling of investors, from the little guy who bought a few shares of Coke stock to large institutional investors and Warren Buffett, who controlled 8 percent of the company's outstanding shares through Berkshire Hathaway. *The New York Times* reported that people who invested $1,000 in Coke stock when Roberto took over in 1980 would have $65,000 at the time of his death, seventeen years later.

Roberto handpicked Doug Ivester, then president and chief operating officer, to succeed him as chairman and CEO. Doug was an accountant by training and became the lead outside auditor with Ernst & Young on the Coca-Cola account. He was then hired by Coca-Cola and rose rapidly through the ranks, from assistant controller to director of auditing to vice president and, finally, to senior vice president and chief financial officer at age thirty-seven. When Don Keough retired in 1993, Doug Ivester was appointed chief operating officer of the company.

Doug was a financial genius. He was the financial engineer who complemented Roberto's vision of ever-increasing shareowner value. His most notable contribution was the creation of the "49 percent solution," wherein the Coca-Cola Company acquired 49 percent of the stock of the publicly traded bottling company Coca-Cola Enterprises, thus buoying the balance sheet of the Coca-Cola Company and adding to its annual earnings. Except in rare circumstances, the company's historical practice had been to act as the franchisor and not the franchisee in its bottling operations.

Upon Roberto's death, the board of directors unanimously approved the appointment of Doug Ivester to replace him. The decision would prove to be a mistake, one that became clear to me almost immediately.

It was common for Coca-Cola executives in Atlanta to work on Saturdays and sometimes on Sundays after church. One Saturday, shortly after Doug became CEO, I walked into his office and found him seated at his desk with a stack of papers about a foot high.

"Hey, Doug," I said. "What are you working on?"

Doug told me in a matter-of-fact tone that he was working on expense reports. He went on, as if it were a point of pride, to tell me he reviewed and approved the expenses of all of his direct reports, all twenty-five.

We chatted a few minutes about Africa bottler restructuring plans, and I left. On my way back to my office, I thought, *Oh, my God, we are in trouble.* If Doug was approving expense reports, who was steering the ship? Who was leading one of the most revered institutions in the history of American business?

There were other warning signs. For instance, in a meeting in Atlanta with the South Africa bottlers, Ivester described himself as a "redneck from Gainesville, Georgia."

As the only person of color in the room, I thought it one of the most embarrassing moments in my entire career. It was an extremely careless remark coming from the CEO of the Coca-Cola Company.

Later that evening, after dinner, some of the South Africa bottlers with whom I had developed strong personal and professional mutual respect took me aside to express their discomfort with the "redneck" comment.

What I did not anticipate was that Ivester's callous insensitivity would seriously damage the reputation of the Coca-Cola Company. There is no doubt that Doug Ivester was a financial wizard, but he was incompetent as a CEO. In my opinion, the board of directors of the Coca-Cola Company did a disservice to the shareowners and employees when they essentially rubber-stamped Roberto's choice of Ivester.

An interesting aside: I received a letter from Ivester, among the many that poured in from all over the world, congratulating me on my twenty-fifth anniversary with the Coca-Cola Company. Ivester wrote to thank me for my service and laud me for my work leading the Africa Group and for my help in focusing the company on communities.

Indeed, in 1998, the Africa Group grew about 7 percent, whereas the European division grew 5 percent, and the Middle East and Asia divisions grew 6 percent. I was proud of the fact that, under my leadership, the Africa Group's operating income had grown from 24 percent of sales to 36 percent of sales in the three years since I took over as group president.

A highly regarded beverage stock analyst at Morgan Stanley was quoted by Andrew Conway in *Beverage Digest* as saying, "Carl Ware has been a very significant player in advancing Coke's agenda in Africa," and, "He's been a major part of the margin expansion and the expansion of Coke's pervasive distribution on the continent. He's very well known to political leaders, and has been very successful at establishing relationships in which Coca-Cola received beneficial tax treatment in exchange for the building of facilities for use by Africans."

Root Causes

Whenever I returned home to Atlanta from my work in Africa in the mid-1990s, I was constantly inundated with racial discrimination complaints from black employees. These men and women came to me informally over lunch, after hours, and often during the weekends at my home. I think they came to me because I was the highest-ranking African American executive, because they knew my reputation as a dedicated mentor, and because they trusted me. For my part, I believed their stories because I had had similar experiences throughout my career.

Eventually, I took the matter to Coca-Cola's COO, then Doug Ivester. I expressed my concern about the low morale and discontent among the company's African American employees, including key managers and executives. Doug said he'd already heard similar stories through human resources channels but, clearly, hearing it from me escalated the seriousness of the issue in his mind.

He asked what I recommended.

I'd given the matter some thought and had discussed it with

some of my African American associates. I told Doug that I'd gather a handful of African American executives to discuss the matter and that I'd bring back our recommendations on how we should deal with the situation. He agreed. And I did just that.

In the fall of 1995, I convened a small group of black Coca-Cola executives at the company's 711 Fifth Avenue office in New York for a daylong session to discuss diversity and how blacks were being treated by the company. The group consisted of executives from several departments, including legal, finance, corporate auditing, human resources, external affairs, and investor relations. This body consisted of highly seasoned, extraordinarily well-trained and experienced executives who were all recognized nationally in their own professions. They were essential members of the company's brain trust.

We wanted to isolate the issues and ferret out the root causes of the problem in order to present Doug with a diversity strategy that the company could act upon immediately. Furthermore, we genuinely wanted Doug to put his own personal stamp on diversity. Every executive in the group signed the report, which I then presented a few days later to Doug in person.

The report, which became known as "The Ware Report," documented a number of areas where changes should be made to improve the company's performance in diversity. Among the key players in its development was my former executive assistant, Terrez Marriott Thompson, an Africa Group financial officer, who today heads global supplier diversity for the Coca-Cola Company.

We pointed out the dearth of blacks in top management and discrepancies in promotions and pay increases. The report I handed to Doug criticized a corporate atmosphere that lacked sensitivity and inclusion and led to conditions wherein African American employees often felt "humiliated, ignored, overlooked, or unacknowledged."

Diversity needed a champion at the top. The report recommended that Doug Ivester, as COO, become that top advocate, leading diversity as a business imperative—a legacy that he would own. The company had everything to gain and nothing to lose in leading by example on diversity, we said.

I advised Doug that this response was not something he should delegate to human resources. "I am the group president of Africa," I said, referring to my job overseeing forty-eight sub-Saharan African nations. "I am not Coca-Cola's affirmative action officer."

The fact that I was being called upon by the company's top white executives every time a racial issue flared up—whether it was employees or external groups—annoyed me greatly. But through a sense of loyalty to the company, I answered the call anyway. I knew my company well enough to know that if I didn't answer the call, it wouldn't get done. I put the company first—always—as long as it didn't put my integrity in jeopardy.

Doug listened to my report, made a few handwritten notes on his copy, and thanked me for the group's efforts. He said he would get back to me, but he never did, even after several nudges for his feedback. In my mind, the mere sending of executive office memorandums on the subject of diversity didn't constitute championing diversity. It requires more direct, hands-on involvement in the manner that we had pointed out in "The Ware Report."

By 1997, racial discrimination within the company began to attract the attention of the US Department of Labor. The Coca-Cola Company maintained federal contracts for military bases, national parks, office buildings, and so forth, which required the company to purge itself of inequities and discriminatory practices and to develop an affirmative action plan. There were even reports that stated the company had violated federal antidiscrimination laws. And, inside the Coca-Cola Company, certain employees were privy to the repeated warnings that the company was vulnerable to litigation, yet they saw little being done to address the extremely subjective review and promotion practices.

This state of affairs eventually led to a class action lawsuit claiming systemic racial discrimination.

In April 1999, four African American employees—some current, some former—indeed filed a federal class action lawsuit against the company. The lawsuit included 2,200 black employees who were similarly affected. A few years earlier, the plaintiffs' attorney, Cyrus Mehri, had sued Texaco on behalf of its black employees and won a $176 million settlement.

The discrimination issues cited in the Coca-Cola lawsuit documented discrepancies in pay, promotion, and performance evaluation.

These issues were identical to ones in "The Ware Report" delivered to Doug almost two years earlier. The most serious of the allegations was that the company erected a hierarchy that kept whites at the top of the pay scale while African American employees were relegated to the bottom of the pay scale.

The plaintiffs also maintained that "glass ceiling" and "glass wall" practices kept African Americans from rising to top positions in particular departments (i.e., marketing, finance, customer relations, bottler operations, sales, and regional management) where salaries and bonuses were more lucrative.

This was not just another race discrimination lawsuit against just another American company. Word of Coca-Cola employees' lawsuit against the company resounded around the world. I felt it firsthand when I went to China to participate in the launch of a new product. In a press conference with twenty-five Chinese reporters, I was grilled on the race discrimination lawsuit and not about the new product I was there to discuss.

For me, this situation underscored the point that a global company operating in 200 countries can ill afford to develop a reputation for racial intolerance.

The lawsuit took its toll on the company upon the international stage but was keenly felt at home in Atlanta. Civil rights organizations including the Southern Christian Leadership Conference, the NAACP, the National Urban League, and People United to Serve Humanity, as well as local black religious and civic leaders gave their support to the plaintiffs. Collectively, they demanded that the company mend its ways.

The company's message defending its handling of the lawsuit was suffocated by the overwhelmingly negative media. Under Ivester's leadership, the company's response to all of this business was, first, to dig in its heels and fight the lawsuit and, second, to establish a Diversity Advisory Council, one of the recommendations of "The Ware Report." The diversity council was a good idea but also too little too late. That one action could not undo the lawsuit.

Ivester asked then-president of Coca-Cola USA Jack Stahl and me to cochair the Diversity Advisory Council. Members of the council were recruited from every department throughout the company and consisted of African Americans, Hispanics, Asians, and other minorities, from secretaries to middle managers to senior executives.

Resigning

In October 1999, I was in London with Mary for the big annual meeting of the Coca-Cola Africa Group, which included bottlers from all over Africa and all of the division and region managers.

I was discussing our strategy to invest in people with the group when someone slid a note in front of me saying that I needed to call Mary. I immediately excused myself and quickly made my way to my hotel room.

Once there, Mary told me, "Doug called and said that it was urgent that you call him."

Moments later, I was on the phone with Doug, who told me about his decision to restructure the company and that I would now be reporting to Doug Daft, who would head up a new Asia/Africa Group. He said the new management committee of the company would consist of seven people reporting directly to him—specifically, the chief financial officer, the chief marketing officer, the HR director, and four group presidents, representing our regions around the world—all of whom were white males.

"Our critics will have a field day with this," I said. "Are you sure you want seven white males reporting to you in the middle of a diversity lawsuit that's tearing this company apart? You should consider our image with our customers, business partners, and other constituents around the world. It doesn't make sense to me for you to do it this way."

"Well, it's not about you," he responded. "It's about what I want."

I said, "Doug, I thought it was about the company."

Even if I was no longer going to be a direct report, I argued, he should still have an African American on the executive committee.

"I don't like it," I said. "I cannot explain this to our constituents who are concerned about the company. I cannot explain this to my Africa staff. I cannot explain it to the media. I will not become a mouthpiece to defend your restructuring. I simply won't do that."

He made it crystal clear that the topic was not up for discussion.

He had made up his mind.

"I'll see you in the office tomorrow," I said.

He interrupted me to say he'd come to London.

"No, no need for you to come here," I said. "We are winding up our conference with the bottlers. I will just jump on a plane and see you on Friday morning."

That Friday morning, I walked into his office and said, "Unless you change your mind, here is my letter of resignation."

He told me he had not anticipated my resigning.

"Well, Doug, I can't look employees in the eye and say that you have done the right thing for the company," I said.

30

THERE IS LIFE AFTER COKE

The headline of *The New York Times* the next day, November 9, 1999, was "Black Executive's Departure to Complicate Coke's Diversity Drive." With my resignation, the highest-ranking African American employees were three corporate vice presidents out of twenty-three vice presidents total. The three corporate vice presidents were Ingrid Saunders Jones, Juan Johnson, and Carolyn Baldwin Byrd.

The press described me as "angry." What they missed was something beyond mere anger. I felt undervalued. The optics of Ivester's action in the midst of a diversity lawsuit revealed a serious lack of judgment: his new senior executive committee consisted of seven white males. Period.

The board members who approved the reorganization were people of high integrity, some of whom I had worked with for decades on important civic and community projects. "Doug led us to believe you were okay with this reorganization," one board member told me.

Another member lamented, "Carl, I wish you would reconsider. The company needs you now more than ever."

In the days following my resignation, a third board member came to me privately and said, "Carl, you are getting more publicity than the brand."

Everyone was upset that my letter of resignation had been leaked to the press. "I didn't ask for it," I said.

"What do we need to do for you to change your mind and retract the letter?" a board member asked. I told them all that I had made my decision. It was final. I further stated Doug Ivester had counteroffered me a diversity consultancy, which was an insult.

Because this development was such an abrupt, unexpected one in my career at the company, I had given no thought to what the future would look like. Ever positive, I thought, *There is life after Coke.*

My resignation came on the heels of a major product contamination debacle in June, in which thirty schoolchildren in Belgium had fallen ill after drinking Coca-Cola products bottled at our plant in that country. A hundred other complaints followed from people who also reported sudden illness from Coke products. Instead of going there himself, issuing a public apology, and ascertaining that our products were safe to drink, Doug Ivester sent a marketing manager to Belgium to handle the contamination crisis.

The reverberation of Ivester's handling of the crisis was felt throughout the Coca-Cola system worldwide. Compounding things was the bottlers' perception of excessive concentrate price increases, which only served to deepen their distrust of the company under Ivester's leadership. The recall cost the company in excess of $100 million in what became the biggest such action in the company's 113-year history.

It wasn't just the diversity lawsuit or mounting pressure from bottlers and European governments that forced the board to take action. On Ivester's watch, earnings declined for two years in a row, and shareholder equity dropped from 56.5 percent in 1997 to 35 percent in 2000.

Four weeks after my resignation, two powerful board members, Warren Buffett and Herb Allen, met Doug Ivester in Chicago and informed him that his services were no longer required.

On December 7, 1999, the *Los Angeles Times* reported, "Coca-Cola Co.'s shares slumped more than 5% on Monday after the world's largest beverage company announced unexpectedly that Chairman and Chief Executive M. Douglas Ivester would resign in April after less than 2 1/2 years on the job."

I don't believe the board conducted a thorough enough search in either the selection of Doug Ivester to succeed Roberto or in the selection of Doug Daft to succeed Ivester. It appeared that the board simply applied its management succession plan without consideration of the total competencies and skills needed to successfully run the Coca-Cola Company.

In the case of Daft, I was not the only veteran Coca-Cola executive who questioned the board's wisdom. I received calls from senior associates around the world, asking, "What on Earth was the board thinking? Did they look beyond the succession plan?" The common theme was that the board was asleep at the switch again.

When Daft was named CEO, I was in the process of bringing my twenty-five-year career with the company to a close. I was spending the majority of my time at our home on Hilton Head Island, playing golf, and thinking about the future. During this transition I continued to receive calls from colleagues, including Jack Stahl, president of Coca-Cola USA, and Neville Isdell, chairman and CEO of Coca-Cola Beverages in Great Britain. Even Don Keough, who was by then retired, stayed in touch, urging me to "keep my powder dry."

Daft later told me that his first act as Coca-Cola's new chairman and chief executive was to contact me with an offer to return to the company. Despite press reports of some tough negotiating, it wasn't much of a conversation. He asked me to put in writing what it would take for me to come back. I told him I wanted to think about it and that I'd get back to him with my answer in a few days.

As I considered my options, I was reminded of a conversation years earlier with International Grocers Association Chairman and CEO Tom Haggai. He had sought my advice on getting IGA launched in South Africa. "Carl, you heading the Africa Group is just too obvious," he said. "You have a much greater value to this company than heading the Africa Group."

Tom's words stuck with me and resonated as I considered Daft's offer to write my own job description. I consulted personal advisors as well as family and friends as I deliberated.

In the end, I wrote a job description that would allow me to fix the daunting problems confronting the company. There was the diversity lawsuit, the Belgium product PR nightmare, bottlers had lost confidence in the Coca-Cola Company, and the wholesome reputation and Coca-Cola brand image had been battered.

Like Roberto Goizueta and Don Keough and Robert W. Woodruff, it was also important for me to leave a lasting mark. I told Doug Daft I would need three years to get this job done. The document I submitted was more than he had asked for. It was a much-needed strategy for rebuilding the company's image as a welcome citizen in every community where we did business around the world.

In its announcement of my return on January 5, 2000, *The Washington Post* carried an extensive story by staff writer Martha Hamilton:

"Doug Daft just made a deft move," said former Atlanta Mayor Maynard H. Jackson. "This new division and Carl Ware will be a match made in Coca-Cola heaven." Ware said he is excited about a job that is in operations and "goes beyond the traditional corporate affairs" role. In fact, Ware is stepping into an area where Coke has suffered some of its worst setbacks in the past year or so, making mistakes such as initially minimizing quality-control problems that produced product recalls in Europe.

"Carl's job is to make sure that, after what they've gone through this year, that the perception of them is a good one," said Emanuel Goldman, an industry analyst at Merrill Lynch Global Securities. Goldman said Africa has shown substantial gains in volume under Ware, even at a time when the company as a whole was experiencing slower growth.

Ware said he and Daft "both agree this business is built on millions of customer relations and community relations and employee relations." The two have worked side by side, said Ware, a veteran of 26 years with Coke, and "are already friends and could have candid conversations about what is best for the business and how to move."

❧

Writing a job description is one thing, but translating it into a day-to-day work plan is something else again. I began my new assignment by figuring out the working relationship between Doug Daft and me.

Soon after I returned to Coca-Cola, Doug Daft asked for my opinion on the appointment of Jack Stahl as the chief operating officer of the Coca-Cola Company.

"Great choice," I responded without hesitation. Jack had done an outstanding job as president of Coca-Cola USA. We cochaired the Diversity Advisory Council and spent a lot of time on business matters. We genuinely liked each other and bonded around our common interests in family, politics, and sports. I admired Jack's intellect and his amazing touch with the employees. Jack succeeded Doug Daft as

CFO and was admired by bottlers and customers. He was also charismatic and persuasive in my decision to unretire. The Coca-Cola Company's board elected Jack as president and COO at its annual meeting on April 19, 2000. The board got it right that time.

※

That was about the extent of the honeymoon. Roughly three weeks after my return, we announced a major restructuring as a result of the losses sustained on Ivester's watch, no doubt exacerbated by the Asian financial crisis that began in 1997. We would lay off 6,000 employees worldwide, or a whopping one-fifth of our global workforce. Forty percent of the jobs to be cut were at our headquarters in Atlanta. It was the largest round of layoffs in the history of the company.

Many of the employees who lost their jobs were people I had worked with for many years. In Atlanta, the layoffs affected people I saw in church and whose children had grown up with my son and played sports with him at Benjamin E. Mays High School. Job losses occurred among some of my close associates in the Africa Group. I knew that the workforce reduction was the right thing to do for the company. But delivering that message to the employees was gut-wrenching at best.

As the company grew in the Goizueta era, so did the layers of bureaucracy, which created redundancy throughout the organization.

Don Keough had a habit of randomly stopping and greeting employees in the hallways. "Tell me about your job in the company," he'd say cheerfully. The employee's response might be "I'm an analyst in the marketing group" or "I'm an attorney in the legal department." He ended every one of those conversations with, "I'm Don Keough, and I sell Coca-Cola."

In senior management meetings, he lamented the fact that we had more people analyzing Coke than selling it. While serving as Africa Group president, I questioned why we needed country, region, and division managers all essentially doing the same job that was being duplicated by staff in Atlanta. By the time of the layoffs, staff at headquarters had mushroomed disproportionately to our operations worldwide. And we didn't sell one case of Coke out of North Avenue.

The discrimination lawsuit only added fuel to the layoff scenario. Among the layoffs was Larry Jones, an African American benefits manager in the human resources department. Larry was in the process of organizing a boycott against the company and planning to take a busload of black employees from Atlanta to the company's 2000 annual meeting in Wilmington, Delaware.

I met with Larry to assure him that employees were welcome to attend the annual meeting and that there would be a place on the agenda for him to speak. The foremost concern of the company was the safety and security of the thirty employees who would be making the bus trip to Delaware. I explained to him that the company would cover all costs associated with the trip and that the company would provide proper security for the protesters.

Larry seemed surprised but agreed to our plan. Neither protesters nor employees were unusual at annual meetings. We welcomed both.

Doug Daft opened the meeting with a few remarks, and then he introduced me. I expressed the company's desire to settle the lawsuit in the most expeditious, amicable, and equitable manner possible and welcomed the employees who had made the long trip from Atlanta. My role was primarily as cochair of the Diversity Advisory Council, though I knew I was speaking as the only African American member of the executive committee. We were as anxious as the employees to settle the lawsuit and get back to business.

At the end of the annual meeting, we were informed by our media relations staff that we needed to meet the press and answer questions. My staff and I thought that Doug Daft as CEO or Jack Stahl as COO should take the lead at this impromptu press conference. But they both deferred to me. The two most senior white executives were using the convenience of the most senior African American executive in the company to do their job.

Both men stood beside me, not fielding any questions. I felt, frankly, used. I felt violated because of my race. I thought to myself, *Why don't you guys do your damn job?* What I had done was what many black people in power are compelled to do. I wanted to save the Coca-Cola Company. But, at the same time, I felt like these guys should be taking the heat for what had gone wrong. It was one of the few times that I personally felt I had been put in a volatile situation.

Later that night, I got a call from Amanda Davis, a Fox 5 Atlanta TV anchor and a mentee. "You handled the Coca-Cola situation well," Amanda assured me. "I was proud of you. But I could see the anguish on your face."

Once we returned to Atlanta, I continued discussions with Daft; Jack Stahl; CFO Gary Fayard, a veteran Coca-Cola man; and Joe Gladden, our general counsel, on the best way for the company to resolve the lawsuit, which was dragging into its second year. We were devoting an inordinate amount of management time to the lawsuit and running out of damage control strategies to address the negative publicity.

The longer we drew it out through costly legal machinations, I noted, the worse it would get. My main objective was to ensure that the Coca-Cola Company would emerge from the lawsuit as the most diverse and inclusive company in the world.

Upon my recommendation, the executive committee decided to settle the lawsuit swiftly.

On June 14, 2000, minutes after settlement of the lawsuit was announced, famed African American attorneys Willie Gary and Johnnie Cochran Jr. filed a $1.5 billion lawsuit in a Georgia state court on behalf of a handful of other African American employees of the Coca-Cola Company. It was an eleventh-hour act of blatant and disruptive legal maneuvering that sought to prolong the process and forestall the real progress we had made. That suit was later thrown out of court.

The final settlement to the original lawsuit was announced on November 16, 2000. It totaled more than $192 million. Each of the four named plaintiffs was awarded up to $300,000 in cash, while the 2,200 then-current and former black salaried employees were awarded an average of $40,000 each, which came to $156 million. The settlement also mandated the company spend $36 million to make sweeping changes via an outside task force.

Days later, a newspaper reporter called me to find out if I, too, would receive an award from the settlement, and if so, how much I could expect. In fact, I did receive an award of $56,000, which I donated to charity and disclosed publicly.

Alexis Herman, former US Secretary of Labor, was recruited to chair the court-mandated Human Resources Task Force to oversee the settlement and to identify ways the company could improve its diversity policies and practices. I was pleased that the court approved the appointment of Alexis for many reasons, chiefly that she had been the independent consultant who helped us settle and implement the PUSH agreement in 1984.

As a direct result of the lawsuit, the company supplier development program was enhanced by a pledge to spend a billion dollars over a five-year period with women and minority vendors. The company also donated $50 million to the Coca-Cola Foundation to support education in diverse communities. The Diversity Advisory Council was institutionalized as a departmental function, with its own staff and budget.

The lawsuit covered only US operations, but the lessons learned were global. As a company, we asked, what does diversity mean in China? What does it look like in South Africa? What does it mean in Europe and Latin America? Managing diversity became a business imperative that would be ingrained in the company culture. It was the right thing to do for our shareowners, our employees, and our customers, no longer simply something "nice" to do.

This outcome was what Woodruff envisioned when he said that the Coca-Cola Company would be a welcomed citizen, a part of every community in which it did business. Roberto often pointed out that excluding minorities and women from key decision-making roles denies a company access to intellectual capital and negatively affects a company's bottom line, an idea since backed by numerous long-term business studies.

31

JUST BUSINESS

Before Doug Daft became CEO, I knew him as a smart marketing executive. He was easy to talk to, and I liked him as a person. But like many of us, Daft had some peculiar habits. For example, Daft and the senior management team would sometimes arrive at a decision on such things as a major corporate reorganization or a new product acquisition. Only later would we learn that someone outside of the executive committee had swayed his mind.

The problem was he rarely came back to the executive committee to inform us that he had changed his mind. His actual management style was difficult to discern. It appeared that he winged his way through the top job by being nice to everyone and indecisive about everything.

My sense was that Doug had a tough time communicating with his board on critical matters concerning the company's growth strategy. Never was this difficulty more evident than in the case of the attempted acquisition of Quaker Oats and its coveted Gatorade brand. After several weeks of intense financial and marketing analysis, we engaged in serious negotiations with Quaker Oats. Our business development, marketing, finance, and legal teams recommended the acquisition, and Doug approved it enthusiastically.

We were convinced that this strategy was the right one, and we were under the impression that Doug had brought the board along each step of the way toward the final decision to acquire Gatorade. At the November 2000 board meeting in our New York office, one of the most powerful board members asked Doug if he was prepared to risk 10 percent of the Coca-Cola Company's value to acquire this one brand. Doug couldn't—or wouldn't—defend his decision. Instead of standing his ground, Doug retreated, and the board quashed the $15.75 billion deal.

The deal team was waiting outside the boardroom when Doug gave us the news. We were stunned. Earlier that day, Doug and Quaker Oats CEO Robert Morrison had posed for publicity shots. A press conference to announce the deal was scheduled for that same afternoon. The episode brought another embarrassing moment for the Coca-Cola Company.

Later, Pepsi bought Gatorade.

≈

In all of our interactions, Jack Stahl never spoke directly about his relationship with Doug Daft or the partnership that we hoped would evolve between the two of them. I sensed their two management styles were not jelling. But because my hands were so full, I never gave it much thought until just before the annual Coke-sponsored Bryant Gumbel/Walt Disney World Celebrity Golf Tournament, held in March 2001 in Orlando. The company invited high-value customers, bottlers, and government officials to participate in the tournament.

On the tournament's second night, I received a call from Jack, who told me he had resigned over irreconcilable management differences with Doug Daft. Again, another bizarre episode at the Coca-Cola Company.

Doug was an interesting character study. As an example, he had an affinity for feng shui, the Chinese philosophical system that purports to harmonize people with their environments. Not long after he became CEO, he hired a feng shui designer to redecorate the executive offices. Despite the perceived value of a makeover, I, for one, declined to have my office redone. I was incredibly busy, and it seemed like an unnecessary expense.

After Jack's departure, Doug did another odd thing. He came into my office and told me he wasn't going to appoint another COO at that time, but he wanted me to move into the COO's office suite.

I said, "Doug, I'm comfortable where I am." But I ended up acceding to his request and occupied the COO's space until I retired. Instead of a view of Emory University and Stone Mountain, my COO suite faced Clark Atlanta University and its iconic clock tower. Another small detail: the COO's suite adjoined the executive dining room, where I once enjoyed Monday lunches with Roberto.

The Belgium Crisis

My role was primarily to serve as the Cola-Cola Company's brand ambassador around the world. Another issue that had plagued the company, of course, was the Belgium contamination debacle under Ivester. It was resolved by our Europe division management team, with whom I met to gain a clear understanding of events leading to the crisis. I was extremely impressed by the division management team's efforts with the Belgium Health Ministry. I was convinced that they were in control of the matter and that the pending report of the government investigation would give us much-needed answers.

The report released by Belgium's High Hygiene Council stated,

> Its conclusion is that this is not a case of intoxication from the consumption of soft drinks. The most probable explanation of the observed symptoms is the presence of a bad odor and/or taste which in sensitive people triggered a psychosomatic reaction with real complaints such as a tendency [to] vomit or actual vomiting and feeling generally ill, as a result.... The entire incident has all the characteristics of a "mass sociogenic illness" (MSI).

Retiring the Confederate Flag and Other Community Service

Although I traveled abroad most of the time, there was a void in the company's traditional leadership role at home. Daft was not well known in the local community and didn't appear to have an affinity for Atlanta, so the role of shadow CEO became part of my identity there. In 2002, I chaired the Metro Atlanta Chamber of Commerce, normally a role for the CEO. For example, Arthur Blank, cofounder of Home Depot and owner and CEO of the Atlanta Falcons football club, succeeded me as chairman. Robert Minkhorst, the president and CEO of Philips Consumer Electronics for North America, preceded me as chairman.

The most controversial issue that took place during my time at the Metro Atlanta Chamber of Commerce was the removal of the Confederate flag as the state's most visible symbol. It was 2002, and the "Stars and Bars" were still flying high over the state capitol. Our discussions at the chamber began with Governor Roy Barnes, who lost his office, in part, over the flag controversy. The discussions continued with newly elected Governor Sonny Perdue. I chaired the chamber board meeting when we told him, in no uncertain terms, that the flag must go.

Six years earlier, Atlanta had hosted the 1996 Olympic Games. The Metro Atlanta Chamber board voted unanimously to support removing the Confederate flag. As one united front, we told the governor that if we were to continue to build an image of an international city and recruit investments from around the country and throughout the world, the rebel flag could not define the Atlanta brand. Some of the most outspoken board members on the subject were Arthur Blank, Juanita Baranco, and Chamber president Sam Williams.

Governor Perdue heard the message from the business community and appointed a commission to design a new state flag, which was adopted by the Georgia General Assembly and is now flying above the state capitol.

❧

My civic involvement in Atlanta continued to expand. I led a $25 million fundraising campaign for the Atlanta Area Council of the Boy Scouts to build a new Atlanta-area Boy Scouts Council headquarters, located at 1800 Circle 75 Parkway in Cobb County.

In preparation for the Olympic Games, the Coca-Cola Company had purchased a swath of property in the heart of downtown Atlanta to house the headquarters of the Olympic Games. Once dubbed the "most valuable piece of urban real estate in the Southeast," the property was located next door to CNN and Philips Arena, among other major attractions. As executive vice president of global public affairs and administration, I oversaw just about everything, including the reuse of the downtown real estate. The big question was, what would be done with the land once the Olympics were over?

Developers came forth with different proposals that included a five-star hotel with shopping and housing, the NASCAR museum, and the College Football Hall of Fame. Some people in the company advocated selling the land. Some even floated the idea of building a new Coca-Cola Company headquarters on the real estate, an idea thankfully quashed by the board. In fact, all of these ideas were reject-ed.

Our guiding principle was to create a lasting legacy for the com-munity. We decided that one of the anchor reuses for the property would be a new World of Coca-Cola Museum, which meant moving the old World of Coke from Underground Atlanta. But the overall vision began to take shape when Home Depot cofounder Bernie Marcus called me to discuss his idea of building the largest aquarium in the Western Hemisphere. It was a visionary idea and would further distinguish Atlanta as an international city.

The entire development came into focus once we decided to es-tablish the National Center for Civil and Human Rights. With it as the third anchor—a world-class civil rights museum set in the cradle of civil rights—the legacy would be complete.

Bernie bought the land for a dollar and spent $250 million to build the Georgia Aquarium, which opened in 2005. The new World of Coke opened in 2007, followed by the Center for Civil and Hu-man Rights in 2014. The center showcases the King papers and con-nects the American civil rights movement to present-day global hu-man rights movements.

Global Ambassador

Much of what I did to restore the Coca-Cola Company's image and relationships with bottlers, business partners, and governments was visiting such places as the Philippines to demonstrate the company's commitment to community uplift, especially education.

The Coca-Cola Company had established a Coca-Cola Founda-tion in the Philippines as a partnership with the government to focus on education. We had been funding a program called the Little Red School House, a project designed to build schools in remote rural are-as. I met with the minister of education to deliver the message that the Coca-Cola Company would be expanding the Little Red School House program. Eventually, fifty-five three-classroom, multi-grade elementary school buildings were constructed, and 500,000 school-children and 12,000 teachers benefitted from the effort.

I traveled to Ho Chi Minh City to announce a commitment of the Coca-Cola Company to a program that would bring technology to communities in Vietnam in the form of Coca-Cola Learning Centers, which offered young people and parents an opportunity to develop their computer skills.

For two years in a row, I served as the Coca-Cola Company's principal representative in Davos, Switzerland, at the World Economic Forum, where world business and government leaders confer and shape global, regional, and industrial agendas. I seized this opportunity to communicate directly with world government leaders about the company's global initiatives, particularly in Africa, through speeches and by hosting lunches and receptions where intimate dialogue could occur between world leaders.

I participated in United Nations forums, where I got to know Secretary-General Kofi Annan. The company worked with the UN on programs dealing with HIV/AIDS in Africa and other humanitarian efforts in areas devastated by natural disasters. For instance, we worked out the details on how Coca-Cola water systems could be better integrated into water relief efforts in the aftermath of a tsunami or other natural disaster.

In 2002, at Daft's request, I flew from the Sydney Olympics to Hong Kong to cochair the Hong Kong–United States Business Council, which is made up of senior executives from some of the most prominent companies in the world. It functions as a forum for business leaders from the US and Hong Kong to exchange views and to advocate policies and programs that foster trade and investment among the US, Hong Kong, and Greater China.

Only a handful of years had passed since the sovereignty over Hong Kong was transferred from Great Britain to China, and the issue of reunification and how it affected doing business in the different economies in the region was the focus. Coca-Cola had a long history there and did business in Hong Kong, Mainland China, and Taiwan. Preparing for this meeting by learning the business issues and players in the region was a fascinating exercise.

Many of the image-rebuilding meetings took place in Washington, DC, where I spoke to the Congressional Black Caucus about the diversity lawsuit and how other companies could get ahead of the curve and instill diversity as a business imperative, versus something nice to do because your workforce consists of women, African Americans, Hispanics, and Asians.

At the request of Jack Straw, member of parliament and home secretary, I traveled to Britain to speak to members of parliament and the staff of the Office of the Home Secretary about diversity. Being invited to deliver this speech was a high honor and the ultimate act of corporate diplomacy.

I would never become the chairman and chief executive officer of the Coca-Cola Company. The question of whether I was the right person for the job aside, I felt I would never be called upon to do that job by the Coca-Cola Company Board of Directors. I didn't believe the board would appoint me or any other African American as CEO. Ironically, they gave me the designated office space of the president and chief operating officer, which I occupied for my last three years. But they would never give me the title of president and chief operating officer.

I never knew where I stood in the hierarchy of the succession plan, though it would have been interesting information. But bitter? I have never been bitter about that.

At the time of my unretirement, I told Doug Daft that I would give the company just three more years. True to my word, I let him know when that time was up.

He commended me for my efforts to restore the company's image and pointed out that we were finally back in the business of selling Coke. After almost three decades of service, he then asked what the company could do for me.

"I don't want a retirement party, Doug," I said. "I don't like retirement parties." Instead, I asked for a million dollars to be donated to Clark Atlanta University to help fund the Carl & Mary Ware Academic Center. It was a nice swan song after twenty-eight-plus years of service.

He didn't hesitate to grant my request, and he made a request of his own—that I stay on as special assistant to the CEO to advise him on all matters that he deemed appropriate. He asked if I would be able to continue to make trips and give speeches on behalf of the company.

"Sure," I said. "If you call me, I'll do it."

I developed a strategic paper for Neville Isdell when he was elected CEO in 2004 and made myself available to him for advice, but he never called. I returned the last check I received in that role to the company.

In those final few years at Coke, I started thinking seriously about what my life would look like once I left the company. The most intriguing opportunity was to use my knowledge to serve as an independent director on boards of global companies that had a reach similar to Coca-Cola's. I had known Carla Hills while she was the United States Secretary of Housing and Urban Development under Gerald Ford and the US Trade Representative under George H. W. Bush. She had served on a number of corporate boards, including Chevron's.

Carla chaired the governance nominating committee of Chevron's board and was the lead director at Chevron. After confirming my interest, Dave O'Reilly, CEO of Chevron, paid me a visit at my office in Atlanta.

Soon after one of my trips to the Davos World Economic Forum, Mary and I flew directly to San Francisco, where Chevron's headquarters were located. There, I was informed that I had been elected to the board. I immediately launched into the process of learning my new responsibilities as a director, which was fascinating because I was learning the ins and outs of a new business sector, the oil industry.

Separately, I had known a number of Chevron executives including George Kirkland, head of the upstream business, whom I had known from his years heading up the Chevron business in Nigeria. I felt that I could I help Chevron in Africa and that I would be among people who were internationalists who would appreciate my Africa experience as well as my other international relationships.

I enjoyed fourteen years on the Chevron board, including two years as chairman of the powerful executive compensation committee, which determines and approves executive earnings. I never stopped learning. At Stanford, I took a special course in executive compensation governance. I attended conferences and consulted experts in the field of executive compensation. Armed with that information, I led the committee to design the most competitive executive compensation plan in the oil industry. The position allowed me to become an expert in an area of corporate governance that was truly fascinating and new to me.

I served on other boards, including that of Coca-Cola Bottling Company Consolidated, a major bottler based in Charlotte, North Carolina. I had a great time helping to steer that company even deeper into markets throughout the Southeast. My experience serving on the Georgia Power board proved invaluable in my role serving on the board of National Life of Vermont, where I learned a tremendous amount about investing. In fact, Tom Williams, CEO of First Atlanta, who served with me on the Georgia Power board, recruited me to the board of National Life of Vermont.

The PGA Tour Golf Course Properties Board was and still is the most pleasant experience of all my corporate board work because it is all for charity and all volunteer. I was recruited to the board by PGA Tour commissioner Deane Beman, who invited Roberto to serve. Roberto, who limited his outside board participation to Ford Motor Company and Kodak, passed up the honor himself and recommended me. I accepted, but I didn't have the time needed to serve on the policy board and instead agreed to serve on a newly formed committee of the board called the Golf Course Properties Advisory Board. This committee was developing a nationwide network of PGA Tour tournament courses, which closely aligned with my background in real estate, marketing, and international business.

The PGA Tour board gave me access to all of the PGA Tour tournaments, including the 2003 President's Cup in South Africa that headlined Ernie Els and Tiger Woods in the closing playoff round. Both putted in stark darkness and made par on the final hole. Gary Player and Jack Nicklaus, the captains of the South Africa team and the US team, respectively, made one of the most memorable and noble gestures in the history of the sport: they declared the match a draw rather than extending the tournament into the next day.

As for joining the Cummins board, Alexis Herman nominated me in 2004, and subsequently Cummins CEO Tim Solso came to Atlanta and invited me to serve on his board. On one hand, the company was working its way out of some very difficult financial and operational challenges. On the other hand, it was also rapidly expanding in Mexico and China and had Africa on its radar screen. Cummins was a good fit.

On July 25, 2011, *The Wall Street Journal* published a story with the headline "Grading Directors by Stock Price." The *Journal* had asked a research firm to find the directors serving on the boards of at least two companies with the highest total shareholder returns among the S&P 500 for at least five years. I was among the twelve outside board directors specifically cited for my contributions to the bottom line of Cummins and Chevron.

The article, by Joann S. Lublin, reported that my work heading the Coca-Cola Company's Africa operation helped open doors for Cummins:

> After pushing Cummins to expand its tiny presence in Africa, Mr. Ware accompanied executives on a 2005 trip there. "We met a lot of people in Nigeria and Angola—including an ex-Coke bottler who became a joint venture partner," says Tom Linebarger, Cummins' president.
>
> Mr. Ware helped Cummins executives realize some African countries were "really starting to boom," Mr. Linebarger says. In 2010, Africa accounted for about $264 million of its sales compared with $13.2 billion worldwide. CEO Tim Solso has said he plans to quadruple sales in Africa to about $1 billion within five years.

In the end, all I ever wanted to be was a businessman.

Afterword

A Few Words about Lucky Feather

As a place, you could say the Ware family farm, now affectionately called Lucky Feather, all started with fifty acres purchased by the hard labor of all of the Ware sons and daughters in the late 1950s.

The first fifty acres were part of the land that my family sharecropped throughout my childhood. In 1980, I bought another 106 acres from a white man named Angelo Grenga.

Over the years, I continued to add acres as land became available. Today, the farm is 250 acres, 222 of which are preserved and managed as natural woodlands.

In an odd way, a visit in the 1970s to Robert W. Woodruff's 36,000-acre Ichauway Plantation in Southwest Georgia served to expand my ideas about land. Mr. Woodruff cultivated only 5,000 acres. The rest he preserved in its natural state so he could engage in his favorite pastime, quail hunting. After visiting Ichauway, I realized that land was not just about toil. It was also a source of enjoyment and beauty.

Unlike Ichauway, remnants of Lucky Feather's farming legacy are still evident. You can easily find piles of rocks in the woods, laid there by bare hands to clear fields for planting, and places where mules plowed terraces into the land to hold topsoil in place. The mule barn I built as a boy with my brother Eugene has been carefully preserved, as has the old family home that we built with our own hands in 1958.

Walking in these sacred woods, I sometimes catch an image of my mother spreading out a blanket for the smallest Wares at the end of a cotton row. Or I hear the pride in my father's voice while calling attention a field he worked as a boy. This is a place where Ma Fanny, Papa Joe, and Grandpa Pete all come back to life for me. It is here that I am left with no doubt that I stand on the shoulders of giants.

Instead of cotton fields, the land is now maintained as a tribute to the hard work, faith, courage, and strength of my ancestors as a multiresource treasure in perpetuity. It is first and foremost a home. It is a sanctuary. And it is a place for gatherings of friends, family, and future generations.

Now, access trails lead into hardwood and pine forests that are used for leisure activities such as game hunting, birding, wildlife viewing, hiking, and trail biking. Abundant wildlife—including deer, turkey, rabbits, red foxes, and squirrels—flourishes there. Our home overlooks Lois Wimberly Lake, which is a habitat on its own that helps to attract many species of animals in large numbers, as well as watering orchards and offering life-sustaining nutrition for wildlife. Among my own favorite pastimes is bird watching around Lois Lake during the early morning and early evening, when wrens, brown thrashers, cardinals, blue jays, tufted ducks, sparrows, and blue heron abound.

Next to our home is a pavilion that is used for family reunions, church and community gatherings, weddings, birthdays, and high school prom and graduation parties. I once hosted a reunion of Coca-Cola African and African American executives. More recently, I hosted a reception for my South African golf buddies, including Zanosi Kunene and Justice Dikgang Moseneke.

The central design features of the home include our vision of a place where our guests could enjoy the many pieces of art that we have collected from around the world. It is a living and growing art collection and a moveable feast of culture that rotates in and out of the Carl & Mary Ware Academic Center at Clark Atlanta University.

All this would seem like a fitting ending to my family story, but, of course, it's not over. This year, my granddaughter, Renita, blessed us with our first great-grandchild, a little boy named Tayden Alexander. He is the first of a new generation, and Lucky Feather is his birthright. Before long, he will begin to learn the names of its animals and trees. I have no doubt that Lucky Feather is where he will learn to hunt and fish. He will become—as we all have—a part of this land, and the land, in turn, will become a part of him.

When I talk about the farm, people often ask what I'm raising, as in what I farm here. I tell them I don't really grow much these days other than grapevines and fruit trees. Down at the farm, I like to tinker with my collection of old automobiles, which I've always had a passion for. For instance, I'm particularly fond of my 1956 Pontiac, which was given to us by Mary's aunt. Even today, that old car still has less than 50,000 miles on it, and I keep it in the barn. There's also my 1979 Cutlass, an automobile that I purchased brand new and later gave to my father. When Daddy passed, it came back to me, still in pretty good shape. Then there's my 1988 Buick Park Avenue and my 1991 Mercedes 600SL, both housed in the same building with my 1980-model Allis Chalmers tractor. I like to ride the tractor around to survey the land, something I look forward to doing with Tayden one day. Watching him the other day, wearing his little sunglasses in the infinity pool that overlooks Lois Lake, I could imagine my parents also smiling down at this happy domestic scene. We are blessed.

And now, the best tribute for last. I am blessed to have enjoyed a life filled with uplifting experiences. I talk a great deal about my life growing up in Oak Grove Baptist Church under the guidance of Pastor E. W. Lumpkin, who bellowed fire and brimstone every time he took the pulpit. But through the years I have been fortunate to count among my best friends a number of pastors including the late Rev. Dr. Cornelius Henderson and Rev. Walter Kimbrough, each of whom led historic Ben Hill United Methodist Church at different times.

My profound thanks to my current spiritual leader, the Rev. Dr. Kevin Murriel of Cascade United Methodist Church for the most extraordinary relationship of them all. Kevin is an author, a renowned Biblical scholar, and an inspiring pastor. Kevin and I also share close extended family relationships and a mentor-mentee relationship (works both ways), and we are both Kappas. On February 9, 2017, Mary and I were shocked and grief-stricken when we woke up that Monday morning and learned our only child, Timothy, had died at age 50. The first call I made was to Pastor Murriel, who was traveling on a church mission in Kenya. Despite his physical distance of some 8,000 miles, we were reassured that we would receive great comfort from our Cascade United Methodist family. The beautiful prayers of Rev. Joyce E. Banks Gross, the songs of lead musician Karen Lowery, and the eulogy of Rev. Kimbrough not only sustained us through those moments of grief, but also helped to inspire me to complete this memoir for Timothy.

ACKNOWLEDGMENTS

This book has been a journey that began shortly after I retired from the Coca-Cola Company in 2003. Working with author and former *USA Today* and *Atlanta Journal-Constitution* journalist John Head, I began to get my story down on paper. I had known John since his days as press secretary for Atlanta mayor Maynard Jackson, when I was Atlanta City Council president, in the late 1970s.

After we were well into the book process, John moved to Berkeley, California, so we conducted our work sessions when I was in town for my Chevron board meetings.

My former secretary at the Coca-Cola Company, Linda Wight, was also retired and living in Tennessee. Linda kept the process moving by transcribing interview tapes and organizing my papers for donation to the Atlanta University Center's Woodruff Library archives, where they would become a permanent part of the institution's collections documenting civil rights, race relations, education, literature, visual and performing arts, religion, politics, and social work.

With guidance from Barbara Masekela, South African ambassador and former chief of staff to Nelson Mandela, John and I completed a first draft of this book. It was a good story. You might even argue that it was a compelling story. Still, a nagging voice in the back of my mind told me it wasn't ready yet. I put the manuscript in the bottom drawer to steep, to allow more time to pass so that I might gain perspective on what it all meant. Besides, I was still adding to my story.

My career transitioned from day-to-day management at Coca-Cola to corporate governance on a national and international stage. I became a full-time director serving on the Council on Foreign Relations, Coca-Cola Bottling Company Consolidated, and the Coca-Cola Africa Foundation; as chairman of the Clark Atlanta University Board of Trustees; as a member of the boards advising the Atlanta Falcons Football Club, National Life of Vermont, and PGA Tour Golf Course Properties; and on the board of directors of Chevron and Cummins. Whew! A whole new career, not covered in my original manuscript.

By 2016, I was even more excited about telling my story. This time, I was fortunate to team up with a fellow Georgia native, author Sibley Fleming. An accomplished journalist in her own right, Sibley also happens to be the granddaughter of an old friend, *Atlanta Journal-Constitution* columnist Celestine Sibley. My goal wasn't to write a bestseller, I explained to Sibley, but to capture as complete an account of the historical events of my life as possible. I hoped that the book would inspire young African American business professionals, but I would also be happy if all we did was create an accurate record of my life for my family and future generations.

I am deeply grateful to Sibley for helping me tell my story and to our editorial assistant, Paulette Carter Jones, a Clark Atlanta University graduate and creator of the online magazine *Talk of Fame 101*. Our successful collaboration was made possible by many others, including not only such librarians and genealogists as Mrs. Jane Strain Ware, author of *The White Wares of Heard County, Georgia*, but also friends, family, and former colleagues, who contributed insight and facts through hundreds of hours of interviews and documentation. Sibley also introduced me to the book's initial copy editor, Edward Austin Hall, who brought a keen eye and a poet's sensibility to the text.

I'd like to acknowledge my older siblings Louise Ware Lynch, Mildred Ware Brown, and Walter Ware for their excellent memories and for transmitting the oral history of our family so that it could be committed to paper. I'd also like to thank my sister Barbara Brown, her daughter Audrey Williams Brown, and my nephew Derwin Ware. I would be remiss if I did not thank my niece Pam Ware, family genealogist and daughter of my brother Thomas.

Thank you to Robert Wood, former Coweta County Commissioner and childhood friend; Octavia Jenkins Mahone and Linette Ward, owners of Roscoe Jenkins Funeral Home in Newnan, Georgia; Jeff Bishop, executive director of the Newnan-Coweta Historical Society; and Gerald Olmstead, a longtime family friend. Thank you to Wilma Long Blanding, Clark College classmate and a founder of the Atlanta Student Movement.

Thank you to my old friends Charles "Chuck" Clifton Andrews

Jr. of San Antonio, Texas, and Eugene McCullers, former community affairs manager for Coca-Cola USA, and to my early readers Zenobia Janine Franklin and Diedra Vanderhall Alexander.

Thanks to my mentor Dr. Eldridge McMillan, retired head of the Southern Education Foundation and longest-serving member of the Board of Regents of the University System of Georgia. My gratitude to Dr. Wiley S. Bolden, who gave an extraordinary interview for the book before he passed, at age ninety-nine, on January 30, 2018.

Much appreciation to my South Africa friends, including Zanosi Kunene, chairman of Coca-Cola Fortune; Phil Gutsche, chairman of Coca-Cola Sabco; and leadership guru Eric Mafuna. All three men filled important gaps in my memory with dates, facts, and figures.

Many thanks to Chief Justice Dikgang Moseneke for his support and his help with matters regarding the Nelson Mandela documents herein.

My heartfelt gratitude to Archbishop Desmond Tutu for being an inspirational part of my work in South Africa and for encouraging me to tell my entire life story.

Many thanks to Father Matthew Esau, Esq., for his invaluable insight and for his stewardship of the EOF legacy.

My sincere thanks to Ingrid Saunders Jones, former senior vice president and chair of the Coca-Cola Foundation and current chair of the National Council of Negro Women. Thanks also go to prominent Atlanta attorney Larry Dingle, a partner of law firm Wilson, Brock and Irby. My sincere thanks also go to former US ambassador and Atlanta mayor Andrew Young for many hours of interviews and insight.

Thank you to Dave "Yummy" Simpson, Shelley Stanley, and Ira Turner, true professionals and lifelong golf buddies.

A special thanks to Clark Atlanta University president Dr. Ron Johnson and executive assistant Crista Monson for arranging an inspiring workroom in the Carl & Mary Ware Academic Center.

Thank you to Atlanta University Center Robert W. Woodruff Library CEO and director Loretta Parham and executive assistant Janice Wiggins for providing a productive workspace. Also, thanks to Renée Marie Cardelli-Contumelio, whose writing on midcentury black life in Pittsburgh public housing proved invaluable to recreating that era.

My appreciation to AUC Archives Research Center staff Sarah Tanner, Brittany Newberry, and the many capable grad students who assisted. The staff at the downtown Capital City Club also deserves a line for hospitality and providing a work environment that was happily enriched by coffee, Cokes, fried butter crackers, and hot gumbo on cold days.

And now, the best tribute for last. I am blessed to have enjoyed a life filled with uplifting experiences. I talk a great deal about my life growing up in Oak Grove Baptist Church under the guidance of Pastor E. W. Lumpkin, who bellowed fire and brimstone every time he took the pulpit. But through the years I have been fortunate to count among my best friends a number of pastors including the late Rev. Dr. Cornelius Henderson and Rev. Walter Kimbrough, each of whom led historic Ben Hill United Methodist Church at different times.

My profound thanks to my current spiritual leader, the Rev. Dr. Kevin Murriel of Cascade United Methodist Church for the most extraordinary relationship of them all. Kevin is an author, a renowned Biblical scholar, and an inspiring pastor. Kevin and I also share close extended family relationships and a mentor-mentee relationship (works both ways), and we are both Kappas. On January 9, 2017, Mary and I were shocked and grief-stricken when we woke up that Monday morning and learned our only child, Timothy, had died at age 50. The first call I made was to Pastor Murriel, who was traveling on a church mission in Kenya. Despite his physical distance of some 8,000 miles, we were reassured that we would receive great comfort from our Cascade United Methodist family. The beautiful prayers of Rev. Joyce E. Banks Gross, the songs of lead musician Karen Lowery, and the eulogy of Rev. Kimbrough not only sustained us through those moments of grief, but also helped to inspire me to complete this memoir for Timothy.

INDEX

ACTION Housing (Allegheny Council to Improve Our Neighborhood), 60-62, 66, 74-75

Activism, 48-49, 50, 76, 107, 193, 219, 258

Addis Ababa bottling plant, 130

Adesanya, Bashorun, 124-125

Affirmative action, 98, 108, 249

Africa Bank, 175

Africa Group of Coca-Cola Company, 57, 205-213, 222-223, 227, 244, 248, 251, 255

African American Institute, 148

African Americans, anti-lynching legislation, 193; Atlanta Police Department, 85-87; citizenship, 6; Coca-Cola Company bottlers, 112-116; graduate degree access, 194; Jim Crow laws, 1, 6, 9, 12, 28-29, 121, 156, 173; Ku Klux Klan, 4, 7, 8, 16, 31-32; lynching, 4-9, 193; racial profiling, 86; See also specific people; student movement, 48-49; voting, 3-7, 48, 77, 123

African National Congress, apartheid, 132; communism, 155; Dakar Conference, 180; Institute for Democratic Alternatives in South Africa (IDASA), 179; leaders and leadership, 143, 144, 178; Mandela association, 131, 184-186; Mozambique support, 232; national anthem, 202; nationalizing industry, 212; PepsiCo, 229; Reconstruction and Development Programme, 213; TransAfrica, 120; violence, 132, 135

African National Congress (ANC), Eminent Persons Group (EPG), 169-170

Africare, 148, 159

Afrikaans, 122, 136

Afrikaners, 136, 147, 182-183

Ahmad-Lewellyn, Shahara, 114, 116

Air Atlanta, 196

Aldridge, Delores, 196

Alfa Laval of Sweden, 172

Aliker, Martin, 234

Allegheny Council to Improve Our Neighborhood (ACTION Housing), 60-62, 66, 74-75

Allen, Herb, 229, 254

Allen, Ivan Jr., 51, 76, 82, 116

Allen, Sadie, 32-33, 44

Amalgamated Beverage Canners, 119, 164

Amalgamated Beverage Industries (ABI), 167

American Banking Institute Internship program, 54

American Express, 196

American Missionary Association, 193

Amin, Idi, 235

Andrews, Chuck, 117

Andrews, Harold, 55

Angelou, Maya, 201

Anglo American Corporation, 179

Angola, 126, 162, 169, 237-238, 270

Anheuser-Busch, 107

Annan, Kofi, 267

Anti-Apartheid Act (US), 171

Apartheid, Coca-Cola disinvestment, 151-166, 169, 205-213; Coca-Cola operations, 112; de Klerk, 182-184; effects, 126; Eminent Persons Group (EPG) probe, 175-177; "honorary whites," 135, 137-138, 161; international sports participation, 224; Leeds Castle Meeting,

169-179; Sullivan Principles, 120; US economic sanctions, 170-171
Apollo Theater, 117
Arnall, Alton Wynn, 4
Arnall, Ellis, 5
Arnall Mills, 4, 20
Arrington, Marvin, 196
Asiko, William, 226
Atlanta Action Forum, 88-89
Atlanta Board of Aldermen, 76, 77
Atlanta Board of Education, 82
Atlanta Charter Commission, 80
Atlanta City Council, African American members, 48; city contracts, 88-92; members, 196; president, 93, 94, 109; Carl Ware election, 80, 81-82; Carl Ware resignation, 100
Atlanta Constitution, 36, 165
Atlanta Daily World, 30
Atlanta Falcons, 263
Atlanta Gas Light Company, 55
Atlanta Hawks, 94
Atlanta Housing Authority (AHA), 78-80, 93, 94
Atlanta Journal-Constitution, 29, 202
Atlanta Life Insurance Company, 112
Atlanta Model Cities program, 75
Atlanta Police Department (ADP), 85-87
Atlanta Student Movement, 48-49
Atlanta University, 48-49, 49, 188-189, 191, 192-196
Atlanta University Center (AUC), 188, 192, 196
Atlanta Urban League, 97
Atlanta's Berlin Wall, 1, 76
Austin, J. Paul, 82, 84-85, 85, 103, 108, 140, 172
Australia, 175, 202
Ayoub, Sam, 129

Babangida, Ibrahim Badamasi, 182
Bacote, Clarence, 192, 194
Bantu Homeland Citizenship Act of 1970a, 121, 136

Baptism, 26-27
Baragwanath Hospital, 141
Baranco, Juanita, 264
Barber, A.C., 5
Barlow Rand, 175, 179
Barnes, Margaret Anne, 4
Barnes, Roy, 263
Baseball, 12-13, 33
Basketball, 42-43
Beasley, Annie, 12
Beasley, Besora, 11-12
Beasley, John, 11
Belgium contamination crisis, 254-255, 263
Beman, Deane, 269
Benn Hill United Methodist Church, 196, 273
Benson, George, 67
Berkshire Hathaway, 245
Berry, George, 90
Beverage Digest, 247
Bhorat, Ebrahim, 159
Big Bethel African Methodist Church, 192, 196
Black Management Forum, 143, 159
Black Panther Party, 67, 70
Black Sash, 170
Blakey, Art, 67
Blanding, Roland, 146
Blanding, Wilma Long, 276
Blandingburg, Leno, 44
Blank, Arthur, 263
Blossomgame, Doshia, 76
Blossomgame, Doshia "Miss Doshia," 55
Boesak, Allan, 143, 157-158, 179, 185
Bohannon, Hamilton "Hamp," 42
Bohannon, John "Fris," 5
Bolden, Wiley S., 56-58, 80
Bond, Julian, 48
Bonner, Fred, 43
Boone, Charlie, 100-101
Boraine, Alex, 159, 180
Borders, William Holmes, 74
Botha, P.W., 120, 157-159, 169-170, 177

Botswana, 126, 135, 162, 169
Bottlers. See Coca-Cola Company; specific bottling companies
Boy Scouts, 264
Boycotts, 76, 107, 219, 258
Brand, Christo, 215
Brawley, James P., 52, 73, 189-191
British Petroleum, 172
Broadnax, Walter, 197-198
Brooks, Stella Brewer, 52
Brown, Ben, 48, 77
Brown, Ernest "Buster," 7-9, 51
Brown, Stella, 52
Brown v. Board of Education of TRopeka (1954), 194
Brown, Willie, 200
Bryant Gumbel/Walt Disney World Celebrity Golf Tournament, 262
Buffett, Warren, 1, 229, 245, 254
Buhari, Muhammadu, 124
Burger King Corporation, 107
Burrell, Tom, 103, 104
Burson, Harold, 149
Burson-Marstellar, 149
Bush, George H.W., 113, 199, 268
Business Roundtable, 186
Buthelezi, Mangosuthu Gatsha, 136, 157
Buthelezi, Mathole, 136
BVS Transport Consultants, 218
Byrd, Carolyn Baldwin, 253

C&S Bank, 53, 94
Cain, Jim, 61
Caine, Michael, 207
Calhoun, Robert, 5
Cambodia, 237
Cameroon, 242
Canadian Coca-Cola, 222
Carl & Mary Ware Academic Center at Clark Atlanta University, 197-199, 267, 272
Carnegie Institute of Technology (Carnegie Mellon University), 57, 59-62
Carter, Jimmy, 48, 93, 112, 148

Carver Homes, 78
Cascade United Methodist Church, 273
Cash, Johnny, 4
Catherine of Aragon (queen of England), 174
CBS Atlanta, 73
Central High School, 42-44
Central Methodist Gardens, 74
Central United Methodist Church, 74
Chafin, Clinton, 85
Chaskalson, Arthur, 147, 158
Chevron, 236, 268
Chikane, Frank, 122
China, 238, 260, 269
Christian Educator, 190
CIA, 157
Citizens Against Slum Housing (CASH), 60-62
Citizens Trust Bank, 89, 193
Citizenship, 6
Civil rights, 3-7, 48, 77, 123
Civil Rights Act of, 50, 57, 1957, 1964
Civil War, 192
Clark-Atlanta University, 56
Clark Atlanta University (CAU), 64, 196-199, 206, 262, 267, 272
Clark College, alumni, 71, 76, 109; Board of Trustees, 188; Committee on the Appeal for Human Rights, 49; grants, 195; history, 190-191; presidents, 73; reputation, 52-53; student movement, 48-49
Clark College Legacy (Brawley), 190
Clark, John Paul, 76
Clark, Laron "Daddy Clark," 55
Clark, Mary Alice. See Ware, Mary Alice Clark
Clark Theological Seminary, 190
Cleaver, Eldridge, 67
Clement, Bill, 112
Clinton, Bill, 158, 198, 199, 235
Clinton, Hillary, 198
CNN, 264
Coca-Cola Bottling Company Consolidated, 269

Coca-Cola Bottling Mpumalanga, 223
Coca-Cola Company, Africa Group,
205-213, 222-223, 227, 244, 248,
251, 255, 257; Belgium contamination crisis, 254-255, 263; Board of
Directors, 227-229, 267; bottling
companies, 112-116, 123-127, 130,
133-134, 138, 167, 216-226, 269;
Dakar Conference, 180; disinvestment in South Africa, 148-149,
151-166, 169, 205-221; Diversity
Advisory Council, 250, 256, 258,
260; Human Resources Task
Force, 259-260; Jesse Jackson activism, 107-112; lawsuits, 249-251,
257-258; Leeds Castle Meeting,
169-179; management, 84-85, 89-
90, 100, 208, 267; Minute Maid,
119, 121, 236; museum, 265; Operation PUSH (People United to
Save Humanity), 107-112, 120; racial discrimination, 247-251, 257-
258; reinvestment in South Africa,
216-231; See also Apartheid, specific employees and managers;
South Africa; specific bottling
companies; specific subsidiaries;
sports sponsorships, 216, 224-225,
241, 262, 266; Sullivan Principles,
120; training programs, 101-103,
221, 225-226; Louise Ware employment, 82
Coca-Cola Femsa, 231
Coca-Cola Fortune, 219
Coca-Cola Foundation, 116-118, 188,
195, 233, 260, 265
Coca-Cola International, 231
Coca-Cola Learning Centers, 266
Coca-Cola Sabco, 167, 217-222, 231-
237
Coca-Cola South Africa, 225
Coca-Cola Table Tennis Festival (Ni-
geria), 241
Coca-Cola University, 102, 221
Cochran, Johnnie Jr., 200, 259
Cole, Brenda, 200

Cole, Thomas W., 189-190, 194, 197,
200, 201
Coleman, Bill, 113
Colgate-Palmolive, 172
Columbia Pictures, 114
Committee of Ten, 143
Committee on the Appeal for Human
Rights, 49
Commonwealth Eminent Persons
Group (EPG), 169-170, 175-177
Commonwealth of Nations, 169
Confederate flag, 263-264
Confederate generals, 109-110
Congressional Black Caucus, 85, 109,
148, 266
Consolidated Gold Fields, 172
Consumer Behavior, 120, 143
Conway, Andrew, 247
Coombs, Fletcher, 97
Cooper, Ralph, 173, 203
Corbett, Michael, 215
Cordy, Tom, 188, 195, 196
Cosby, Bill, 114-116
Cote d'Ivoire, 242
Cotton, 5, 20, 52
Council on Foundations, 117, 159
Cox, John, 89, 97
Crawford, Vernon, 195
Crossroad-KTC Holocaust, 170
Cruver, Wilbur, 44
Cuba, 238
Cummings, Alex, 241
Cummins Foundation, 116-117, 269-
270

Daft, Doug, 203, 251, 254-256, 258-
259, 262-262, 266, 267
Dahlberg, Bill, 106
Dakar Conference, 179-180
Daley, Richard, 66
Dalzell Place, 65, 71
Daniels, Grandison B., 192-193
Davis, Amanda, 73, 258-259
Davis, Art, 59
Davis, Brant, 148, 149, 152, 159, 204
Davis, Charlie, 98

Davis, Myrtle, 196
Davis, Ossie, 51
Davis, Ovid, 84, 89, 103
Davos World Economic Forum, 268
Dawson, Harold, 89
de Klerk, F.W., 182-185
Dee, Ruby, 51
Delta Airlines, 83, 89, 90, 97, 103, 142
Delta Beverages, 133-134
Democratic National Committee, 48
Detroit riots, 66
Diana (Princess of Wales), 207
Dingle, Larry, 85, 97
Discrimination. See Segregation and
    discrimination; African Americans
Diversity Advisory Council, 250, 256,
    258
Dobbs, John Wesley, 77-78, 112
Dodson, F.A., 41
Douglass, Frederick, 193, 198
Dove, Pearlie, 52
Dubois, W.E.B., 193
Dunston, Edmond, 13

East Lake Meadows, 78
Eastwood, Stuart, 131, 236
Ebenezer Baptist Church, 74
Ebony (magazine), 113, 197
Edmunds, Art, 69-72
Education, Central High School, 42-
    44; Coca-Cola management train-
    ing, 101-103, 221; Harvard Uni-
    versity International Senior Man-
    agement Program, 205-206;
    Mount Zion Elementary, 31-33;
    racism, 31-32; Roscoe Elementary,
    33; See also specific educational in-
    stitutions; segregation and discrim-
    ination, 32-33, 57-58, 194; South
    Africa managers, 225-226; specific
    institutions and schools; statistics
    on black college graduates, 52;
    Ware, Ulas B., 14
Egbe, Bill, 241
Eisenhower, Dwight D., 33
Elder, John, 53

Els, Ernie, 269
Eminent Persons Group (EPG), 169-
    170, 175-177
Emory University, 148, 193, 196, 199,
    260
England, 1, 206-213
Equal Justice Initiative, 6
Equal Opportunity Foundation, 154-
    161, 159, 164
Equal Opportunity Fund, 215
Equitable Real Estate Investment, 196
Ernst & Young, 221-222, 245
Erving, Julius "Dr. J," 115-116
Erwin, Alec, 187
Ethiopia, 120, 122, 126, 129-130, 231,
    236
ExxonMobil, 236

Fair Housing Act of, 62, 1968
Fayard, Gary, 259
Fedco Foods Corporation, 113-114
Federal Housing Administration, 74
Felder, James (Jim), 53, 109
Ferrari, Eddie, 131
FIFA World Cup, 224
Fifteenth Amendment, 6
First Atlanta, 269
First Corporate Merchant Bank, 223
First Georgia Bank, 98
Fisk Cottage, 190
Fisk University, 193
Flamingo Bottlers, 234
Flores, Tony, 107
Forbes, 113
Ford Foundation, 69
Ford, Gerald, 268
Ford Motor Company, 269
Fountain, Hiawatha, 67
Fourteenth Amendment, 6
Fowler, Wyche, 82, 85, 93
Fox 5 Atlanta, 258-259
Franklin, Allen, 106, 196
Franklin, John Hope, 193
Fraser, Malcolm, 175
Fraternal Order of Police, 87
Frazier, Jim, 72

Freedmen's Aid Society, 190
Freedom National Bank, 114
Freeman, Cody, 5
Frenette, Charlie, 241
Frontline States, 169
Funderburg, Owen, 97

Gammon Theological Seminary, 192
Gary, Willie, 259
Gatorade, 261
Geechee, 19-20
General Motors, 85, 120, 165-166, 172
Georgia Aquarium, 265
Georgia Association of Black Elected
    Officials (GABEO), 94-95
Georgia Gulf Corporation, 196
Georgia-Pacific, 89
Georgia Power Company, 17, 89, 103,
    104, 106, 196, 269
Georgia State University, 98, 102-103
Georgia Sunshine Law, 88
Georgia Tech, 50
Gerwel, Jakes, 158, 187, 215
Ghana, 238-241
Gladden, Joe, 259
Glover, Danny, 200
Godwin, Lamond, 53, 195, 196
Goizueta, Olguita, 172-173
Goizueta, Roberto, Atlanta ACTION
    Forum, 89; boards of directors ser-
    vice, 269; Coca-Cola Company
    growth, 108, 119, 257; Coca-Cola
    Foundation, 117; Coca-Cola in
    South Africa, 119, 123, 143, 151,
    156, 172-179; death, 245-246; di-
    versity attitude, 260; Leeds Castle
    meeting, 171-179, 244; legacy, 255;
    Nelson Mandela relationship, 202-
    203, 217; Operation PUSH, 1;
    Peachtree Golf Club membership,
    115-114; public relations advisor,
    149; successor, 254
Goldman, Emanuel, 256
Goldston, Nate, 206
Golf Course Properties Advisory
    Board, 269

Good, Johnny B., 93
Gordimer, Nadine, 147
Gourmet Services, 206
Grady Homes, 78
Grady Memorial Hospital, 46-47, 49-
    50
Graham, Lewis, 86
Graves, Earl, 229
Great Depression, 191
Green, Ernie, 112
Grenga, Angelo, 104-105, 271
Griffith, Andy, 4
Gross, Joyce E. Banks, 273
GSPIA (University of Pittsburgh
    Graduate School of Public & In-
    ternational Affairs), 65-67, 74
Guber, Peter, 200
Guillaume, Robert, 200
Guthman, Richard, 93
Gutsche, Phil, 167, 232-234, 236

Haggai, Tom, 255
Haley, Leon, 69, 72
Hall, Arsenio, 200
Hall, Mike, 208-209
Hall, Prince, 5, 46, 74, 123
Hall, William "Hook," 42
Halle, Claus, 130, 143-144, 154, 171
Ham, Clifford, 66
Hamby, Garth, 173, 178
Hamilton, Grace Towns, 97, 194
Hamilton, Martha, 256
Hamilton, Robin, 168
Hardy, Willie T., 45
Haregot, Bereket, 236
Hart, Barbara, 67
Hart, Chuck, 67
Hartsfield International Airport, 83, 90
Hartsfield, William B., 51, 84
Harvard University's International
    Senior Management Program, 205-
    206
Haygood, Atticus G., 191
Heath, Edward, 175, 177
Henderson, Cornelius, 196, 273
Henderson, Vivian, 73

284

Hendricks, Cliff, 67
Henkel of Germany, 172
Henry VIII (king of England), 174
Herman, Alexis, 112, 198, 259, 269
Herndon Homes, 78
Highveld Coca-Cola Bottling Company, 219
Hill, Genevieve, 79
Hill, Jesse, 50, 89, 97, 113
Hiller, Richard, 113-114
Hills, Carla, 268
HIV/AIDS, 266
H.J. Russell & Company, 91
Holder, Bob, 106
Hollis, Michael, 196
Hollowell, Donald L., 97
Holmes, Alfred "Tup," 77
Holmes, Hamilton, 48
Holyfield, Evander, 201
Home Depot, 265
Hong Kong–United States Business Council, 266
"Honorary whites," 135, 137, 161
Hooks, Benjamin, 109
Hose, Sam, 7
Houston, Thomas, 44
Houston, Whitney, 229, 230
Howard University, 193
HUD, 62, 67, 74, 75, 79
Hugh Spalding Hospital, 49
Human Resources Task Force at Coca-Cola Company, 259-260
Hunter-Gault, Charlayne, 48
Hunter, John, 200, 202-203, 223, 232
Hyde, Rex, 34, 37

Iams, John, 170
IBM, 172
Ichauway Plantation, 271
Ide, Bill, 93
Ikekube, Laolu, 124-128
Inkatha Freedom Party, 137, 154, 157
Inman, John, 86-87
Inner City Broadcasting Corporation, 117

Institute for Democratic Alternatives in South Africa (IDASA), 179
Integration. See Segregation and discrimination
Interdenominational Theological Center, 49
International Cadbury Schweppes, 172
International Grocers Association (IGA), 255
International Monetary Fund (IMF), 211, 240
Isdell, Neville, 203, 208-210, 212, 222, 230, 255, 267-268
Ivester, Doug, 233, 245-246, 250, 253-254, 257
Ivory Coast, 207

Jackson, Esther, 52
Jackson, Ira, 87
Jackson, Jackie, 109
Jackson, Jesse, 107, 159
Jackson, Jesse Jr., 109
Jackson, Maynard Holbrook, affirmative action, 89; assistants, 112; Coca-Cola rehiring Carl Ware, 256; death, 92; Georgia Sunshine Law, 88; Hartsfield International Airport, 91-92; inclusive policies, 100; Nelson Mandela honorary degree, 201, 203; mayoral candidacy, 80; Urban Fellows Program, 96; Carl Ware relationship, 94, 251
Jacob, John, 206
Jansen, Martin, 233
Jenkins, Octavia, 9
Jennings Supermarket, 41
Jet (magazine), 113
Jim Crow laws, 1, 6, 9, 12, 24, 28-29, 121, 156, 173
Johannesburg Stock Exchange, 164
Johnson & Johnson, 172
Johnson, James Weldon, 193
Johnson, John, 109, 113
Johnson, Johnny, 75
Johnson, Juan, 253
Johnson, Leroy, 50, 97

Johnson, Lyndon B., 62, 75
Johnson, Magic, 229
Johnson Publishing Company, 113
Jones Hill United Methodist Church, 19, 22, 137
Jones, Ingrid Saunders, Africa Group, 244; Atlanta City government, 96-98; Carl & Mary Ware Academic Center at Clark Atlanta University, 198; Coca-Cola Foundation, 117-118; Coke/PUSH agreement, 112; Equal Opportunity Fund, 164; manager at Coca-Cola, 253; Desmond Tutu honorary degree, 200
Jones, Larry, 258
Jones Quarter, 16-18, 21
Jonesboro Heights, 78
Jordan, Pallo, 215
Jordan, Vernon, 109
Joseph, James, 116, 159
J.T. Knight's Scrap Yard, 34
Julius, Corey, 138-139

kaDinuzulu, Magogo, 136
kaDinuzulu, Solomon (king), 136-137
Kahn, Meyer, 167
Kappa Alpha Psi, 56
Kathrada, Ahmed, 155
Kelley, Mary Francis, 43
Kennedy, John F., 53
Kent, Muhtar, 209
Kentucky Fried Chicken, 107
Kenya, 122, 129, 210, 231, 233, 236, 242
Kenyatta, Jomo, 130
Keough, Don, Africa Group management, 204-205; Coca-Cola in South Africa, 119, 123, 140, 143, 151, 156, 165; Jesse Jackson activism, 108-109; Leeds Castle Meeting, 171; legacy, 255; management style, 208, 255, 257; operating committee meetings, 212; Philadelphia Coca-Cola Bottling Company, 114; retirement, 245; Carl Ware mentor, 103

Kessler department store, 29
Kilimanjaro Holdings, 168, 219
Killingsworth, J. Dekoven, 46
Kimbraugh, Walter, 273-274
King & Spalding, 93
King, Coretta Scott, 163, 201
King, Don, 113
King, Lonnie, 48
King, Martin Luther Jr., 49, 71, 81, 88, 90, 100, 111, 186, 265
King, Martin Luther Sr., 74
Kirk, Rahsaan Roland, 67
Kirkland, George, 268
Kirkland, J.W., 5, 39
Kirshman, Neville, 222-223
Knox, Simmie, 198
Kodak, 269
Ku Klux Klan, 4, 7, 8, 16, 31-32
Kunene, Keith, 218, 220
Kunene, Zanosi, 223, 272
Kuse, James R., 196

LaBord, Susie, 79
Land, A.J., 19
Land purchases, 33-40, 104-105
Lane, Mills B., 53
Lawrence, David, 60, 223
Lawsuits, 249-251, 257-258
Lee, Spike, 73
Leeds Castle Meeting, 169-179
Leon, Kenny, 73
Leonard, Sugar Ray, 200
Lesotho, 162-163, 169
Lewis, Dave, 138-139
Lewis, John G., 74, 201
Liberty Baptist Church, 11
Lincoln University, 193
Linebarger, Tom, 270
Linver, Sandy, 227
Little Red School House program, 265
Little Rock Nine, 111
Llewellyn, J. Bruce, 113, 115-116, 221, 223
Lois Ware Lake, 105, 272
Long, Carolyn, 48

Long Walk to Freedom (Mandela), 121
Long, Wilma (Blanding), 48
Los Angeles Times, 165, 254
Lovelace, Bobby, 25
Lowery, Joseph E., 74, 109, 201
Lowery, Karen, 273
Lublin, Joann S., 270
Lucas, C. Payne, 148, 159
Lucky Feather, 105, 271-272
Lugar, Dick, 171
Lugar, Richard "Dick," 95
Lumpkin, E.W., 273
Lynching, 4-9, 193

Machel, Graca, 234
Machel, Samora, 232-234
Macozoma Sakumzi "Saki," 226
Maddox, Jim, 80-81
Maddox, Lester, 50-51
Mafuna, Eric, 120, 139, 143, 148-149, 171, 218
Makhathini, Johnny, 144, 147, 179
Makuno, Paul, 130
Malcolm X, 67
Malcolm X: Struggle for Freedom (movie), 67
Mandela, Nelson, advisors, 215; African National Congress association, 131, 184-186; autobiography, 121; communism, 186; Goizueta relationship, 217; governance of South Africa, 158; honorary degree, 200; imprisonment, 131, 138, 155, 169, 183-186; inauguration, 214-217; nationalizing industry, 212; Pepsi-Co, 229; Rubgy World Cup, 225; Carl Ware relationship, 203, 212, 214-217
Mandela, Winnie, 181, 185
Manuel, Trevor, 187
Maponya, Marina, 140
Maponya, Richard, 140, 143, 167-168
Marcus, Bernie, 265
Marshall, Thurgood, 198
Martin Luther King Jr. Village, 74

Masekela, Barbara, 144, 201, 203
Masons, 5, 46, 74, 123
Massell, Sam, 75, 77, 80, 87
Mauritius, 162
Mays, Willie, 33
Mbeki, Govan, 155, 187, 214-215
Mbeki, Thabo, 122, 144, 155-157, 179
Mboeni, Tito, 187
McClendon, Betty, 44
McClure, Bill, 146
McDonald, Norma, 84
McDonald's Corporation, 204
McHenry, Don, 147, 157, 163, 166, 184-186, 220, 229
Mchunu, Ernest, 139, 143, 159, 171, 181
McMillan, Eldridge, 188, 195, 196
Mehri, Cyrus, 249
Mellon National Bank, 63
Mellon, Richard King, 60
Mellow Yellow, 102
Mengi, Reginald, 233
Mercer University, 193
Merrick, John, 193
Merrill Lynch Global Securities, 256
Methodist Episcopal Church, 190
Metro Atlanta Chamber of Commerce, 263
Mexico, 269
Meyer, Fred, 139-140, 144, 181
Mgadi, Subu, 226
Midnight Star, 25
Millard, Charlie, 116
Miller, J.C., 39
Miller, Zell, 201
Minkhorst, Robert, 263
Minute Maid, 119, 121, 236
Mitchell, Danny, 48
Mitchell, Lester "Mitch," 67
Mitchell, M.C., 39, 42
Mitchell, Sandra, 71
Mitchell, Wade, 53
Mkapa, Benjamin, 233
Mncube, Gertrude, 158
Mobil, 172
Mocumbi, Pascal, 232

Mogoerane, Simon, 135
Mohanoe, Pali Francis, 158
Morehouse College, 48, 49, 50, 59, 86, 192
Morris Brown College, 49, 192
Morrison, Chuck, 166
Morrison, Robert, 262
Moseneke, Dikgang, 272
Mosololi, Jerry, 135
Motaung, Marcus, 135
Moten, Dan, 8
Motlana, Nthato, 143, 147
Motsuenyane, Sam, 143, 175
Mount Zion Baptist Church, 16
Mount Zion Elementary, 31-33
Moye, Rute, 226
Mozambique, 126, 162-163, 169, 231-232
Mozambique Children's Fund, 232
Mozley Park, 67
Mswati III (king of Swaziland), 162-163
Mugabe, Robert, 132
Mugabe, Sally, 132
Muldawer & Patterson, 75
Muldawer, Paul, 75
Murder, 4-9, 51, 86
Murder in Coweta County (Barnes), 4
Murriel, Kevin, 273
Museveni, Yoweri, 234-236
Mutizwa, Joe, 133-134
Mutual Federal Savings and Loan Association, 193

Nairobi Bottlers, 130
Namibia, 163, 184-185, 230
NatBev, 217, 218-220, 223
National African Federated Chamber of Commerce, 144, 175
National Association for the Advancement of Colored People (NAACP), 10, 109, 193, 250
National Beverage Services, 164, 239
National Center for Civil and Human Rights, 265

National Conference of Black Mayors, 148
National Conference of Black State Legislators, 148
National League of Cities, 95, 171
National Life of Vermont, 269
National Urban League, 10, 109, 206, 250
Naude, Beyers, 143, 147
Ndegwa, Philip, 131
Neighborhood Reinvestment Corporation (NeighborWorks America), 62
Nepal, 237
Nestle of Switzerland, 172
New African Investments Limited, 147
New York Times, 159, 165, 245, 253
New York University, 193
Newnan Colored Hospital, 43
Newnan Hospital, 43, 46, 123
Newton, Bill, 171-172
Nicklaus, Jack, 269
Nigeria, 122, 175, 182, 210, 241-242, 268, 270
Nigerian Bottling Company (NBC), 123-126
Nkomo, Joshua, 132
Nobel Prize, 90, 147, 149
North Carolina Mutual Life Insurance Company, 193
Nujoma, Sam, 185
Nunn-Lugar Act, 95
Nunn, Sam, 95, 196, 201

Oak Grove Baptist Church, 5, 26-28, 44, 46, 55, 82, 123, 124, 273
Obasanjo, Olusegun, 175
Office of Economic Opportunity internship, 57, 59-62
Oil, 123
Olympic Games, 224, 225, 241, 242, 264, 266
Onque, Earle, 67
Operation Equality, 69-70
Operation PUSH (People United to Save Humanity), 107-112, 120, 250, 260

Opportunities Industrialization Centers of America, 85-87, 120
O'Reilly, Dave, 268

Paige, Alfonzo, 22, 30, 39
Parks, P.H., 191
Parks, Rosa, 194
Patrick, Deval, 206
Patterson, Pickens Andrew, 74, 75
Peachtree Asset Management, 195
Peachtree Golf Club, 115-116
Peanuts, 20
Peniston, Ellis, 4
People United to Save Humanity. See Operation PUSH (People United to Save Humanity)
PepsiCo, 228-231, 260
Perdue, Sonny, 264
Perry Homes, 78
Perry, William, 53
PGA Tour Golf Course Properties Board, 269
Philadelphia Coca-Cola Bottling Company, 114-115, 167, 221, 223
Philippines, 265
Philips Arena, 264
Philips Consumer Electronics for North America, 263
Pickard, Marc, 84
Pickrick Restaurant, 50
Pienaar, Francois, 225
Pillsbury International, 241
Player, Gary, 269
Poitier, Sidney, 200
Police, 85-87
Poll tax, 5
Population Registration Act of 1950a, 122
Porter, Jimmy, 71
Portman, John, 89
Potts, J.H., 3-4
Potts, Lamar, 3-7, 19
Powell, Colin, 1
"Prayer rock," 22
President's Award, 199
Price, Helen Smith, 118

Prince Hall Masons, 5, 46, 74, 123
Princeton University, 57
Profiling, 86
Purcell, Lester, 78, 80
Puskar, George, 196

Quaker Oats, 261-262
Quilting, 39

Racial profiling, 86
Racism. See Segregation and discrimination; African Americans; Apartheid; Ku Klux Klan
Rainbow Coalition, 159
Ramphal, Shridath, 176
Rawlings, Jerry, 238-240
Reagan, Ronald, 41, 108, 157, 171, 204
Reconstruction and Development Programme of ANC, 213
Reid, Jacque, 73
Religion. See specific churches
Richardson, Dorothy Mae, 60-62
Riley, Pat, 200
Riordan, Richard, 200
Riots, 66, 72, 95
Road Dogs, 146
Robert W. Woodruff Library, 193, 195
Robinson, Ann, 194
Robinson, Jackie, 33, 114
Robinson, James, 73-74
Robinson, Jim, 75
Robinson, Randall, 148
Rooney, Patrick, 134
Roosevelt, Theodore, 193
Roscoe Elementary, 33
Roscoe Jenkins Funeral Home, 8-9
Rosen, Peter, 148, 160
Rosholt, A.M., 175
Royston, Graham, 222-223
Rugby World Cup, 224
Rukwava, Charles, 133, 226
Runcie, A.K., 163
Russell, Herman, 89, 97, 106, 109, 113
Rutledge, Pinky, 96

Sabco, 167, 217-222, 231-237

Sandford, Mary, 79
Santos, Eduardo, 238
Saudi Arabia, 123
Savimbi, Jonas, 238
Scherer, Bob, 106
Sebukema, Davis, 235
Segregation and discrimination, Atlanta city contracts, 88-92, 98; banking, 70, 98-99; Civil Rights Act of 1964a, 51; Coca-Cola Company, 247-251; education, 32-33, 57-58, 194; hotels, 64; housing, 60-62, 69-70, 76; Jim Crow laws, 1, 6, 9, 12, 24, 28-29, 121, 156, 173; lawsuits, 249-251, 257-258; medical care, 43, 49-50; mortgages, 70; police, 85; racial profiling, 86; restaurants, 29
Selassie, Haile I, 129
Seldon, Henry, 44
Sempala, Edith, 234
Senegal, 10
Senior citizen centers, 80
Seven7-Eleven, 107
Shagari, Shehu Usman Aliyu, 123-124
Sharecropping, 23-26
Sharp Advertising, 104
Sharp, Bill, 103-104
Shell Oil Company, 185
Singh, Prittipal, 131
Sisulu, Mlungisi, 158
Sisulu, Sheila, 158
Sisulu, Walter, 155, 158
Sit-ins, 50
Slavery, 10, 23, 121, 193
Smith College, 148
Smith, Gambrell & Russell, 196
Smith, Martha, 46
Smith, Paul, 23-24, 34, 37, 41
Smith, Roger B., 172
Smith, Sam, 6
Smith, Ted, 74
Smith, Willie George, 45
Smuts, Jan, 136
Snyder, David, 148
Sobhuza II (king of Swaziland), 162

Solso, Tim, 269
Sons of Calvary, 45
Sony Entertainment, 200
Sorrell, Doug, 205
South Africa, Afrikaans, 122; apartheid, 112, 119-122, 126, 135, 137-138; Coca-Cola Company disinvestment, 136-140, 151-166, 171, 205-213; Coca-Cola Company reinvestment, 216-231; corruption, 229; democratic elections, 202, 211, 213; labor strikes, 228; Sullivan Principles, 120, 175, 177
South African Breweries (SAB), 167, 226
South African Defense Forces (SADF), 135, 169-170
South African Reserve Bank, 232
Southern African Development Community, 163
Southern Center for Studies in Public Policy, 73
Southern Christian Leadership Conference, 250
Southern Education Foundation, 188
Soviet Union, 1, 238
Soweto Uprising, 149-150
Spaghetti, 62-63
Speakeasy, 227
Spelman College, 49, 192
Spence, Junior, 86
Sports sponsorships, 216, 224-225, 241
Sri Lanka, 237
Stahl, Jack, 203, 250, 255-259, 262
Stealing, 40
Steel, Mike, 226
Stegall, Leroy, 29
Steyn, J.J., 175
Story of Atlanta University (Bacote), 192-193
Strain, Jane Ware, 10-11
Straw, Jack, 266
Strickland, C.J., 86
Sullivan, Leon, 85, 120, 171-172, 175
Sullivan, Lucias, 95

Sullivan Principles, 120, 140, 151, 171, 175, 177
South Africa application, 175, 177
Summers, Jack, 81
Sunshine Law, 88
Surtee, Yusuf, 139, 150, 158, 203
Sutton, Percy, 117
Suzman, Helen, 147
Swaziland, 162-163, 169
Switzerland, 266
Sybia, Eunice, 149

Talmadge, Eugene, 4-5
Talmadge, Herman, 77
Tambo, Oliver, 136, 144, 155-157, 179
Tanzania, 170, 210, 231, 233, 241
Tate, James, 192-193
Tayden, Alexander, 272-273
Teltsch, Kathleen, 159
Texaco, 249
Thayer, E.O., 190
The Resurgent Neighborhood (Ham), 66
Thompson, Fletcher, 79
Thompson, J. Walter, 120
Thompson, Terrez Marriott, 248
Thugwane, Josia, 225
Thula, Gibson, 143, 167
Title 16a, 80
Towns, George, 194
Trailor, Rose, 14
TransAfrica, 120, 148
Truman, Harry, 33
Truth and Reconciliation Commission, 122, 159
Tucker, Robert, 53
Turner, Cody, 5
Turner Communications Company, 94
Turner, Ted, 94
Turner, Wilson, 4
Tutu, Desmond, apartheid opposition, ix-xii, 143, 149-153, CAU dinners, 206; Coca-Cola disinvestment in South Africa, 152-153, 165; Crossroad-KTC Holocaust ceasefire, 170; Equal Opportunity Founda-tion, 154-161, 164; honorary de-gree, 200; Lord Archbishop of Cape Town, 163; Sullivan Princi-ples, 179; tailor, 139; Truth and Reconciliation Commission, 159; Carl Ware relationship, 1, 206
Tutu, Leah, 151, 200
Tyler Perry Studios, 98

Uganda, 231, 236
Unilever Limited, 172
United Democratic Front, 158
United Nations, 93, 147, 266, 267
United Negro College Fund, 198
University Homes, 71
University John-Hope Homes, 78
University of Georgia, 48, 193, 194
University of Pittsburgh Graduate School of Public & International Affairs (GSPIA), 65-67, 74
University of the Western Cape, 215
Urban community development, 60-62
Urban East, 73-78
Urban Fellows Program, 96
Urban Foundation, 175
Urban League of Pittsburgh, 69-70
US Anti-Apartheid Act, 171
US Chamber of Commerce, 186
US Congress, 6, 62, 93, 95, 120
US Constitution, 6
US Department of Health, Education, and Welfare, 79
US Department of Labor, 249
US National Register of Historic Plac-es, 117
US Secretary of Housing and Urban Development, 268
US Secretary of Labor, 259
US Steel, 68
US Supreme Court, 77, 194

Van Stavel, Brendon, 217-218
van Zyl Slabbert, Frederik, 170
Vietnam, 237, 266
Viljoen, Hennie, 136-139, 144, 148, 181

Voting, 3-7, 48, 77, 123
Voting Rights Act of, 48, 77, 1965

Wade, Lyndon, 97
Walahaja Hotel & Ballroom, 64
Wall Street Journal, 270
Wallace, John, 4
Walton, Mary, 11
Walton, Peter, 11
Ward, Felker, 97
Ward, Haskell, 53
Ward, Linette, 9
Ware, Aaron, 198, 206
Ware, Barbara, 16, 25
Ware, Besora Beasley, 10, 11
Ware, Carl, Africa Group, 206-213,
    222-223; baptism, 26-27; birth, 1,
    21; boards of director service, 268-
    270; career overview, 1; education,
    31-33, 42-43, 205-206; England,
    206-213; Roberto Goizueta rela-
    tionship, 1; Lucky Feather, 105,
    271-272; Nelson Mandela relation-
    ship, 203, 212, 214-217; marriage,
    64; philanthropy, 197-199, 268,
    272; rehire at Coca-Cola, 256; res-
    ignation from Coca-Cola company,
    251-252; retirement, 268; spaghetti
    eating, 62-63; Desmond Tutu rela-
    tionship, 1, 206; Ware Report,
    248-251
Ware, Crawford, 83
Ware, Derwin, 145
Ware, Eddie Benjamin, 14
Ware, Eddie Lee, 51
Ware, Ernest, 45
Ware, Eugene, 16, 24, 26, 35, 38, 40,
    44-46, 144, 271
Ware, Evelyn, 16
Ware, Henry, Sr., 11
Ware, John, 11
Ware, Joyce, 16
Ware, Julia, 16, 17, 25, 27
Ware, Lois Missouri Wimberly
    (Mamma), 2, 16-18, 24-26, 39-40,
    44, 141-146

Ware, Louise, 15, 16, 19, 28, 34-35,
    56, 82, 109
Ware, Lucy, 11
Ware, Mary Alice Clark, background,
    54-55; education, 68, 76; employ-
    ment, 80; England, 206-213; Leeds
    Castle Meeting, 172-173; Nelson
    Mandela, 184-187, 214-217; mar-
    riage, 59, 64, 67, 145, 149; philan-
    thropy, 197-199, 268, 272
Ware, Mildred, 8, 15-17, 31-32, 56,
    81-85
Ware, Peter Walton (Grandpa "Pete"),
    10-14, 19-20, 26, 36, 83, 271
Ware, Renita, 198, 206, 272
Ware Report, 248-251
Ware, Robert, 11
Ware, Robert, Jr., 11
Ware, Thomas, 16, 24, 26, 35, 40
Ware, Timothy, 64, 65, 67, 76, 81,
    144-145
Ware, Ulas B., birth, 10;children, 16;
    death, 273; debt, 38; education, 14;
    employment, 16-18, 20; family
    cabin, 144; fiftieth wedding anni-
    versary, 146; marriage, 16; prayer
    rock, 22; property purchase, 33-40;
    sharecropping, 23-26; values, 2;
    voting, 3-7, 123
Ware, Ulas B. Jr., 16
Ware, Walter, 3, 5-6, 8-9, 14, 16, 22,
    26, 31-32, 35, 42, 44
Ware, William Henry, 15
Ware, Willie, 16, 34, 51
Washington Post, 165, 255-256
Watergate scandal, 84
Waters, Maxine, 200
WCLK radio, 73
Weaver, Robert C., 62
Whatley, Louise, 79
Wheat Street Baptist Church, 74
Wheat Street Gardens, 74
Wheatley, Phillis, 193
White House Fellows program, 96
William L. Bonnell Company (Bonnell
    Aluminum), 41, 43

Williams, Chester, 224
Williams, Hosea, 82, 93
Williams, Kevin, 226, 241
Williams, Sam, 264
Williams, Tom, 269
Williamson, Q.V., 97, 98
Wimberly, J.S., 7
Wimberly, Lamar, 7
Wimberly, Levi, 7
Wimberly, Lois Missouri. See Ware,
    Lois Missouri Wimberly
Wimberly, "Ma Fannie" Pollard, 18-20
Wimberly, "Papa Joe," 18-20, 271
Wimberly, Sam, 7
Winfrey, Oprah, 198
Woertz, Patricia, 236
Wolf, Millie, 59
Wood, Robert, 3, 32
Woodruff Foundation, 116
Woodruff, Robert W., Ichauway Plan-
    tation, 271; legacy, 193, 195, 199,
    245, 255; management style, 165,
    260; Carl Ware first meeting, 89-
    90
Woods, Tiger, 269
Woolworth's, 48
World Alliance of Reformed Churches,
    158
World Bank, 211, 240
World Economic Forum, 266
World of Coca-Cola Museum, 265
Wright, Linda, 188
Wright, Richard, 193
WSB-TV, 54
WXIA television station, 84

Yancey, Prentiss, 188, 195, 196
Yates & Milton Drug Store, 48, 49,
    193
Yates, Clayton R., 193
Yates, Gene, 17
Young, Andrew, 79, 93, 200, 201, 206

Zambia, 126, 132, 135, 147, 169, 210
Zimbabwe, 122, 126, 131-135, 169,
    210, 226

Zulu, 136, 137, 154, 157-158
Zulu Methodist Church, 137